6-52

REFORMERS
IN PROFILE

REFORMERS IN PROFILE

edited by
B. A. Gerrish

FORTRESS PRESS   PHILADELPHIA

5739G67

1–682

TABLE OF CONTENTS

FOREWORD

This collection of essays is designed as an offering for the 450th anniversary of the Protestant Reformation. The reasons why it takes the form of a series of historical "profiles," from John Wyclyf to Ignatius Loyola, are explained in the Introduction. Some readers may pick the volume up out of straightforward historical curiosity, wishing only to stroll through a gallery of intriguing personalities. And it must be affirmed at the outset that these studies are all historical, not propagandist, in design. They are written by, though not for, historical specialists, and they may serve as an introduction to an important and fascinating period of the church's history. Certainly, the contributors share no party platform: like the subjects of their essays, they represent a variety of viewpoints. This very diversity may itself convey something to the reader. The editor hopes that this volume may be of service to the ecumenical fellowship by broadening horizons and improving communications — perhaps also by correcting partisan misrepresentation of the church's past.

Acknowledgments are due to my assistant Mr. Joseph Fitzer, for preparing the index, and to the Mennonite Publishing House, Scottdale, Pennsylvania, for the extensive quotations (in chapter viii) from the *Complete Writings of Menno Simons,* translated by Leonard Verduin and edited by J. C. Wenger (corrected edition, 1966).

The University of Chicago   B. A. Gerrish

REFORMERS
IN PROFILE

INTRODUCTION

It has been said often enough that the purpose of historical knowledge is to let us act more wisely in the present. But if the past is able in this way to reach into the present, the reverse is equally true: our historical knowledge is already shaped by our present experience. Both processes can clearly be seen in our current picture of the Reformation. Fresh historical research has opened our minds to once-neglected traditions such as Anabaptism, and the new freedom of exchange among different confessions has in turn made us more willing to take another look at the history of them all.

One could present the Reformation strictly from the standpoint of a chosen hero — Martin Luther, say, or John Calvin — and divide the rest of the *dramatis personae* into forerunners, disciples, adversaries, and reactionaries. Often enough Reformation history has been written in this manner. Indeed, the threefold pattern of "forerunners, Reformers, and Counter-Reformation" has attained something like the status of textbook orthodoxy among "mainline" Protestants. But such a perspective makes it hard to treat the forerunners and rivals with any kind of historical sympathy. They were, after all, men with their own programs of reform, and the integrity of each one's individual vision cannot be preserved as long as it is viewed as merely, so to say, adjectival to some other more substantive vision. The sixteenth century was the age of reformations (in the plural), and precisely as such it forms a unity with the preceding two centuries. Perhaps, indeed, we are moving toward a view of reformation less as a once-and-for-all event in the history of the church and more as a permanent aspect of the church's existence. Even when reformed, the church is always in need of reform: *ecclesia reformata* is *ecclesia reformanda*. It is from some such perspective as this that the year 1967 looks back on the events of 1517.

Our concern here has been more with typology than with historical influence (or theological valuation). That is to say, the reformers profiled here have been selected, for the most part, as representatives of distinctive concepts of reform. We begin with two late medieval reformers, then distinguish in the sixteenth century four main patterns of reform: humanistic, Protestant, radical, and Roman Catholic. The categories could no doubt be extended and subdivided. One could even look beyond the Western church to the remarkable figure of Cyril Lucar, who sought (without success) to import Calvinism into the Eastern Orthodox tradition. But the line has to be drawn somewhere, and we have provided a sufficiently diverse gallery of profiles.

The compilation of long lists of abuses is a characteristic feature of the period (1300–1600). Such lists appear, for instance, in d'Ailly's *Treatise on the Reform of the Church,* in Erasmus' *Praise of Folly,* in Luther's *To the Christian Nobility,* and in the "decrees on reform" of the Council of Trent. But reform was seldom just a matter of correcting abuses. Even where strictly doctrinal matters were not expressly included in the idea of reform, the question "How shall we achieve the reformation?" posed theological problems. Leadership ought logically to have come from the popes, who were acknowledged as the vicars of Christ upon earth. But the popes themselves were entangled in the web of corruption, so that the cry had to be for reform "in head" as well as "in members." Moreover, the course of events in the later Middle Ages undermined the administrative power of the popes, even though they grew rich at the same time. The fourteenth century began with a sweeping assertion of papal claims in the Bull *Unam Sanctam* of Boniface VIII (1302); but the prestige of the papacy declined sharply in the period which followed. Wyclyf and d'Ailly lived in the age of the "Babylonian Captivity," during which the papacy was located not in Rome but at Avignon and existed under

French domination (1309-77). They both shared in the general shock of Christendom when the return of the papacy to Rome (1377) and the subsequent papal elections (1378) led to the "Great Western Schism," by which the Roman church found itself with two lines of claimants to the throne of St. Peter. By the end of the century the bold assertion of Boniface, that "it is altogether necessary to salvation for every human creature to be subject to the Roman pontiff," had acquired an ironical and taunting ring. Which Roman pontiff? The schism was not healed until 1417, and in the meantime yet a third papal line had been created.

The Englishman, John Wyclyf, and the Frenchman, Pierre d'Ailly, represent two strikingly different types of *later medieval reform*. Wyclyf (*ca.* 1325-1384) was a radical who derided the Roman dogma of transubstantiation, supplied theological warrant for disendowing the church, and identified the pope as the Antichrist and his adherents as the "twelve daughters of the diabolical leech." But he was more than a flamboyant ecclesiastical gadfly. S. Harrison Thomson gives a portrait of the whole Wyclyf — "a philosopher, a theologian, a reformer and a political thinker, all at the same time" — and surveys the entire range of his impressive literary output. Though it is of interest to compare him with the later Protestant Reformers, Professor Thomson makes it plain that the cardinal principles of Continental Protestantism do not provide an appropriate measure of Wyclyf's stature as reformer and thinker.

Vehemently opposed to Wyclyf, yet equally dedicated to the cause of reform, was Pierre d'Ailly (1350-1420), who proposed to mend a divided Christendom and purify the church by the summoning of a general council. Francis Oakley presents d'Ailly as "a staunch advocate of the establishment theology of his day" and examines his conciliarist ideas as both a program of reform and a doctrine of the church. For the strict conciliarist, final authority lay not with the pope but with the universal church or a general council representing it. Since the Protestant Reformers called for a general council to settle the religious dispute of the sixteenth century, they have often been viewed as the inheritors of the conciliarist program. Be that as it may, Professor Oakley maintains rather that d'Ailly's ideas point toward the Roman Catholic Council of Trent (1545–63) — and toward the Second Vatican Council of our own day.

The revived interest in classical antiquity, which we know as the "Renaissance" (a French label for an Italian product!), proved itself an ambiguous force in the life of the church. It appeared that pagan values could hasten the degradation of the papacy, and yet that the new learning could itself be harnessed to the cause of reformation. The alliance of scholarship and piety lies at the heart of the *humanistic reform*. Lewis W. Spitz examines Erasmus (1469–1536) as the representative of a humanistic program, "in part critical, for the most part constructive." A loyal Roman Catholic without being one of the "party men," Erasmus exposed the follies of church and society to his merciless criticism, but sought, above all, to open up the treasures of the New Testament by applying the key of Renaissance scholarship. His aim was to permit the original "philosophy of Christ" — a matter of life more than of dogma — to renew a church which had mislaid the one thing needful amidst a host of unessentials.

The *Protestant reform*, as Luther himself perceived, was explicitly doctrinal in a manner foreign to Erasmus. Luther (1483–1546) "wanted a gracious God and a sound theology," as F. Edward Cranz expresses it. And his theology carries with it not just a correction of abuses but "a whole new universe of thought." Professor Cranz describes the change in Luther's thinking as a reversal of direction, by which the Christian no longer thinks forward to a future salvation in heaven, but lives out of a heavenly righteousness which he possesses already by faith. A fresh and vigorous understanding of the Christian's existence in society was implicit in Luther's "rediscovery of the gospel."

Outside of Germany, Protestantism assumed a variety of forms. The leaders of the Reformation in Switzerland and in England, for example, owed much to Luther, yet chose (in greater or lesser degree) to go their own way. The Swiss churches were styled "Reformed." Bard Thompson depicts Ulrich Zwingli (1484–1531), the Reformer of Zurich, as "one of the eminent Reformed theologians, the first of that tradition." He sketches the making of the Reformer, the first and second phases of his work in Zurich, the content of his thought, and the bitter conflicts of his closing years. Unquestionably a reformer of the "evangelical," or Protestant, type, Zwingli was more drastic in his reformatory program than Luther, less radical than the Anabaptists. Professor Thompson sets Zwingli's work in the context of its complex relations with other patterns of reform — humanistic, Lutheran, and Anabaptist — as well as in the context of its opposition to Rome. Zwingli liked to stress his independence from Luther. He was, he claimed, a Paulinian, not a Lutheran, and he had begun to preach the gospel of Christ "before any man in our region had so much as heard the name of Luther." He came to the Reformation from Humanism, and his evangelical awakening was in large part intellectual. In his application of the biblical norm and in his understanding of the Spirit's working he represented a distinctive variety of Protestantism. "It was typical of him to say, 'None but the Holy Spirit gives faith, which is trust in God, and no external thing gives it.' "

Closer to Luther than to Zwingli was John Calvin (1509–64), whose inclusion among our profiles rests more on his historical stature than on peculiarities of religious typology. Calvin has been a highly controversial figure from his own day until the present, and his name may conjure up the image of a morose predestinarian and a meddler in the private lives of the citizens of Geneva. Our attempt has been to show that his theology — at least in his own intention — was an affirmation of the pre-eminence of Jesus Christ, not a gloomy predestinarianism nor a new legalism. All corruptions in religion, according to Calvin, have their source in the refusal to abide in Christ alone. From this christological center he moved out to the problems of Church reform, and took his stand under the Lutheran banner. But he insisted that in so doing he was no schismatic, but one who lived, with the ancient Fathers, in the bosom of the Catholic church.

Thomas Cranmer (1489–1556), the English Reformer, has sometimes been handled roughly by historians. He has been made to appear as a man of indecision of whom it has been remarked that had he lived a few hours longer he might well have been converted once again. Geoffrey W. Bromiley helps us toward a more balanced impression of Cranmer in a series of five sketches: the scholar, the ecclesiastic, the reformer, the theologian, and the martyr. Although Cranmer died in the Marian persecutions, "the essential features of the church of the Elizabethan Settlement were still the features impressed upon it by this most unassuming and apparently least effectual of all the Reformers." It is for this reason — because, like Luther and Calvin, he shaped one of the three main non-Roman communions of the Western church — that Cranmer has his profile in our gallery of reformers. As a theologian, he cannot be judged original. (To only one doctrinal theme, the eucharist, did he devote extensive labors.) Yet Professor Bromiley finds something distinctive in Cranmer's emphasis upon the identity of the reformed church and the patristic church, and he points out that this emphasis "became an integral part of the Anglican position."

No area of sixteenth-century research has made more significant advances in recent times than the study of *radical reform*. The concept of a "radical reformation" covers a variety of movements which are loosely linked in the historian's mind by a shared contrast with the conservatism of the Lutheran, Calvinistic, and Anglican reformations. Menno, the gentle pastor, and Muentzer, the revolutionary, are representatives from opposite ends of the radical spectrum. J. C. Wenger portrays Menno Simons (1496?–1561) as "in all essential points . . . an evangelical believer on Christ. . . . " (One recalls Harold Bender's description of Anabaptism as "consistent evangelical Protestantism.") But there were points at which Menno differed from Protestants and Roman Catholics alike; these points, too (such as the practice of believers' baptism), are illustrated by Professor Wenger through selections from Menno's writings. To the Mennonite the Protestants had failed chiefly in the matter of moral reform. As Menno himself severely charged, "They sing, 'We are free!' while the smell of beer and wine issues from their drunken mouths and noses." Nothing stands out more clearly in Professor Wenger's citations than the austere and uncompromising demand for Christian obedience and the living of a new life. Reform, for Menno, included the gathering of genuine fellowships of the saints after the model of the primitive church.

Thomas Muentzer (1498?–1525) is the youthful hero of Marxist historiography who confessed himself a communist and a revolutionary and paid with his life. In him spiritual reform is linked with the cause of social reconstruction. Hans J. Hillerbrand, however, finds in Muentzer a much more complicated and enigmatic figure who first became a Protestant, then ventured into apocalyptic paths of his own. (The transition is marked by a change in his language about Luther: his "sweetest father" becomes "the pope of Wittenberg" and even worse.) Apparently, Muentzer came to think of himself as an inspired prophet, the "new Daniel," and, though not the ringleader or spokesman of the peasants, he identified their cause with his because his appeal to the rulers had failed. He was a reformer, inspired by zeal for "poor, miserable, wretched Christendom," who wanted to see the empirical consequences of faith. Professor Hillerbrand brings to light the strong mystical vein in Muentzer's thought, with its emphasis on obedience and suffering with Christ. But Muentzer will be remembered above all for his remarkable hints that the redemption purchased by Christ's blood establishes social equality and freedom among his people.

The Roman church was not sleeping while all these critics and rebels were trying to bring renewal to Christendom, though it must be admitted that the popes in general dragged their feet when challenged to lead their people in reform. By the time a reforming council was assembled under the pope (1545), the Western church had already been divided. Nevertheless, between Martin Luther and us stands the *Roman Catholic reform,* which should not be described merely as a "counter-reformation," as though its interest had been simply to undo the reformation of others. The Roman church of the second half of the sixteenth century cannot be identified with the institution which Luther attacked in the turbulent years of the Protestant revolt. And yet it was not a new church either, for the Roman Catholic reform tapped the great spiritual resources of the Middle Ages, which had never run dry in the years of degradation and decline. In a sense, the Roman revival was no less diverse and comprehensive than the reform movements outside the Roman church. It had its "liberals," like Contarini, and its "conservatives," like Caraffa (Pope Paul IV); and its program ranged all the way from covering the naked art in the Sistine Chapel to defining the doctrines which Luther had placed in question. Ignatius Loyola (1491–1556) is presented in our final chapter, by Robert E. McNally, S.J., as a typical figure of the Roman Catholic reform. Professor McNally finds in Ignatius' loyalty to the hierarchical church "the very epitome of Tridentine papalism." Ignatius did not seek to change the church's existing structures or inherited theology, but rather to renew the church by reforming the Christian people within it. And for such a program the resources of divine grace were already available. The Society of Jesus, as Father McNally suggests, was to serve as a model for the reform of the church.

Part One

LATER MEDIEVAL
REFORM

CHAPTER ONE

JOHN WYCLYF

S. HARRISON THOMSON

I

The thought and personality of John Wyclyf have been matters of controversy since he first came to public notice in the middle of the fourteenth century. There are many gaps in our knowledge of his life and career. We do not even know with any degree of certainty where or when he was born. Scarcely any two of his biographers have agreed on date or place, and there seems at this point little likelihood that the future will bring any more precise conclusions.

What is now generally agreed upon is that he was born between 1320 and 1330 somewhere in the North of England. In 1720 John Lewis (who took his information from Leland) stated his surmise that Wyclyf had been born in "Wicliffe near Richmond in Yorkshire about the year 1324." This was generally accepted without any contemporary documentation until relatively late in the nineteenth century, when 1330 was suggested by H. Rashdall and Rudolf Buddensieg. G. Lechler, author of a monumental study of Wyclyf's life and thought (German edition, 1873), made no attempt to choose between 1320 and 1330. The author of the classic life of Wyclyf, H. B. Workman (1926), suggested 1328 as a reasonable compromise. The vagueness of Wyclyf's birthdate holds for the place of his birth as well. Several villages have been suggested, one of which, Spresswill, never existed. We must be content with knowing that John Wyclyf was a Yorkshireman, born around 1325, who came up to the University of Oxford around 1340 and spent most of the rest of his life there in the town which he loved. His was a family of some importance in Yorkshire and a career in the church was a normal expectation.

In general, students went to the university between the ages of fourteen and sixteen. The usual minimum period for the Bachelor of Arts degree was four years of rigorous study. Many students took longer. Here another factor of time enters the calculations. From late 1348 to 1353 the university was virtually disbanded because of the Black Death, and we have no inkling of what Wyclyf was doing during that time. He may have left Oxford for his Yorkshire home. Once back in Oxford he resumed his academic career, taking his B.A. degree and in 1356 becoming a probationary fellow of Merton College. Three years later, according to the rules of the university, he could supplicate for the M.A. He became a master in 1361, and that same year he was Master of Balliol College, a post he held for only a year and several months. He accepted the rectorship of the church of Fillingham, a parish in the gift of Balliol College, and continued to lecture at Oxford. In 1362 he accepted, in addition, a prebend at Aust which did not call for residence. He received the degree of Master of Theology in 1363.

In December, 1365 Wyclyf was appointed Warden of Canterbury Hall in Oxford by Islip, the Archbishop of Canterbury. The archbishop planned to organize the hall on a new basis: four of the students were to be seculars and eight were to be regulars, at best a very delicate arrangement. Islip died shortly thereafter and the students protested the irregular nomination of Wyclyf. The papal curia decided in favor of the regulars. Wyclyf was probably not deeply disappointed. He had a weak case, and made no pointed reference to the incident in his writings. In April, 1368 he was granted permission to be absent from his parish for another two years of study in Oxford. Later in that year Wyclyf exchanged the rectorate of Fillingham for that of Ludgershall, which was nearer Oxford, a matter of sixteen miles, though its stipend was much less.

Soon after this Wyclyf entered the service of the king. He speaks of himself as *peculiaris regis clericus* ("the king's special cleric"). It was not as a tried and trained civil servant that he was recruited, for that he was not. But for King Edward's son, John of Gaunt, the Duke of Lancaster, to have on his side the most prestigious scholar at Oxford was of great value. Previously unfamiliar with the world of politics and diplomacy, Wyclyf attended the Parliament of 1371 as a spectator. It was a tense and contentious parliament. The issues between the clergy and the crown were tightly drawn and Wyclyf must have learned much from the acrimonious sessions. Soon thereafter (April, 1374) he was appointed by the crown to the rectorate of Lutterworth, an obvious compensation for his services as a consultant on matters of church and state. Resigning Ludgershall, he served the parish of Lutterworth until his death.

Wyclyf took his doctor's degree in 1372. This degree, by common practice, called for lectures on Peter Lombard's *Four Books of Sentences*. By the fourteenth century it had become acceptable for a candidate for the D.D. to take one of the four books or a prominent doctrine treated by Peter. Wyclyf chose to deal with the doctrine of the incarnation, in a treatise known to us as the *De benedicta incarnacione* ("On the Blessed Incarnation"). For the most part the work is not heretical in intent, though we are able to find a few phrases that could be labeled "dangerous." It is, moreover, clear that he was not completely happy about the accepted scholastic doctrine of transubstantiation, and his whole argument was subjected to some attack.

England was involved in an expensive war with France, and the constant papal demands on England met with stubborn resistance from the English people and their leaders. A conference was set for the late summer of 1374, to meet at Bruges and iron out questions at issue between the "French" (Avignonese) papacy and the English crown. Wyclyf was a member of the small English delegation. The conference was a failure. Wyclyf, as a theologian, took no leading part in the negotiations, and after a few weeks returned to England. He made no secret of his disgust at the venality of both sides. On his return he set to work feverishly on his study of dominion, divine and civil. He had seen at close range the implications of the powerful posture of the papacy. His life before 1374 had been peaceful and serene compared with the ten years from his first involvement in politics and polemics until his death in 1384.

During these years Wyclyf was the focus of a papal bull, of formal trials and hearings, and of broad and bitter attacks on his teaching and preaching. For his part he was so productive that even his enemies were amazed. He conceived and completed a *Summa theologica* in twelve volumes, at least six other books, and numberless pamphlets. He instigated a translation of the Vulgate Bible into English, preached hundreds of sermons, kept up his lecturing at the university until his health would no longer allow it, and kept in touch with the popular movement sometimes called the "poor priests."

The implications of Wyclyf's thinking on the relations of the church to the crown in England had been realized by the hierarchy since before he took his D.D. — that is, previous to 1372. Whether he committed his thought to writing at this early date or not, we can sense the deep, almost frantic desire of the church leaders to stop the growth of Wyclyf's influence among the people and indeed (in certain quarters) among the clergy. From about the fall of 1374 he was deeply involved in his treatise on dominion, a theology which, once broached, carried with it the thorough re-examination of the functioning and relations of church and state. The *Determinacio de dominio,* (late 1374–early 1375), was the first careful, if tentative, statement of his concept of dominion. It was less a polemic than a programmatic sketch, forecasting the lines along which Wyclyf had decided to proceed. He had by this time organized in his own mind the plan of his second *Summa*. To a remarkable degree he kept to his schedule. We can trace the development of his thought through the next decade as he covers the whole theological and ecclesiological spectrum. He followed the *Determinacio* with the interesting *De dominio divino* (1375), intended to lay a broad basis for the *Summa theologica*.

The Good Parliament of 1376 instituted some desired and salutary measures. The sentiment of the Commons was anti-Gaunt and anticlerical. Wyclyf, in his preaching, had asked for many of the reforms parliament was now putting forward. The long bill of *gravamina,* containing 140 headings of specific grievances, met with his approval. But the implementation of this program of reform could not be put through. The king was in his dotage, and his eldest son Edward, the "Black Prince," was dying. Under these circumstances John of Gaunt was very powerful, but he also had powerful enemies. A reform program could not be expected to succeed in the face of obstacles of such deadening effect.

When the Good Parliament was adjourned Gaunt's enemies, along with those who opposed Wyclyf, were able to proceed against him. William Courtenay, the new Bishop of London, cited Wyclyf to appear before the bishops on the afternoon of February 19, 1377. Courtenay, a representative of the landed families and the conservative element in the church, was also a bitter enemy of John of Gaunt. The duke realized that the proposed hearing was directed as much against him as against Wyclyf. He did not come to the hearing unprepared. He brought along four Oxford friars, representatives of the four mendicant orders, to be his counsel in matters of theology. Courtenay and the regular orders were on very unfriendly terms; thus the friars could be counted on to defend Wyclyf against their enemy. In addition Gaunt brought with him Henry Percy, recently appointed king's marshal, and a small squad of armed retainers. The chapel was crowded with citizens of London, all anxious to defend the honor of their bishop and of Sudbury, Archbishop of Canterbury. Percy asked Wyclyf to be seated, whereupon Courtenay protested that Wyclyf, the accused, should stand. Gaunt muttered threats that he would humble all English bishops, particularly Courtenay. After these courtesies the meeting broke up. Wyclyf had not uttered a word throughout the whole proceedings. The London citizenry, loyal to Courtenay, managed to get the bishop safely out of the chapel, while Wyclyf's adherents carried him to safety. He made no mention of the incident in any of his later works.

Wyclyf's enemies, momentarily defeated, had no intention of leaving him free to continue spreading his heresies. Detailed reports of his teaching and preaching were sent to Pope Gregory XI, now returned from Avignon to Rome. Pursuant to these reports, the pope on May 22, 1377 issued five copies of a bull against Wyclyf. One copy was sent to the Archbishop of Canterbury, a second to Courtenay, a third to Edward III, a fourth to the Chancellor of Oxford University, and a fifth to the whole university. The bull was not published in England until December 18. Its content was specific. Wyclyf's writings had been combed with care. Eighteen theses, taken from the *Determinacio* of 1374, from his works on dominion, and perhaps from sermons preached in Oxford or London, were specified. He was summoned to appear in Rome within thirty days. Courtenay and Sudbury ordered the Chancellor of Oxford to examine the charges, and the chancellor, unwilling to disobey either the pope or the Duke of Lancaster, settled on a compromise. He told Wyclyf to stay in Black Hall under a sort of house arrest, and passed a copy of the bull on to the regent masters in theology for their study and judgment. The consensus of the referees was that the theses of Wyclyf listed in the bull "were true but sounded badly to the ear."

Wyclyf's popularity among the people was at its height. Several months later, in January of 1378, Wyclyf was summoned to be tried at St. Paul's in London. He chose, probably at Gaunt's suggestion, not to go, but when the meeting place was moved to Lambeth Palace, the episcopal seat, he decided to go. Once again the tension between the hierarchy and the crown was great. The government party received the open support of the queen mother, regent for the boy-king Richard II. The queen ordered the bishops to avoid any judgment against Wyclyf. This order virtually ended the trial. Wyclyf was under no obligation to say anything, but he did publish a reply to the charges against him under the title of *Protestacio* ("Protest"). The London populace made several angry demonstrations against the clergy, but the trial petered out for lack of substantial support, realistic analysis of the issues, and intelligent guidance.

Gregory XI died in Rome on March 27, 1378, and Urban VI

was promptly elected to succeed him. The Great Schism may be said to have broken out in September, when the same cardinals who had elected Urban disavowed obedience to him and elected one of their number, Robert of Geneva, in his stead. Robert took the pontifical name of Clement VII. The English church accepted Urban, as might have been expected from the fact that Robert was a Frenchman and England and France were at war. The split in the Christian church was deeply disturbing to Wyclyf and gave him grounds for much of his subsequent criticism of the whole institution.

In the same summer of 1378 an incident occurred that gave Wyclyf an opportunity to formulate his thinking about the relations between church and state, with special regard to the English establishment. Two knights who had been held in the Tower of London escaped and took sanctuary in Westminster Abbey. Government soldiers entered the church, pursued one of the knights around the nave, killed him and threw the corpse out of the abbey. The archbishop excommunicated the commander of the troops engaged in the fray, and services in the abbey ceased. The incident posed the question of whether the secular power had real jurisdiction over a church or the traditional sanctuary held against the needs of the crown. Wyclyf was at the moment deeply immersed in his *De ecclesia* ("On the Church"). He was asked by the king (at Gaunt's suggestion) to discuss the matter from the point of view of church law. His defense before parliament of the action of the crown was worked into the seventh chapter of the *De ecclesia*. It was a useful example — to Wyclyf at all events — of the need for revision of the relations between the church and the English crown.

Within the next six months Wyclyf published three of his most important treatises: *De ecclesia, De officio regis* ("On the Office of the King"), and *De potestate pape* ("On the Power of the Pope"). In all three the case for the predominance of the secular power over the church in temporal matters was clearly and cogently stated. From this step, a near-rejection of any papacy, Wyclyf moved in the summer of 1379 to a study of the nature and relevance of the eucharist. The conclusion he reached was radical and led to a heated controversy with the friars. The rejection of transubstantiation, one of the central doctrines of the church, was certain to bring sharp and bitter attacks. Wyclyf was quite aware that the stakes were high, and that he would have to face the loss of support and amity from many quarters. His logic and the implications of his realism drove him to publish his conclusions at any cost. He was at this time (1378 to 1382) in the full swing of his theological studies. He had now essentially retired from politics and was developing as rapidly as possible his theological *Summa* in its many contexts.

We may properly assign to this period — early 1380 — his first efforts at translation of the Bible into the vernacular. It is probable that Wyclyf did not personally take part in the actual work of translation, but was rather the prime instigator. He was extremely busy with his own writing and the frequent annoyances of his enemies. The second attempt at translation was not undertaken until some years after Wyclyf's death. His whole corpus of writing is infused with a deep conviction that all truth and guidance may be found in the Scriptures alone. The Bible for him was the rule of faith.

A new chancellor, William Berton of Merton, an old enemy of Wyclyf, undertook in 1380 to constitute a council of twelve clerics to examine Wyclyf's works. Of the twelve, four were seculars, six were friars, and two were monks. Some had already engaged in polemics with Wyclyf. Only one, Robert Rigg, several times Chancellor of Oxford University, was of any eminence. They were ordered to concentrate on Wyclyf's teaching on the eucharist. The verdict of such a packed jury was a foregone conclusion. Nevertheless the vote was close, seven to five, against Wyclyf. Wyclyf appealed their judgment to the king. John of Gaunt, fearing that Wyclyf's position as the holder of condemned doctrines would involve the government adversely, came to Oxford and asked him to be silent concerning the eucharist. Wyclyf felt he could not in conscience be silent on a question of such importance to the faith, although he was aware that his refusal would cost him Gaunt's support. To clarify his position he published in May, 1381 a *Confessio* ("Confession"), an academic document obviously intended to keep the matter within the limits of university discussion. A number of clergy and scholars replied to the *Confessio* in moderate terms. Then there was silence for several months. Wyclyf apparently was sick during the summer and then was ill in London for a time. On recovery he moved to his parish at Lutterworth, never to leave it again save for a few very short stays in Oxford.

On May 13, 1381 the Peasants' Revolt broke out. There is no reliable evidence connecting Wyclyf with the movement. John Ball, one of the leaders, allegedly confessed that he had been a student of Wyclyf for two years. If such a confession was actually made, which may be doubted, not many people took it seriously. Yet this popular movement damaged Wyclyf's image because it allowed his enemies to say that this disaster was implicit in his heresies. The reformer still had supporters at Oxford, although some of them were in danger because of him. In addition there was unmistakable evidence that his teaching was finding support among the common people. The chronicler Henry Knighton, no friend of Wyclyf, remarked in 1382: "The sect has multiplied so widely that on the road every second person you meet will be a disciple of Wyclyf."

Early in May, 1382 Courtenay, secure in his position, called a synod to meet at Blackfriars to consider Wyclyf's heresies. It was a mixed, handpicked group: nine bishops; sixteen doctors of divinity; eleven doctors of laws; seven bachelors of theology; and two bachelors of laws. They were almost all friars, some of whom had had some contact with Wyclyf or with his followers. Wyclyf was not invited. Twenty-four conclusions from his works were examined and condemned. Just as the synod was ready to adjourn, a serious earthquake shook all of England. Courtenay, with great presence of mind, held the council together by declaring the earthquake to be a sign of God's approval of their action. Wyclyf took the opposite position.

Courtenay and his party were gaining strength. The court had by now given up support of Wyclyf, and his adherents at Oxford had become objects of Courtenay's pursuit. At one point Courtenay was temporarily blocked. He was giving orders to Oxford University, and the whole university rose to defend itself. The last word, however, was Courtenay's. At the second synod at Blackfriars he was able to silence several defenders of Wyclyf. He obtained on June 26 a patent from the Privy Council to imprison any defender of the condemned theses. One of the defenders escaped to Rome; three others were forced to recant in November, 1382.

In this same month Wyclyf suffered a stroke. It may not have been a massive stroke, as he continued to write, finishing some of his most important works, among them the substantial *Opus evangelicum* ("A Study of the Gospel") and the *Trialogus* ("Trialogue") which was a sort of distillation of his theology and philosophy. His acerbity and his continued interest in what was happening in England and abroad may be seen in his indignant protest against the so-called crusade of Bishop Henry Despenser (May, 1383). The crusade, shamefully mismanaged, profited no one. The bishop lost his temporal positions and his popularity generally, largely because of Wyclyf's attacks. On December 28, 1384, while hearing mass, Wyclyf suffered a second stroke; he died three days later. He was buried in the Lutterworth church graveyard, still in communion with the church. In 1428 his remains were exhumed and burned, and the ashes were thrown into the Swift River.

II

The preceding section has given a bare outline of the life of a brilliant, provocative and controversial personality. But Wyclyf was more than that. Early in his career at Oxford he was recognized by many as destined to be one of the leading minds of his time in England — this on the basis of his lectures and writing in the field of logic and metaphysics. He was a student in the Oxford of FitzRalph, Bradwardine, Thomas Buckingham, and Walter Burley, when the opinions of William Ockham were being hotly discussed. Ockham had his adherents, but the temper of Oxford leaned against his nominalism. Wyclyf in any event found the Augustinianism of Bradwardine and Burley more congenial to him than the nominalism of the "doctors of signs," as Ockham's followers were called.

His first work, *De logica* ("On Logic"), was divided into three consecutive treatises. *De logica I* is purely introductory, a manual to guide the beginner. The introductory sentence makes this purpose clear: "I have been urged by some friends of God's law to compile a treatise to demonstrate the logic of Sacred Scripture . . . . I am putting forward, in order to sharpen the minds of the faithful, proofs of propositions which may be deduced from the Scriptures." This early declaration of his purpose in producing a Christian-focused logic suggests that he intended to build a formal understructure which would be used in his theology. His grand plan was a *Summa de ente* ("On Being") in thirteen tractates. It was intended to cover selected subjects in philosophy which he thought needed more thorough treatment than had been given them theretofore. In general, the first part of the *Summa* has a certain reference to the problems of Man, while the second part is pointed toward God's attributes and actions. The clearest case of this dual focus is the discussion of universals in the first part as the concern of Man and its counterpart in the second part, the treatise on ideas, which emphasizes the origin of these seminal ideas in the mind of God. A similar parallelism may be noted elsewhere in the *Summa*, if not throughout.

Wyclyf was probably the most articulate philosopher of his time. It is perhaps strange to find so vigorous a presentation of the *via antiqua* ("old way") in the late fourteenth century. The other case, that for the nominalistic *via moderna* ("modern way"), was popular and brilliantly argued by thinkers like Woodham, Buridan, Swineshed (Sevenset), Strode and others, but none equaled Wyclyf in breadth of conception and briskness of presentation.

A large part of Wyclyf's thought and writing in the earlier stage of his life concerned the hotly debated question of universals and ideas. A question which had absorbed the thought of Christian thinkers since the time of Augustine, it was occasioned by a few sentences in Boethius' translation of Porphyry's *Isagoge* ("Introduction") to the *Categories* of Aristotle. Along the way from the time of Augustine to the time of Wyclyf and later, the road was marked by periodic outbreaks of conflict between the Augustinian-Platonic strain and a more materialistic approach to the problems of being and becoming.

To Wyclyf universals exist as separate entities in the mind of God. One may say that these universal ideas constitute the mind of God as archetypes. Wyclyf relied on his realist logic in every study he made, whether in philosophy, in theology, or in politics. In his battles over the doctrine of transubstantiation, for example, we find that his whole case for rejecting the church's doctrine of the mass rests upon his realism. Because individuals are subsumed under the universal idea which is real in the mind of God, the annihilation of any *res* ("thing") is impossible. God cannot destroy a part of himself.

The application of this conclusion to the doctrine of transubstantiation is obvious. According to the teaching of the Roman church, at the words of the ministrant *Hoc est corpus meum* ("This is my body"), the substance of the bread ceases to exist and gives way to the substance of the body of Christ; only the accidents of the material bread remain. Wyclyf rejected this explanation, insisting that the accidents must have a substance. If the accidents do not change, neither can the substance change. The sacrament is in its own nature real bread and is sacramentally the body of Christ.[1] Wyclyf was quite aware from the beginning that

---

[1] That is, the body of Christ is present "in" the consecrated element, which is not itself changed into the body, but is an efficacious sign of it. Cf. *De eucharistia*, I, paragraphs 11 and 14. (Footnote references are to Wyclif Society editions.)

his views on the nature of the sacrament would be rejected sharply by the hierarchy, and on many occasions, in English and in Latin, he restated and explained his views on the eucharist. But the establishment would not accept any of his explanations. From a distance it would appear that Wyclyf was using dialectic exposition to explain a theological mystery, a difficult transfer of vocabulary in any age. Obviously, few besides the educated clergy could understand the scholastic terminology and most of those who could were afraid of the disturbance which would result from changing the sacramental institutions of the church.

For a realist in philosophy to accept the doctrine of predestination would appear logical. For one who looked to Augustine for guidance, acceptance would even seem imperative. In Oxford of the mid-fourteenth century, Augustine had his loyal disciples, among whom Thomas Bradwardine loomed large. Bradwardine had firmly argued for predestination but had not excluded the believer from some limited freedom of choice. Wyclyf was directly influenced by Bradwardine's predestinarianism, although his reasoning was somewhat different. In this special branch of theology it is quite clear that Bradwardine and (perhaps less certainly) Wyclyf harbored no discernibly heretical doctrine. Both, moreover, were strong trinitarians; both accepted the Scriptures and the basic doctrines of the Fathers. But to several of the sacraments, apart from the eucharist, Wyclyf pronounced open opposition. Confirmation he rejected as unscriptural; baptism he accepted as scripturally based. Ordination he accepted, but he hedged it with conditions limiting its expansion. He saw evil in the church's misuse of this sacrament to increase its wealth and power. Confession he regarded as a modern innovation. Marriage he saw as a divine institution. Like a juggler who keeps three or four balls in the air at a time, Wyclyf must have been hard put to avoid substantial confusion. This very versatility makes our goal of profiling him here in his true stature as a philosopher, a theologian, a reformer and a political thinker—all at the same time—extremely difficult to attain.

III

We have spoken of Wyclyf's *Summa de ente* (also called *Summa intellectualium*) which was probably completed by about 1369. By that time he had begun to find his interest in theology absorbing his studies. He would obviously have been reading FitzRalph, who was highly regarded in England and abroad as a great scholar and churchman of the generation before Wyclyf (in the 1340's and 1350's). Wyclyf may quite easily have listened to his lectures or sermons. One of FitzRalph's leading doctrines was that of dominion, upon which he elaborated in *De pauperie salvatoris* ("On the Poverty of the Savior," 1356). To Wyclyf dominion was the guiding element in the relationship of God to all his creation. All God's creatures, sharing in God's being, have dominion (lordship). One who sins becomes as nothing, because sin has no being, and the sinner ceases to be able to participate in God's being. Lordship is through grace. God delegates dominion to individuals to be used during his good pleasure. There are two kinds of lordship, civil and spiritual, and the two must not be confused.

This conclusion was the basis for Wyclyf's drive for disendowment of the church in England. Property (dominion) could not rightly be held by those in a state of sin. The possession of lands and other material property obstructed the clergy in the fulfillment of God's law. In much of his writing Wyclyf approved the idea of Franciscan poverty as an ideal state. In his later writing, after he broke with the mendicant orders, he propounded the complete disendowment of the church. The question of who was to decide whether or not a priest was living in accord with God's law was not easy to answer. At first he left the question open but later, in his treatise *De officio regis* ("On the Office of the King"), he accepted the principle that it was a decision which the king should make. In any event it was the king's responsibility to see that physical properties should be in the control and disposition of the civil power and that the clergy were living in accord with God's

law. The practical difficulty of finding laity able to judge the clergy
was hardly grasped by Wyclyf in his planning. He might have
answered that the planning stage is bound to meet with obstruc-
tion, but we must strive for the ideal. He was unafraid of the ideal
in his planning.

It seems probable that the several years prior to and subsequent
to his doctorate (1370–74) were years of reading and organizing. He was in progress from a philosophical *Summa* written along
original lines to a theological *Summa,* also along original lines. His
lectures must have been giving some indication of how his
thought was developing. The call from the government to become
a policy consultant — for that is what he was, "the king's special
cleric" — came as a natural result of his eminence in Oxford, supplemented by conversations with civil officials in London. The
government certainly would not have appointed him to a position
of confidence without knowing precisely what his ideas on the
power and policies of the government were.

Wyclyf's trip to Bruges in the summer of 1374 forced him to
bring his thoughts on church and state into focus. He began to
utilize his unhappy experience at Bruges to compose his second
Summa, this on separate theological and political subjects. The
whole was to be in twelve books and an introduction. The introduction, *De dominio divino,* places the discussion on a high plane.
This treatise is strongly theological. In it he rephrases some of his
previous arguments, softening here, clarifying there. Yet the scholastic philosopher is still present in his method and assumptions.
In Books II and III of the *De dominio divino* he specifically
examines the concept of dominion through grace, in preparation
for the longer treatise on civil dominion. The first treatise in the
Summa, written about 1375–76, was the treatise on the Ten
Commandments (*De X mandatis divinis*). The commandments
are examined as the *vetus lex* ("old law") and the changes that
arose in the Christian era are seen to be the *nova lex* ("new law").
Wyclyf's purpose seems to be to show that the Ten Commandments should be understood as a necessary basis for the *nova lex*

and that the *nova lex* is a fulfillment and perfection of the *vetus lex*. The Middle Ages saw many treatises on the Ten Commandments. Wyclyf was doubtless quite aware of that fact. His treatment differs in being a part of a whole, composed on different bases, especially in view of his over-all theme of dominion.

The next treatise in this *Summa* is the *De statu innocencie* ("On the State of Innocence"), shorter and perhaps inserted later, after the composition of the *De civili dominio* ("On Civil Dominion"). He smoothed out the scriptural framework on which to build the later works in the *Summa*. Wyclyf confidently stipulates that the civil power can control the church, secular or monastic. On the other hand, no cleric should lay claim to any civil and therefore inferior lordship. Wyclyf distinguishes between dominion, which God alone has in full measure, and use, which many may have. The individual may appear to possess dominion but without grace he does not really have it.

The *De civili dominio,* in three parts, constitutes Books III, IV, and V of the *Summa theologica* and is followed by the *De veritate sacre scripture* ("On the Truth of Sacred Scripture"), in which Wyclyf defends Holy Scripture from every criticism, extols its sufficiency for every need in the life of the individual Christian and in the life of the church as a whole. It is the gauge for all moral and spiritual problems. Early in the treatise he says: "All law, all philosophy, all logic and all ethics are in Sacred Scripture." He holds that individuals, even some of the doctors of the church, fail because of a lack of attention to the Scriptures. In one place he says: "I say that my conclusions took their origin neither from him [Ockham] nor from me, since they are irrefutably established in Scripture and often repeated by holy doctors who cite them." He insists on the priority of the literal interpretation of Scripture over the other three senses, allegorical, tropological and anagogic, all of which open the doors to confusion for the faithful. Pursuant to this deep conviction of the unique significance of Scripture over all other writings, he wanted the common people to have the Scriptures in the vernacular. The translation of the text into

English may not have been his work, but it certainly was begun at his inspiration and was a realization of his dreams.

As one reads the *De veritate* it becomes evident that Wyclyf's opinion of the papacy changes between Book I of the treatise and Book III. This change was more clearly marked as news of the Great Schism and of the behavior of Pope Urban VI reached England. Wyclyf's attitude toward Urban cooled but he did not declare for Clement VII. Basically he deprecated the whole situation, yet was able to point out that this schism was a product of an evil system. A new approach to the life of the church was a crying necessity. He felt a growing confidence in his position, and for the remaining five years of his life he maintained his tempo of polemics against the evils in the church and in its organization. Living quietly at Lutterworth, he was busy with his writing but it is quite likely that he was visited by former students and friends who looked to him for counsel. The old account of his inspiring and guiding the "poor priests" has little real verification in any of the reliable contemporary sources. There is little doubt that Wyclyf was aware of the basic principles of propaganda, but during the last years of his life he was in failing health and too busy with the remaining treatises in his *Summa* to be able to direct any such organization that would have demanded an energetic leadership.

Book VII of the *Summa theologica* is the large treatise *De ecclesia,* which has been the occasion of many studies. As a work of scholarship it lacks clarity. It is not well organized, it is frequently repetitious, and its line of argument is often interrupted by the introduction of seemingly extraneous matter. One must assume that the work was thrown together under the stress of a continuing polemic with the establishment.

Because of all his involvement in the dispute over the relations of church and state, Wyclyf set about treating the institution of the church on a theological basis. The church exists as a tripartite body: the *ecclesia triumphans,* made up of the saints who have gone to rest; the *ecclesia dormiens,* those in purgatory (literally, "asleep") awaiting final salvation; and the *eccelesia militans,* consisting of those in the world, active in the visible church. The church militant is in turn tripartite: the clergy, the lords temporal, and the people. The head of the church in all its three degrees is Christ, and the members are known only to Christ. In the church militant there may be members "judged by their present righteousness," but still not finally predestinate. The foreknown and the predestined are mixed in the visible militant church. The membership of the visible church, with the pope at Rome as its head, contains many reprobates known only to God. The severe doctrine of predestination rules Wyclyf's ecclesiological thinking. On this basis, if it were argued consistently, there would be little need to maintain the elaborate and costly establishment. If everybody here below were saved or damned by God's election before he was born, regardless of his efforts or the ministry of the sacraments and the acceptance of the creed of the visible church, no one, from pope to peasant, could be sure of his salvation. Wyclyf was not himself sure of being one of the elect.

In Wyclyf's day the large issue of the relations between church and state was every Englishman's daily intellectual diet. Wyclyf had seen and lived with enough of the government in action to have opinions as to the propriety of either side's claims and actions. But if the church, headed by the pope, was in fact as evil and pointless as Wyclyf made out, some corrective must be found. In Wyclyf's judgment the king, as God's elect, should assume the task of governing the church according to the Scriptures through his responsible ministers. This, he claimed, was not only the best kind of government, but God's planned rule. The first thing the king should do on assuming his rule of the English church would be to revoke the endowments of the clergy and re-establish the church on a basis of conformity to the law of Christ.

He undertook to prove his convictions to the English people and to the hierarchy of the English church. This proof forms the burden of Book VIII of his theological *Summa, De officio regis* ("On the Office of the King"). The argument is fully as theological and scholastic as that in the *De ecclesia*. The pages are heavily weighted toward Scripture, the Old as well as the New Testament. Here Wyclyf quotes canon law more frequently than in any other work he composed. It is as if he wanted particularly to convince those who, by training and temperament, were not open to philosophical and reform arguments. For breadth of erudition it is by far the most impressive of his works. His thesis is that the king, elected by the people, is subject to the law, some of which he himself may have declared. The people should obey the law, even if it does not please them. The community, however, may depose a ruler who steadily violates the law.

Wyclyf does not flatly advocate a national church existing completely apart from the Roman church, but the arguments he puts forth could readily be understood in that sense: England has not been subject to the Roman Empire as other European states have been. Her historical independence is a matter of record. Furthermore the nexus of the Roman Empire to the Roman church is completely wanting in the case of England. For this and for similar reasons the Christian church in England has her own existence. The tragic schism now scandalizing Christendom, Wyclyf argues, is a result of the evil connection of the Empire and Rome, whose head could easily be the Antichrist.

In the ninth book of the *Summa, De potestate pape,* Wyclyf continues to analyze the relationship of the pope to the true church of Christ. He studies the papacy as a historical phenomenon and concludes that the papacy has come to its present position of wealth and power by very un-Christian means. He lists the abuses in detail and asserts that the church would do much better if the pope would return to the simple life and thought of the earlier scriptural form. It will be noticed that he does not yet advocate abolition of the papacy but he does say that the papacy is not necessary to salvation, and the church should return to its state during the three centuries before Constantine, when there was no pope and there were no endowments.

The three treatises *De simonia, De apostasia,* and *De blasphemia* ("On Simony," "On Apostasy," and "On Blasphemy") conclude this *Summa*. The papacy is accused of all three. Wyclyf would have had no difficulty in proving the curia's guilt in the case of simony. It was an open sore, both in Rome and in Avigon.

The *De apostasia* brings no new element into the discussion. However, it appears that Wyclyf wants to clear up some points which were too hastily or inadequately put forward in earlier works. Specifically he reformulates his thinking on the confrontaticn of God and sinful man. The term *apostasia* is an inclusive expression meant to cover every sin or failure that separates God from man. Then Wyclyf proceeds to discuss the whole matter of the eucharist in terms slightly less metaphysical than those he had used earlier. Yet this section is redolent of the philosopher's podium rather than of the preacher's pulpit. Wyclyf is obviously trying to maintain a moderate position, using scholastic canons of dispute to keep the discussion alive.

The twelfth and last treatise in the theological *Summa*, under the title *De blasphemia*, appears to bring most of his religious thought from the high theoretical and philosophical arena to a level of practicality. Almost every doctrine he has hitherto advanced is discussed here in terms understandable to the layman. His favorite ideas — the prideful vanity of the prelates, disendowment, the power claimed by the pope and his defenders, the vices of the clergy, the evils of the friars, the venality of the rural deans, the blasphemies of the Antichrist, the involvement of the higher clergy in secular affairs — all these were the objects of Wyclyf's reforming anger.

The achievement of two weighty *Summae*, one philosophical and the other theological, was an impressive corpus. What makes them even more significant is the fact that each made a revolutionary impact upon its respective discipline at the time and in a later age. Wyclyf wanted the impact of his thought upon the church and upon the state to be wide and deep. His *Summae* are in Latin, an idiom normally available to the literate circles in England. For the perhaps wider group who knew only English he wrote a body of separate pamphlets and pronouncements in the vernacular on issues which he regarded as important in his program. In addition he left, well-organized and (as it were) proofread, a corpus of sermons in Latin, which may have been preached in English and which, as now printed, occupy four octavo volumes. There is another corpus of sermons and pamphlets also in four printed volumes. In some cases the authorship may be dubious, but they must properly be assigned to members of Wyclyf's circle, either students of his or others related to the Lollard movement. There has been discovered recently a voluminous commentary on the *Physics* of Aristotle, existing in only one manuscript, but it adds little to our estimate of Wyclyf.

To his friendly contemporaries and students Wyclyf was known as *Doctor Evangelicus* and sometimes as *Johannes Augustini*. Somewhere along the line he took time to compose a commentary or *postilla* on the whole Bible. A number of copies of his commentary on the New Testament are extant, in Prague and in Vienna. Until very recently none of the Old Testament commentaries appeared to have survived. Within the last decade a commentary on a number of Old Testament books was discovered in an Oxford library. Wyclyf's name had been erased in several places, attributable no doubt to the desire of some student or colleague to save the manuscripts from burning, as ordered in the decree *De heretico comburendo* of 1401.

IV

The fate of Wyclyf's work in England was not glorious, if we may judge by its acceptance and propagation. The firmness with which his work and his followers at Oxford and among the common people were sought out and purged was remarkable. He was not excommunicated, but died in communion with the church. However, during the last two years of his life he was essentially out of active touch with his followers. We may assume that a large factor in his isolation was his illness, which made contacts with his former students so trying that he had to live a very quiet, retired life. One by one his former students were silenced, forced into exile, or obliged to recant. The establishment was relentless in its pursuit, and, we may conclude, almost completely successful. The connection of Wyclyf and his movement with the Lollards was very minor. The English establishment in its search for heresy found very few suspects who knew or professed to know the tenets which Wyclyf held.

Wyclyf's beliefs may have been crushed in England, but they found acceptance on the continent, in faraway Bohemia, where reform in religious thought and practice had been openly under way from the middle of the fourteenth century and indeed found local support from Emperor Charles IV and his son Wenzel IV. The conditions in the church in Bohemia had so deteriorated that they were about as bad as in Wyclyf's England. Wyclyf's ideas of reform were then welcome. John Hus and his supporters found satisfaction and validation for their own reform in Wyclyf's writings, which they copied out and circulated with enthusiasm. The two men, Wyclyf and Hus, are almost universally bracketed together and they do have many things in common. There remain, however, several differences between them. Not the least of these is that Wyclyf's reform effort died with him, whereas Hus's hopes and aspirations became the voice and the spirit of a whole nation for generations after his martyrdom.

It has often been questioned whether Wyclyf was really in the reform tradition or simply a medieval philosopher of the schools, vainly wrapped up in the fatuous obfuscations of scholastic inanities. His motivation has been asserted to be rooted in ambition to make for himself a name as a schoolman. In the course of his voluminous writings he was in some matters inconsistent. Students of his life and thought can find almost anything they want. Wyclyf was aware that his ideas developed and changed. In a number of places he said his thoughts when he was young were different from his later convictions. On some points in theology and in philosophy he changed little, if at all; on others he made radical modifications. But by 1382, the height of his constructive intellectual labors, his thought may be regarded as stable.

It may be convenient to assess Wyclyf's place in the reform tradition by setting up his record against the conventional notes of the Continental Reformation: the supremacy of Scripture over tradition; justification by faith alone; and the priesthood of all believers. While there is some danger in using such broad terms, it is valid to apply some such familiar patterns to see if it is possible to fit Wyclyf into a tradition which has its own history in another country and in another century.

There has been hardly a person in the whole of Christian history who was so intent as Wyclyf upon the universal applicability of the Scriptures to all problems that could arise in all walks of life — in church, in state, and in the life of the individual. The "law of Christ," the "law of God," the "law of Grace," are terms which are found on almost every page of his writings. "The law of Christ, that is Sacred Scripture, infinitely surpasses other laws."[2] Or again: "For Scripture is the rule by which heresy can best be distinguished from its opposite."[3] Or again: "Since our Jesus is God and man who taught both testaments."[4] Or again: "Whence the writings of other great teachers — however true — are called 'apocryphal' and are not to be believed except in so far as they are founded upon the Scripture of the Lord."[5] The quotations could be multiplied manyfold. Wyclyf took every opportunity to emphasize his conviction of the ultimate value of Scripture for the Christian world. The later Reformers could not have expressed their evangelical convictions more strongly.

On the principle of justification by faith alone Wyclyf was less eloquent. The thought can be found in his writings after assiduous searching, but it does not come out clearly. In his *Postilla in totam Bibliam* ("Commentary on the Bible"), where one might expect to

---

[2] *Trialogus*, p. 238.
[3] *De veritate sacre scripture*, III, p. 274.
[4] *Ibid.*
[5] *Trialogus*, p. 239.

find so determinative an idea expressed in the interpretation of Romans and Galatians, it must be said that his comments are rather pedantic and medieval.

From the beginning of his theological career Wyclyf had consistently been firmly opposed to the hierarchical organization of the Roman church. The whole burden of his thought and action had been that the individual Christian was to live and be judged at the last day according to his obedience to the law of Christ. This left little room for the interposition of the clergy in the process. Indeed the frequent tirades against the clergy, secular and regular, would lead us to believe that Wyclyf thought the church would be better off without the clergy to absorb the vitality and usefulness of the individuals composing the church.

Of the third principle of the Continental Reformation, the priesthood of believers, we find no formal expression. As Wyclyf looked about him he came to the conclusion that the great chasm between the individual Christian and the clergy as a class was insuperable. The privileged status of the clergy was beyond the reach of the simple *viator,* regardless of how moral or immoral the clergy might be. The layman was eternally stopped from bridging that chasm, however moral and obedient to the law of Christ he might be. Wyclyf had long been shocked by this unjust and indissoluble relationship. Much, if not most, of his writing and preaching was pointed precisely at a correction of this evil. He pursued his aim both on a practical and on a theoretical level. His theological *Summa* took up all relevant functions of the church as he knew it, as, on a practical level, did his preaching, pamphleteering and service of the crown. In the course of his stormy ministry he crossed and sometimes recrossed boundaries. Much of his writing was *ad hoc* — an answer to an attack or a longer treatment of a point in philosophy or in theology which seemed to him relevant or needed.

Wyclyf was asking questions of the fourteenth century. Some questions asked in the sixteenth century or indeed in the twentieth century he did not pretend to answer. We have seen how his

answers on the matter of "faith alone" were at some distance from
Luther and his contemporaries. The same reserve will be apparent
if we consult him about the priesthood of all believers. At times
he seems to be avoiding the issue. But there are two statements
which might well indicate the direction his thought was taking. In
his treatise on the power of the pope he says, "From this it is manifest, first, that a woman is a priest . . . . It is manifest, secondly,
that just as all holy men and women who are members of Christ
are also priests . . . so only the predestined are members of Christ
or a part of Holy Mother Church and Christians in the proper
sense."[6]

Wyclyf does not come out badly from a confrontation of his
thought and action with the cardinal principles of the Continental
Reformation. He did not answer all the questions which were put
to him explicitly or implicitly in his own century, let alone those of
the sixteenth century. Yet under almost any set of criteria he has
made a basic impact in a number of significant areas of the development of Western life and thought. He may have failed to reform
the English church in the direction he hoped and planned, but the
English church was never quite the same after Wyclyf.

If we try to estimate Wyclyf's achievements we shall have to use
a large canvas. He had ideas — often revolutionary, often creative
— on a wide range of political and religious questions, backed up
by highly competent expertise in social and philosophical dialectic.
If we may judge from his career and occasional remarks, he first
chose to gain recognition as a realist logician. Once earned, this
recognition stayed with him throughout his career, long after he
had built a philosophical *Summa de ente,* unique in structure but
in the Augustinian tradition. This *Summa* marked him as the leading philosopher of the England of his day, and to this day commands the respect of historians of philosophy. Unlike others of the
Augustinian tradition, he was no mystic. Of his private religious
life we know almost nothing. He never speaks of a conversion, nor

---

[6] *De potestate pape,* p. 312.

of any profound religious experience. He was, however, a voluble exegete of the text of the Bible, both Old and New Testaments, and shows a wide range of reading in the Fathers. In general his interpretation is conservative and literal. The appellation of *Doctor Evangelicus* was well won.

Wyclyf would have to be called a nationalist in politics, perhaps even an Erastian in his contention that the king was the master of the church, could properly correct the spiritual hierarchy for heresy or immorality of life, and should control completely the secular properties of the clergy. The doctrine of dominion, though not original with Wyclyf, received added cogency from his support and diffusion. It fitted easily into the English constitutional structure at a time when the popes were Frenchmen and thereby enemies of the English crown. The weighty treatises on divine and civil dominion were written with deliberate intent to bring political and theological points of view into a legal unity.

Wyclyf's writings may have touched the lives of many people in England in the last decades of the century, but they found no lasting welcome in the land of their beginnings. The afterlife of Wyclyf's labors was to be worked out in a land far from England. In England the heretical roots of the movement were destroyed by the governmental pursuit of all those who had any connections with Wyclyf or with his disciples. The Act of 1401 on the burning of heretics (*De heretico comburendo*) was effective. What failed in England was successful in Bohemia. Whereas in England the establishment, laity as well as hierarchy, was firm in its determination to root out the evil heresy, in Bohemia the leadership of the movement was favored by many of the clergy and by many of the nobility as well as, spasmodically, by the crown. The Council of Constance in 1415 was aware of the issues: a universal, sacramental church against a national, individualistic state. There could have been no other decision than the one that was made at Constance. Wyclyf was the personification of the unforgivable heresy of a supra-clerical national church. The fathers of the council saw, or thought they saw, lurking behind Hus as he stood before the council to be condemned, the sinister ghost of John Wyclyf, arch-heretic and monstrous blasphemer. In condemning Hus the council was confident that it had uprooted the heresies of both men.

BIBLIOGRAPHY

Wyclyf was first published in 1525 when his *Trialogus* saw the light in Basel (?), probably through Froben, Erasmus' printer. In 1753 the work was again published, in Bayreuth, with an amazingly well-informed introduction by L. P. Wirth. It is to be regretted that this edition has been overlooked by subsequent bibliographers. Matthew Flacius Illyricus gathered much bibliographical material about Wyclyf in his *Catalogus Testium Veritatis* (Frankfort, 1572), pp. 725–26, and the Appendix to his *Auctarium,* pp. 162–66. For data concerning Wyclyf's life the English chroniclers are most helpful: Henry Knighton, Thomas Walsingham, Anthony à Wood, Thomas Netter of Walden, John Foxe, and John Leland. Knighton, Walsingham and Netter are in the Rolls Series. These chronicles and other records are indispensable to any sound research on Wyclyf. The libraries of Prague and Vienna are the real storehouses of original Wyclyfiana, possessing more of Wyclyf's manuscripts than there are in all of England. Manuscripts are found in strange places besides these repositories. Several very fine copies of some of Wyclyf's works are to be found in the library of the Escorial, and they are the work of English scribes. It is not known whether Philip II read them or not.

In general Wyclyf has been well treated by bibliographers. John Bale (1557) listed many titles and the Incipits of many works. Thomas Tanner (d. 1735) greatly increased the details and specified the manuscripts he had seen — a prodigious labor. His work, *Bibliotheca Britannico-Hibernica,* was published posthumously in 1748. John Lewis, a country parson, wrote a *Life of Wyclif* (1720) which he enriched with many documents. In 1820 the work was reprinted with some hitherto unpublished addenda found in Lewis' own copy. Scholars have paid too little attention to this second edition of Lewis' already very sound work. W. W. Shirley, im-pressed by the material he found in editing for the Rolls Series the *Fasciculi Zizaniorum* (1858), composed a *Catalogue of the Original Works of John Wyclif* (1865), based, for the most part, on the several catalogues of Wyclyf's works in manuscripts of the National Library of Vienna (then known as the *Hofbibliothek*). I have argued elsewhere that these catalogues were probably the work of Peter Payne of Oxford.

In 1869 the *Trialogus* was edited for the third time by Gotthard Lechler of Leipzig at Oxford. Soon thereafter a society was formed with the explicit purpose of publishing the works of Wyclyf. Its first publication was in 1882. From then until its disappearance in 1924 the society published thirty-five volumes. The general level of editing was high. One editor, Dr. Johann Loserth, of Graz, was responsible for thirteen of the thirty-five, a prodigious accomplishment, as anyone familiar with the scholastic scripts will readily concede. Three volumes of Wyclyf's works have appeared since 1924: the first two books of the philosophical *Summa*, ed. S. H. Thomson, (1930), and the *De trinitate*, ed. A. D. Breck (1962). Several others of the same *Summa* have been edited but not published.

A convenient listing of the publications of the society may be found in H. B. Workman's classic biography, *John Wyclif* (2 vols.; 1926), pp. xxxv ff. The best of the minor studies of Wyclyf is that of B. L. Manning in Volume VII of the *Cambridge Medieval History*, pp. 900-7.

In recent years several monographs have appeared that merit mention: Gunnar Westin, *Wyclif och hans Reformidéer* (Uppsala, 1936); J. H. Dahmus, *The Prosecution of John Wyclyf* (New Haven, 1952); K. B. McFarlane, *John Wycliffe and the Beginnings of English Non-Conformity* (London, 1952); L. J. Daly, S.J., *The Political Theory of John Wyclif* (Chicago, 1962); J. A. Robson, *Wyclif and the Oxford Schools* (Cambridge, 1961); E. A. Block, *John Wyclif: Radical Dissenter* (San Diego, 1962); John Stacey, *Wyclif and Reform* (London, 1964).

A number of serious articles have appeared in journals on both sides of the Atlantic: Paul de Vooght, "La notion wiclévienne de l'épiscopat dans l'interprétation de Jean Huss," *Irénikon*, XXVIII (1965), 290–300; Beryl Smalley, "John Wyclif's *Postilla super totam bibliam*," *Bodleian Library Record* (April, 1953), 186-205; James Crompton, "*Fasciculi Zizaniorum* I," *Journal of Ecclesiastical History*, XII (1961), 35–45; Michael Wilks, "Predestination, Property and Power: Wyclif's Theory of Dominion and Grace," *Studies in Church History*, II (1961), 220–36; Margaret Aston, "John Wyclif's Reformation Reputation," *Past and Present* (April, 1965), 35–45.

CHAPTER TWO

PIERRE D'AILLY

FRANCIS OAKLEY

Pierre d'Ailly (Petrus de Alliaco) was a tireless writer. Despite the extent of his involvement in practical affairs, he left behind him over one hundred and seventy works — books, tracts, letters, poems, sermons — covering an astonishing variety of subjects. These works have never been gathered together into a single collection but if one has the energy and patience to run them down and to read them with attention one can get a clear impression of the way his mind worked. About the man himself, however, one can learn much less. If he was a systematic and fairly coherent thinker, he was also very much the medieval academic. His writings reveal little of his personality. The numerous biographical attempts of the last century and a half have taught us much about d'Ailly the philosopher, the theologian, the churchman, but they have also made it clear that d'Ailly the man has successfully eluded his historical pursuers. As is so often the case in medieval studies, the biographical picture one constructs is marred by an irremediable externality.

I

D'Ailly was of bourgeois stock. The family name was drawn from the village of Ailly in Picardy but it was at Compiègne in the Ile de France that he himself was born in 1350. Little or nothing is known of his childhood years. He entered the University of Paris in 1364 as a bursar at the Collège de Navarre. This college had been founded sixty years earlier by Jeanne de Navarre, wife of Philip IV, and it is perhaps worthy of mention that with it during the three centuries following its founding were to be associated a notable series of Conciliarists and Gallicans, among them d'Ailly himself and his pupil, Jean Gerson, as well as Jean Courtecuisse (Brevicoxa), John Major, Jacques Almain and Bishop Bossuet.

It was as a student in the Faculty of Arts and as a member of the "French" nation, one of its four subdivisions, that d'Ailly began his academic career at Paris. Even after becoming a Bachelor of Arts in 1367 he remained with the faculty as a teacher and it was only in 1368 that he moved on to the higher Faculty of Theology and confronted the successive hurdles of the long and arduous "graduate" course in theology. Like all of his fellows he was obliged to spend the first six years studying the Bible and the *Sentences* of Peter Lombard — the standard textbook of theology during the later Middle Ages — and after examination he was admitted to the rank of *baccalaurius cursor*. As a cursor, he now became a teacher of theology and was required to lecture on the Bible to the junior members of his own faculty. The next rank, that of *baccalaurius sententiarius*, came in 1377, and with it the duty of lecturing on the *Sentences*. This duty he fulfilled, revealing in the process his firm commitment to the nominalist theology of William Ockham (d. 1349), with its overriding stress on the omnipotence of God and its concomitant denial of any extra-mental reality to universal concepts.[1] In 1378, having finished his course on the *Sentences*, he was admitted to the rank of *baccalaurius formatus* and, in 1381, after the necessary series of formal disputations, he was granted the *licentia docendi* (authority to teach) and became a Doctor of Theology. Already in 1372 he had been chosen "proctor," or representative, of the "French" nation. In the years that followed, he became successively canon of the cathedral chapter of Noyon (1381), rector of his old College of Navarre (1383), chaplain to the French king (1389) and Chancellor of the University of Paris (1389) — this last a papal appointment.

---

[1] On this point, see Francis Oakley, *The Political Thought of Pierre d'Ailly: The Voluntarist Tradition* (New Haven, 1964), pp. 14–32, 180 ff.

The closing years of d'Ailly's theological studies and his entry into public life coincided, therefore, with the termination of "the Babylonian Captivity," the return of the papacy from Avignon to Rome, and the tragic onset of the Great Schism of the West.[2] The first papal election after the return to Rome took place in April, 1378, to the accompaniment of rioting outside the conclave and sharp dissension within. It ended with the election of the Archbishop of Bari, a compromise candidate who took the title of Urban VI. The Roman mob had clamored noisily for the election of a Roman. The cardinals, unwilling to accede to this demand, but divided among themselves, had been forced, for the first time in over half a century, to choose a non-French pope. The Archbishop of Bari was an Italian but not a Roman and many of the French cardinals had come to regard him almost as one of themselves. They were able, therefore, to agree on his candidacy. But his subsequent behavior led to a rapid worsening of relations and in May and June of 1378 all the cardinals, with the exception of the four Italians, made their way to Anagni. There, by the end of September, they had not only repudiated Urban's election as made under duress and therefore invalid, but had also gone on to choose in his place Robert of Geneva, a French cardinal. He assumed the name of Clement VII and took up residence at Avignon.

Since neither of the rival claimants was able to displace the other or to command the allegiance of all the Christian nations, the schism thus engendered was of a far more serious nature than its many predecessors, and, despite all efforts by churchmen and temporal rulers to terminate it, endured for almost fifty years. During those years both claimants obdurately refused to withdraw, either individually or concurrently. During those years, too, their rival curias strove to perpetuate their claims — Benedict XIII being elected at Avignon to succeed Clement VII, and Boniface IX, Innocent VII, and then Gregory XII to succeed Urban VI at Rome. Finally, in 1409, the abortive attempts of the Council of

---

[2] For a recent account of the events leading up to the schism, see Walter Ullmann, *The Origins of the Great Schism* (London, 1949).

Pisa to end the schism led to the addition of a third line of papal claimants, in the persons first of Alexander V and then of John XXIII.

Such were the events that were to do much to shape the course of d'Ailly's career. After some hesitation, the French king, Charles V, had recognized the Avignonese pontiff, and, under royal pressure, the University of Paris had followed suit. The "English" and "Picard" nations of the Faculty of Arts, nevertheless, had chosen to remain neutral, and, as early as 1379, two members of the "English" nation, Konrad von Gelnhausen and Heinrich von Langenstein, had boldly advocated the summoning of a general council to put an end to the schism. With the death of Charles V in 1380 and the succession to the throne of a minor, the university itself shifted its position. In 1381 it openly indicated its preference for the *via concilii* (conciliar solution) and in that year d'Ailly himself may have defended this position before the royal court — at least, he himself later claimed to have done so. Such a position was by no means in accord with the policy of the regent, Louis of Anjou, who hoped for Avignonese assistance in furthering his own ambitions in Italy, and it is perhaps because of this that d'Ailly retired for a while to his canonry at Noyon. During the course of the same year, nevertheless, in his *Epistola diaboli Leviathan* ("Letter of the Devil Leviathan"), he once again advocated the conciliar solution. Despite later shifts and hesitations this seems to have been the solution closest to his heart, and in the years after 1403, when other solutions had failed and when the obduracy of the rival claimants was becoming increasingly apparent, he began once more to advocate the conciliar solution.

In the years that intervened he became one of the leading prelates of his day. During the course of his rise to fame, he fluctuated in his attitudes toward the Avignonese papacy and the problem of ending the schism. In 1383 he returned to the university as Rector of Navarre and busied himself with academic matters until 1394 when, after a referendum had revealed it to be overwhelmingly the opinion of the university, he openly committed himself to supporting the *via cessionis,* or simultaneous abdication of the rival pontiffs, as the most practicable way for ending the schism and the one most likely to succeed. This approach, adopted by the French court, served for the next few years as the focus of the national ecclesiastical policy, and led in 1398 to the unilateral French withdrawal of obedience from the Avignonese pontiff in an unsuccessful attempt to coerce him into abdicating.

D'Ailly himself, though sent to Avignon by both the university and the king, and charged on successive embassies with the task of securing the adoption of the *via cessionis,* seems to have become somewhat less than enthusiastic in his advocacy of the cause — possibly because of a succession of favors heaped upon him by the Avignonese popes. Only the refusal of the royal permission had prevented Clement VII from making him Bishop of Laon as early as 1389, and, to an impressive series of minor benefices, Benedict XIII was able in 1395 to add the bishopric of Puy. These favors were interpreted by d'Ailly's colleagues at Paris as an attempt — regrettably successful — to purchase his support; and when he became Bishop of Puy at least one of the nations of the Faculty of Arts decided to exclude him from its meetings, especially those in which the ending of the schism was to be discussed. It is difficult to assess the extent to which such suspicions were justifiable, but it is certain that d'Ailly opposed the withdrawal of obedience in 1398, was active in bringing about a partial restoration of obedience in 1403, tried to absent himself in 1406 from the clerical assembly at Paris which sought to institute proceedings against Benedict XIII, and, when coerced into attending, insisted against opposition on speaking in defense of that pontiff.

D'Ailly never visited Puy and his successor was to be critical of his administration of the diocese. He did not remain Bishop of Puy very long, for in 1397 he was appointed to the more important bishopric of Cambrai which he retained until his elevation to the cardinalate in 1411. This diocese was an immense one, divided both by language and by the borderline between the two papal "obediences," and witnessing very strikingly, therefore, to the damaging effects of the schism. Despite numerous obstacles, d'Ailly's administration seems to have been both effective and enlightened. In an attempt to restore unity he held three diocesan synods, and from 1399 to 1402 he withdrew from the French ecclesiastical and political scene and concerned himself wholly with his diocesan duties. Much of this time he devoted to the initiation and implementation of a wide-ranging program of reform, attempting, among other things, to root out simony and clerical concubinage, to improve the level of clerical education, and to discourage the multiplication of saints' days. In so doing, he was anticipating in practice many of the ideas he was to include in the program of reform that he presented to the Council of Constance in 1416. Similarly, he did much during these years to encourage the activity of the Brethren of the Common Life whom he was later to defend against their detractors at Constance.

The end of 1402, however, brought renewed involvement in matters of high ecclesiastical policy and d'Ailly was forced gradually to spend more and more time away from Cambrai. His conviction of the sincerity of Benedict XIII led him in 1406 to defend that pontiff at the Council of Paris, but the subsequent years of fruitless negotiation in which he himself was deeply involved finally led him in January of 1408 to break with Benedict and to return to Cambrai. This break became definite in the course of the following year.

By that time, the collapse of negotiations between the Roman and Avignonese pontiffs had led dissident cardinals from both obediences to forswear their allegiance to their respective pontiffs and to summon a general council of the whole church to meet at Pisa. This news d'Ailly had welcomed, and, aligning himself formally with the dissident cardinals, he had set off for Pisa. He had sent ahead of him an important series of letters and suggestions, but he cannot be said to have played a prominent part at Pisa as he was absent on a diplomatic mission for the council during the two fateful sessions that witnessed the attempted deposition of the Roman and Avignonese popes and the election of their successor,

Alexander V. The troubled years that followed saw the deflation of the hopes raised by Pisa, which now seemed to have done little more than add a third line of claimants to the papal office. During these years, d'Ailly became increasingly prominent in ecclesiastical affairs. In 1411, John XXIII, successor to Alexander V, made him a cardinal, and there can be no doubt about the importance of his position when the Council of Constance met. His role during the early sessions of the council was clearly a dominant one. From his opening sermon on December 2, 1414, until the election of the new pope, Martin V, in 1417, d'Ailly was involved in most of the great events of the council — notably, in the condemnations of John XXIII, of the propositions of Jean Petit, the apologist of tyrannicide, and of John Hus, with whom he seems to have shown little patience and less charity. At the close of the council, Martin V sent him as legate to Avignon, and there he died on August 9, 1420.

He had absented himself from the fourth and fifth general sessions of the council, the critical sessions which formally asserted the superiority of council to pope, and the illness with which he excused his absence may well have been strictly diplomatic. In his relations with John XXIII, as in his work on the reform commission of the council, he reveals himself to have been more flexible and conciliatory in practice than his theories might lead one to expect. Indeed, despite the radical nature of many of his ideas, the over-all impression given is that of excessive prudence.

II

Ideas often, however, live longer than deeds. During the course of the late-fifteenth and sixteenth centuries, the bulk of d'Ailly's writings were to appear in print, some of them reappearing in successive editions right on into the eighteenth century. The largest group of these writings is devoted to matters relating to the schism and to ecclesiastical reform. The most notable of these are his

Tractatus de potestate ecclesiastica ("Treatise on the Power of the Church", 1416) and his *Tractatus de reformatione ecclesiae* ("Treatise on the Reform of the Church," *ca.* 1416).[3] Sandwiched between this group and another fairly large group of philosophical and theological works are to be found works on biblical matters, such as his *Epistola ad novos Hebraeos* ("Letter to the New Hebrews"), some rhetorical, pietistic and political works, and an imposing set of tracts on geography and astronomy. This last set includes his *Imago mundi* ("Image of the World," 1410), perhaps the best known of all his works because Christopher Columbus studied and annotated it before embarking on his historic voyage, and his *Exhortatio super kalendarii correctione* ("Exhortation on Correcting the Calendar," 1411), in which he advocated in vain the reform that was later to be adopted by Gregory XIII.

Many of these works were widely read, and as as result d'Ailly's name occurs frequently in the theological, ecclesiological, and even political literature of the sixteenth and seventeenth centuries. The works that attracted most attention were his commentary on the *Sentences* of Lombard, his conciliar tracts and his *Tractatus de reformatione ecclesiae*. This last treatise seems to have been used by Protestants as anti-Romanist propaganda, being republished at Basel in 1551 under the significant title *De squaloribus ecclesiae Romanae* ("On the Squalors of the Roman Church").[4] This, together with the fact that Luther cited approvingly d'Ailly's heterodox views on the eucharist[5] led some historians to view d'Ailly as

---

[3] The latter being a redaction of the third part of his *Tractatus de materia concilii generalis* (1402–3), a work rediscovered less than a century ago. See Oakley, *op. cit.,* App. III, pp. 243–342.

[4] See Louis Salembier, *Petrus de Alliaco* (Insulis, 1886), p. xxxii.

[5] In *The Babylonian Captivity of the Church,* where he said: "Some time ago, when I was studying scholastic theology, I was greatly impressed by Dr. Pierre d'Ailly, cardinal of Cambrai. He discussed the fourth book of the *Sententiae* very acutely, and said it was far more likely, and required the presupposition of fewer miracles, if one regarded the bread and wine on the altar as real bread and wine, and not their mere accidents — had not the church determined otherwise." Cited from John Dillenberger (ed.), *Martin Luther: Selections from His Writings* (Garden City, N.Y., 1961), p. 265.

very much "a Reformer before the Reformation." In this they were helped by a failure to comprehend the central thrust of the nominalist theology or the complexity of its relationship with the mature thought of Luther. They were helped also by a widespread tendency to regard conciliar theory as a revolutionary doctrine pointing again in the general direction of the Protestant Reformation.

In light of the scholarship of the last half-century, however, it is no longer fashionable to view either the nominalist theology or the conciliar theory as channeling in any *direct* way into the mainstream of Protestant thinking. D'Ailly emerges, then, as a man who appears less an innovator in matters pertaining to dogmatic theology than a staunch advocate of the establishment theology of his day. Illustrative of this is his vehement opposition to Wyclyfite and Hussite ideas and his rejection of any attempt to derive the totality of the church's doctrine from Scripture alone, unsupplemented by an oral tradition stemming from the apostles.

Reformer he certainly was, but it is in his conciliar thinking that one must seek his reforming ideas. And these ideas do not point in the direction of the Protestant Reformation. Instead, they point in the direction of the reforms of the Council of Trent in matters concerning ecclesiastical discipline; they point in the direction of the Gallican ecclesiology taught for centuries by the theologians of the Sorbonne; they point also (and one is tempted to say "therefore") in the direction of the ecclesiology that has emerged from the deliberations of the Second Vatican Council.

The legacy of his ideas, then, was a complex one, and this complexity reflects the complexity of conciliar theory itself. For the conciliar thinking of the "classical age" dominated by the Councils of Constance and Basel betrays many more variations than we tend to think — too many, indeed, and too elusive to trap within the framework of any simple classification. But it is possible to discern within the pattern of that thinking three broad strands, distinct in their origins, distinct in their subsequent careers, but woven momentarily and fatefully into a meaningful and historic configuration. And this configuration is more clearly evident in the thinking of d'Ailly than in that of any other Conciliarist, with the possible exception of Nicholas of Cusa.

The first of these three strands is the demand for reform of the church "in head and in members" and the belief that this reform could best be initiated and consolidated through the periodic assembly of general councils. Official ratification was to be given to this point of view in the decree *Frequens,* promulgated in 1417 at Constance and providing for the assembly of councils at frequent and regular intervals. Already in 1402–3, however, d'Ailly himself had given clear expression to this demand in the third part of his *Tractatus de materia concilii generalis,* ("Treatise on the Subject Matter of a General Council"), later revised and presented as a program of reform at Constance under the title of *Tractatus de reformatione ecclesiae.*[6]

It begins with a rather portentous introduction denouncing the corruption of the church of his day and predicting further calamities if something is not done about it. Six sections follow, in the first of which d'Ailly insists that if the whole body of the church is to be reformed at all it will be necessary to hold both general and provincial councils far more frequently than has been customary in the past. Among other things, the badly needed reform of the Roman curia can be undertaken only by a general council, and it is the failure to hold such councils that accounts for the long duration both of the Western schism and of the schism between the Orthodox and Latin churches, and for many other evils as well. He proposes, therefore, that provision be made for provincial councils to assemble at least once every three years, and for general councils to assemble automatically at intervals of thirty or, at most, fifty years without the necessity of any specific papal convocation or mandate.

In the second section he denounces, among other things, "that detestable abuse from which the present schism drew its origin" — namely, that the papacy should be attached to any nation or kingdom for such a long time that the nation could almost claim it as

---

[6] Printed in Oakley, *loc. cit.,* pp. 314–42.

its own. This should be remedied and it should also be decreed that no two successive popes be drawn from the College of Cardinals since it is not to be presumed that non-cardinals are ineligible. As for the cardinals themselves, the greater part of them should never be drawn from a single nation or kingdom, there should not be more than one cardinal from any single ecclesiastical province, their number should be reduced, and something should be done to eliminate the scandalous pluralism so prevalent among them. D'Ailly deplores the tendency of the curia to multiply the number of excommunications attached to its penal constitutions and to burden the faithful with an excessive number of statutes and canons obliging on pain of mortal sin. He ventilates the possibility that the cardinalate, not being of divine institution, might well be allowed to lapse into desuetude, and the place of the cardinals as papal assistants taken by prelates from the several kingdoms and provinces. When revising the work for delivery at Constance, however, he omitted this passage and replaced it by one denouncing as erroneous the idea that the cardinalate was useless or that it was not of apostolic origin — a shift reflecting his growing conservatism and, at the same time, the fact that he himself was now a member of the Sacred College.[7]

The third section concerns the state of the episcopate, pleading that new provision be made to prevent the underaged, the ignorant and the unworthy from being made bishops and to prevent bishops from involving themselves too deeply in secular affairs. Provision should also be made to cut down the evil of nonresidence, to prevent corruption and the imposition of unfair financial burdens on the faithful, and to improve episcopal administration in general. The multiplication of saints, feast days, images, and devotional novelties should be eschewed; liturgical reforms should be instituted. Finally, an attempt should be made to prevent the collection of any fees for the administration of orders or of the sacraments in general, or for burials, or for the performance of anything pertaining to spirituals.

---

[7] See Oakley, *op. cit.,* p. 251 and App. V, pp. 346–47.

In the fourth and fifth sections d'Ailly addresses himself to the need for reform among the monastic clergy and the secular clergy respectively. There were too many monastic orders and religious communities — far more than the available revenues could support or the existing need justify. The activities and numbers of the mendicants should be curtailed and monastic exemptions from episcopal jurisdiction eliminated. It is clear that his sympathies lie with the secular clergy, but here again reform is needed. Widespread clerical ignorance and a deplorable system of promotions have to remedied — the former by providing theological libraries and teaching in theology at the cathedral churches, the latter by the appointment to major positions of the learned rather than the well-connected and of theologians rather than lawyers.

The sixth and final section concerns the need for reformation in the lives of the laity, especially princes. It consists of a traditional and rather prolix lecture on the duty of Christian princes to set a good example to their subjects; to eschew immorality, blasphemy, the practice of the magic arts, and heresy; to attack the Saracens and to keep the Jews in their place; to rule their people, in sum, not for their own selfish ends but on behalf of Christ.

This discourse contained, then, a comprehensive and practical program of reform, one that not only anticipated many of the reforming decrees of the Council of Trent but also on some issues pointed forward to the Roman Catholic *aggiornamento* of the 1960's. That this should be the case is indicative less of d'Ailly's prescience than of the persistent nature of the problems that have plagued the Latin Catholic church. Few of his specific proposals for reform were entirely new. Even the connection of the demand for reform in head and in members with the proposal that general councils should be assembled at regular intervals dated back to the work of William Durantis the Younger in the early years of the fourteenth century. What was new was the linking of this demand for conciliar reform with the second strand in conciliar thinking, namely, the strict conciliar theory itself. Not that this was an innovation of d'Ailly's, but, as Jedin has said, it had required "the pitiful situation created by the Schism to bring about the alliance of conciliar theory with the demand for reform."[8] This alliance should not be taken for granted. By the mid-fifteenth century it was crumbling, and in the years after the Council of Basel even those who believed that the necessary reforms in head and in members could be achieved only by means of a general council increasingly recoiled from advocacy of the strict conciliar theory. At the same time, advocates of that theory, most of them Gallican theologians, were not necessarily themselves very interested in reform.

In thinking of most of the Conciliarists of the classical era, however, both strands are present, and in intimate juxtaposition. And this is true of D'Ailly himself. But what was the strict conciliar theory? Although it took more than one form, basic to it was the insistence that the final authority of the church lay not with the pope but with the whole body of the faithful and that the pope possessed, therefore, not an absolute but merely a ministerial authority delegated to him for the good of the church. The authority inherent in the church, d'Ailly argued, is not exhausted by the mere act of electing its ruler. Like any other community, the church retains by natural law the power to prevent its own destruction and it can exercise this power, if necessary, against the command of its ruler. For if the pope, whose power is ordained to the "edification" and not to the "destruction" of the church, tries to subvert it by manifest heresy, open tyranny, or other notorious crime, it must be possible to chastise him, since otherwise the church would not be a perfectly ordained community. It follows therefore that in such cases "which touch the destruction of the church," the pope can be judged and condemned by the universal church or by the general council representing it. And, as he pointed out in his *Tractatus de potestate ecclesiastica* (1417), "this conclusion has been acted upon in the condemnation and

---

[8] Hubert Jedin, *A History of the Council of Trent,* trans. Ernest Graf (2 vols.; London, 1957–61), I, 9.

deposition of Pope John XXIII by the general council, the decision of which it is forbidden to gainsay."[9]

The immediate practical importance of the strict conciliar theory, then, lay in the fact that it opened the way for an appeal from the obduracy of the rival pontiffs to the decision of the faithful as expressed through their representatives assembled in a general council. But its long-range significance sprang from its enduring constitutional implications. For it called into question the whole late-medieval drive toward the creation of an absolutist papal monarchy, stressed against it the communitarian and collegial aspects of ecclesiastical authority, and pointed the way to the creation of constitutional machinery designed to prevent at least a catastrophic abuse of papal power. The precise nature of these constitutional implications has often been misunderstood, partly because historians have not always been aware of the crucial distinction between "power of orders" and "power of jurisdiction" that was a commonplace of canonist and conciliarist thought, partly because the council fathers assembled at Basel later in the century extended conciliar theory into a claim to erect a parliamentary regime for the day-to-day government of the church.

D'Ailly's thinking may serve as a good corrective to such distortions. For him, conciliar theory has nothing to do with the "power of orders," the sacerdotal power which comes directly from above but which is, after all, possessed in no higher degree by the pope than by any other bishop. Nor (at least for him)[10] does it necessarily hinge upon the *magisterium* or teaching authority of the church, for his denial of papal infallibility is not predicated on any ascription of doctrinal inerrancy to the general council. This he dismisses as no more than a "pious belief." What conciliar theory concerns, instead, is the jurisdictional power in the church, the *potestas regiminis*, the truly *governmental* power. More pre-

---

9 Printed in Louis Ellies Dupin (ed.), *Johannis Gersonii Opera Omnia* (5 vols.; Antwerp, 1706), II, 951.

10 Though not all Conciliarists would agree with him on this. For his views, see Francis Oakley, "Pierre d'Ailly and Papal Infallibility," *Mediaeval Studies*, XXVI (1964), 353–58.

cisely, what it concerns is the location within the church of the *plenitudo postestatis*, the plenitude of power to which d'Ailly referred also as the "plenitude of jurisdiction."

Against the claims of the high papalists, the Conciliarists of the classical era denied that the plenitude of power resided in the pope alone. But that they did not wish thereby to deny the divine origin or the permanent nature of the papal primacy, or, indeed, to encroach upon the normal day-to-day working of the papal monarchy is evident from the marked caution with which d'Ailly expressed himself on this very point. Though in one place he can speak of the *plenitudo potestatis* as pertaining *separably* to the pope, *inseparably* to the body of the church, and *representatively* to the general council, no sooner does he do so than he qualifies his position by saying that, "properly speaking," this plenitude of power belongs to the pope alone, for he is the one who generally exercises it, and as a result it is possessed by the church and the general council representing it merely "figuratively and in some equivocal way."[11] Not very clear statements, but certainly indicative of a rather anxious moderation, and, as affiliated arguments reveal, designed above all to support the basic conciliar contention that while plenitude of power normally resides in the pope, it is to be used for no other end but the good of the whole church, and that the church or the general council representing it retains, therefore, the right to intervene to prevent its abuse.

D'Ailly had already argued, it is true, that general councils should in the future assemble automatically every thirty or fifty years with or without special mandate from the pope, and he had gone on to assert that in order to prevent the abuse of the papal plenitude of power the general council could restrict its use. This would suggest that what he had in mind was not only institutional machinery capable of remedying (on extraordinary occasions) papal abuses of power, but also some more continuously operating restraints. It was not to the council, however, that he looked most

---

[11] For d'Ailly's discussion of the plenitude of power see especially his *Tractatus de potestate ecclesiastica,* Dupin, II, 945–46, 950–51.

directly for such limiting machinery, but to the Sacred College, for d'Ailly was one of the minority of Conciliarists in whose thinking there was present the third, least prominent, and most frequently overlooked strand of conciliar thought — namely, that which envisaged the constitution of the church in oligarchic terms, its government ordinarily in the hands of the Roman curia, the pope being limited in the exercise of his power by that of the cardinals with whose "advice, consent, direction and remembrance" he had to rule.[12]

D'Ailly flatly asserted that the College of Cardinals inherited this task from the "sacred college or senate of the apostles," which it had replaced in the hierarchical order but which had exercised the office of the cardinalate. But Peter was head of the universal church before he became Bishop of Rome, and the apostles were "cardinals of the world" before they became cardinals of that city. It follows, therefore, that the cardinals are co-assistants and "as it were, special collaborators" of the pope "in the place and name of the universal church as well as of the Roman church." Because of this it is fitting that the election of the pope should pertain to them for in this they act as vicegerents of the universal church. Indeed, they act as vicegerents of the church not only in electing the pope, but in anything that they legitimately do with the object of promoting the union of the church. Thus when, for the conservation of the faith or the well-being of the church, necessity or utility demands the convocation of a general council, and the pope fails to act, then the authority to convoke the council devolves upon the cardinals "not so much by human as by divine institution, in the name and place of the whole universal church."

By arguing in this way, d'Ailly betrays the influence of an old curialist tradition that predated the conciliar movement and that had its origin in the de facto share increasingly taken by the cardinals from the investiture struggle onwards in the day-to-day government of the church. This tradition had received explicit theoretical formulation in the glosses of the thirteenth-century

---

[12] *Ibid*, pp. 929–30, 935–36.

canonists, Hostiensis and Joannes Monachus, who had maintained that the cardinals shared with the pope the exercise of the *plenitudo potestatis*. In its origin such a view was of course not necessarily related to conciliar ideas at all, and although at Constance both d'Ailly and the Italian cardinal, Franceso Zabarella, synthesized it with the more "democratic" conciliar theory, the fifteenth century saw the disintegration of the synthesis. The old curialist oligarchic tradition persisted, but it found its home now where it had found it before — not among the advocates of the strict conciliar theory but in the Roman curia itself. There it was espoused by the cardinals of the era of papal restoration who seem to have sensed that the growing absolutism of the papal monarchy posed a threat, not only to their own vested interests, but to the well-being of the whole church. And thus, in his great *Summa de ecclesia*, Torquemada, the dean of papalists himself, reproduced verbatim (though without acknowledgment) much of d'Ailly's discussion of the role of the cardinalate in the government of the church.

D'Ailly's importance as a reformer, then, springs very much from the fact that he combined in his thinking, just as he reflected in his career, all three of the elements that went to make up the mature conciliarist position of the classical era. His program for reform in head and in members found its most direct echo in the disciplinary legislation of Trent, but it is one that continues to generate harmonics even to the present day. His advocacy of the strict conciliar theory, while it reverberated most strongly among the Gallican theologians of the sixteenth, seventeenth and eighteenth centuries, has evoked among Roman Catholic theologians and historians in the last half-dozen years or so new and unexpected chords. And in the wake of the Second Vatican Council and the formal and permanent establishment by Paul VI of a representative Synod of Bishops at Rome, one may be excused, perhaps, if one is tempted to interpret d'Ailly's adhesion to the old curialist tradition less as an oligarchic archaism than as a confused anticipation of the principle of episcopal collegiality.

BIBLIOGRAPHY

D'Ailly's works and their locations are listed in Louis Salembier, *Petrus de Alliaco* (Insulis, 1886). A full bibliography of the secondary literature on d'Ailly may be found in Francis Oakley, *The Political Thought of Pierre d'Ailly: The Voluntarist Tradition* (New Haven, 1964), pp. 350 ff. To this should now be added Francis Oakley, "Pierre d'Ailly and Papal Infallibility," *Mediaeval Studies*, XXVI (1964), 353–58. The same bibliography lists appropriate background material in late-medieval ecclesiastical history and in the history of philosophy and theology.

Two biographies should be mentioned here: Paul Tschackert, *Peter von Ailli* (Gotha, 1877) and Louis Salembier, *Le Cardinal Pierre d'Ailly* (Tourcoing, 1931). The most recent biographical sketch is that of A. Coville in the *Dictionnaire de biographie française*, s.v. "d'Ailly, Pierre.

The literature in English is not extensive: see especially A. E. Roberts, "Pierre d'Ailly and the Council of Constance: A Study in 'Ockhamite' Theory and Practice," *Trans. Royal Hist. Soc.*, 4th series, 18 (1935), 123–42; J. P. McGowan, *Pierre d'Ailly and the Council of Constance* (Washington, 1936); and Francis Oakley, *The Political Thought of Pierre d'Ailly*.

Of d'Ailly's conciliar writings, the most valuable are the *Tractatus de materia concilii generalis*, ed. Francis Oakley, in *Political Thought of Pierre d'Ailly*, App. III, pp. 244–342; the *Tractatus de potestate ecclesiastica*, in *Johannis Gersonii Opera Omnia*, ed. Louis Ellies Dupin, (5 vols.; Antwerp, 1706), II, 925–60; and the *Propositiones Utiles*, in Dupin, II, 112–13. This last tract is a valuable epitome of conciliar theory; an English translation may be found in Francis Oakley, "The 'Propositiones Utiles' of Pierre d'Ailly," *Church History*, XXIX (1960), 378–403. One other conciliar tract of d'Ailly's has been translated into English by I. W. Raymond, "D'Ailly's 'Epistola Diaboli Leviathan,'" *Church History*, XXII (1953, 181–91. Brian Tierney, *Foundations of Conciliar Theory* (Cambridge, 1955), is by far the best work on the general topic of conciliar theory, but those unacquainted with the subject will find J. Neville Figgis, *Political Thought from Gerson to Grotius: Seven Studies* (New York, 1961), Chapter 2, a valuable and stimulating introduction.

PART TWO

HUMANISTIC REFORM

CHAPTER THREE

DESIDERIUS ERASMUS

Lewis W. Spitz

The prince of the Christian Humanists, Desiderius Erasmus, was a man of vision and a man of hope. His vision was that of a reformed Christendom in which men had turned to follow the Master in faith and love, in which the church had returned to the simplicity and purity of New Testament times, and in which nations had learned to live together in peace and harmony. His hope was that through Christian scholarship and wholesome instruction the philosophy of Christ could be so clearly portrayed that plowboys and prelates, citizens and kings would at last understand the meaning of the gospel and would be moved to revive the whole darkening world. "I dreamed," wrote Erasmus, "of a golden age and the fortunate islands: and then, as Aristophanes said, I awoke."

Erasmus' rude awakening was not so great a shock as he pretended, for he had been sleeping with only one eye closed. No one had a keener eye for the foibles and follies, the maladies and wrongdoings of mankind. Nevertheless, once he had determined to devote his life to scholarship as his chosen instrument for doing what could be done for the reform of Christendom, he never wavered from his announced program. He could not be prevented by illness, tempted by offers, intimidated by threats, enervated by self-doubts, discouraged by failures, or frustrated by circumstances from working with single-mindedness and zeal to purify the church with water from the ancient wellsprings and to inspire mankind with the philosophy of Christ. In the century and a half before the Reformation the common cry for reform meant many different things to many different people. To Erasmus it meant the

DESIDERIUS ERASMUS   61

realization of his program for the *restitutio Christianismi* through
the cultivation of the new learning and the spread of the ideals
and principles of Christian Humanism. He worked for this goal
literally until the very end, for when he was virtually lying on his
deathbed he dictated a treatise *On the Purity of the Church*.

The year 1516 saw Erasmus, as a mature man of forty-seven at
the height of his powers, enjoy two major publishing triumphs. In
March of that year his critical edition of the New Testament in
Greek with a substantially new Latin translation attached saw the
light, and in the fall of that year his nine-volume edition of
Jerome's writings appeared at Froben's in Basel. Men should learn
pure religious precepts directly from the sources in Christian
antiquity — from the Scriptures and from the Fathers. His books
were read in homes throughout northern Europe. All the world
paid him homage as he became virtually the literary and intellectual arbiter of his age. "Every day," he once exclaimed, "letters
come to me from the most distant regions, from kings, princes,
prelates, from learned men, and even from people of whose very
existence I did not know!"[1] Although he denied that the motto on
his coat of arms, *concedo nulli* ("I yield to none"), referred to himself and was therefore an arrogant statement, it was fully evident
that nearly all intellectuals did defer to him as their acknowledged
leader. His rise to such pre-eminence was by no means predictable,
for the circumstances of his birth and his beginnings were inaus-
picious indeed.

I

Erasmus was born in 1469, in Gouda in the Netherlands, the
illegitimate son of a priest, Rogerius Gerardus. Herasmus, as he

---

[1] The monumental edition of the correspondence provides a massive
documentation for the extent of Erasmus' exchanges with people in all
walks of life, but especially with Humanists and Reformers: P. S. Allen
(ed.), *Opus epistolarum Desiderii Erasmi Roterodami* (12 vols.; Oxford,
1906–58).

was christened, had such a complex about his birth that he later set the date at 1466 in order to imply that his older brother and he had been born in wedlock before his father took orders. Erasmus' complexes make his unusual sensitivity and his desire to equal and excel psychologically explicable.

He was schooled under the Brethren of the Common Life at nearby Deventer, 1475–84. There he learned the simple piety and devotion reflected in that great masterpiece of voluntaristic mysticism which was produced in those very years, Thomas à Kempis' *Imitation of Christ*. There he also developed an invincible love for the "safe" classics — those works of virtuous men of antiquity, such as Cicero and Seneca, that were useful for moral instruction — and for Jerome and other Latin Fathers. The year before Erasmus left Deventer, Alexander Hegius, friend of Rudolph Agricola, the father of German Humanism, came as headmaster of the school.

When their father died in 1484, Erasmus and his brother Peter were sent by their guardians to school in S'Hertogenbosch. After two or three years their guardians persuaded them to enter into monasteries. In 1492, while an Augustinian canon at Steyn, Erasmus was ordained a priest. During these formative years Erasmus developed certain patterns of thinking, metaphorically and moralistically, which he retained ever after.

Two years after his ordination Erasmus devised an escape from the galling seclusion with unintellectual monks: he traveled as secretary to the Bishop of Cambrai. In August of 1495, he entered the Collège de Montaigu of the University of Paris, a severe center for scholastic study. His secular interests grew more evident during his stay in Paris, where he came into contact with intellectuals such as the French Humanist Gaguin. He first broke into print with a small contribution to one of Gaguin's historical volumes; this infected him with a pride of authorship that never left him.

In the spring of 1499, as tutor to William Blount, Baron Mountjoy, he made that first trip to England which proved so portentous for his whole career. During the two or three months which he spent at Oxford he heard John Colet's lectures on the Epistle of St. Paul to the Romans and became Colet's close personal friend. Colet was both a man acquainted with the Italian humanist ideal of the return to ancient sources of wisdom and a man of great theological concern. He was deeply imbued with Paul's sense of the depth of man's sin and his absolute dependence upon God's forgiving grace.

Colet's influence upon Erasmus was decisive, for he won him for the cause of religion and Christian letters. Erasmus resisted Colet's suggestion that he do a commentary on Moses or Isaiah, protesting that "this task demands not a tyro but a highly experienced emperor!"[2] Once the idea of applying his humanistic scholarship to biblical studies and to the revival of Christian antiquity had been planted in Erasmus' mind, however, it grew — slowly at first, but with an irresistible power through the years until it became his all-consuming passion. As a thirty-year-old man he took up the intensive study of Greek in order to possess the key instrument for his studies, above all for an understanding of the epistles of Paul. Five years later he could write to Colet how eagerly he was "pursuing sacred letters and chafing at every hindrance and delay."

Those five years were years of penury and sacrifice during which he eked out a precarious existence dependent upon doles from patrons, gifts from friends, and a small income from the publication of a collection of eight hundred Latin *Adages* in 1500. In a monastic library he came across a book of tremendous importance for his intellectual development, Lorenzo Valla's *Annotations on the New Testament*, which he had Badius publish in 1505. In the preface to that edition Erasmus argued, on the example of Jerome and Valla, for the importance of philology in the study of the Scriptures.

Erasmus was soon to see Italy, the homeland of Valla. On a visit to England he was engaged by the king's physician as a companion for his two sons. In September of 1506 they left for the South.

---

[2] *Opus epistolarum*, I, 248.

After spending a year at his tutorial duties in Bologna, he went to live with the famous Renaissance publisher Aldus Manutius in Venice. Aldus published an edition of the *Adages* enlarged to more than three thousand entries, many of them Greek proverbs. "Together we attacked a work," Erasmus recalled later, "I writing while Aldus gave my copy to the press." With a new pupil, Alexander Stuart, the illegitimate son of James IV of Scotland, he traveled to Siena and Rome before returning to England. In England he stayed at the home of Sir Thomas More and then taught at Cambridge University.

Erasmus already enjoyed a European reputation so that his trip in 1514 to Basel, where he had decided to live in order to be near his publisher Johannes Froben, took on the nature of a triumphal procession. In Strassburg the humanist sodality led by Jakob Wimpfeling welcomed him in ecstasy, and the city of Basel stirred with excitement when the greatest man of letters passed through its gates to make his home there. Except for a brief period in Louvain, which he found uncongenial because of ignorant monks and "sophists," and short excursions to England and elsewhere, he lived and worked in Basel for many years.

But Basel itself was rapidly developing into a center of Swiss Reformed Protestantism under the leadership of Oecolampadius. In 1524 Erasmus was pressured into writing his treatise *De libero arbitrio*, on free will, against Luther. But he found the Basel reformers even more radical than Luther, with their highly spiritualized sacramental doctrine, their dismissal of ancient rites and ceremonies, and their refusal to acknowledge the supremacy of the Roman See. In April of 1529 he left Basel, going down the Rhine on a river boat to Freiburg im Breisgau and the security of orthodox Hapsburg lands. The relative quiet of that lovely city, with its beautiful cathedral, set in the Black Forest with its rushing mountain streams appealed to weary Erasmus. He stayed there six years, then returned to Basel in the summer of 1535 to see his work on Ecclesiastes through the press and to continue his work on Origen. Too, he hoped to find medical help in Basel, for he was now dreadfully ill and was preparing to die. The end came in June of 1536, and he died, though unattended by a priest, with a prayer on his lips. The prince of the Humanists and philosopher of Christ died with the comfort of that elemental wisdom of faith which he shared with many common men throughout the centuries. He was honored by Protestant Basel with a magnificent funeral and he lies buried in the left aisle of the great cathedral.

II

The German philosopher Schopenhauer once asked whether it is necessary in order to praise the dead to deceive the living. Erasmus was a great intellectual and an outsized man of history, and yet he was a man with obvious faults. It must be said, to his credit, that he was aware of more of his weaknesses than most men are willing to admit to themselves.

Erasmus looks out from those familiar portraits by great artists such as Holbein, Quentin Metsys, or Dürer with alert, somewhat quizzical eyes. He had the blue eyes and yellow hair of a genuine Dutchman and added the style "Roterodamus" to his Latinized names, Desiderius Erasmus, in order to stress his loyalty to his native land. "His manner and his conversation," wrote his young Basel admirer Beatus Rhenanus, "were polished, affable, and even charming."

And yet to someone as rough and ready as Elector Frederick the Wise of Saxony there seemed to be something a bit indirect and devious about Erasmus' manner. During their famous meeting in the Cologne inn, at the time of the coronation of Charles V, Erasmus assured Frederick that Luther's only mistake was in attacking the crown of the pope and the belly of the monks. Frederick commented afterwards that Erasmus was a curious little man, for one never quite knew how one stood with him. Erasmus was extremely sensitive to his environment and open to immediate impressions. For this reason, with the orthodox he could sound like a good churchman, with the Humanists he could be gentlemanly, and with the reformers he could begin speaking of his *philosophia evangelica.* It was less a matter of calculated duplicity than it was of his ability to see so much positive good in the views of all the men around him.

His personality was a complicated *complexio oppositorum.* On one hand, Erasmus had enormous perseverence and drive, living an ascetic and carefully regulated life in the interest of his scholarly production. On the other hand, he was a real valetudinarian, he pampered himself, he loved the amenities of life and the comforts wealth provides, and he was almost a genuine hypochondriac. He secured a dispensation from the requirement of eating fish on Friday, for he believed fish made him sick. His heart, he wrote was Catholic, but his stomach was Lutheran. He was capable, in the interest of his personal freedom and intellectual independence, of turning down positions which would have brought him the highest worldly honors: an appointment by the duke of Bavaria, a pension from Archduke Ferdinand of Austria, and possibly a cardinal's hat from Pope Paul III. Then again he could be vainglorious and condescending, mean and petty, cruel and cutting in controversy against foes great or small.

At ease among the intellectuals of all nations, he was a genuine cosmopolitan who could say that he preferred to be "a citizen of the world, common to all, or rather, a stranger to all." And yet he felt most secure in the Empire, whether on the lower or the upper Rhine, and managed to arouse the hostility of French Humanists such as Guillaume Budé and Etienne Dolét, who labeled him "a jealous detractor of the French name." A certain sense of northern cultural rivalry with the Italian Humanists played a part in his crusade against the pedantic Ciceronians. He could boldly attack the crimes and follies of pontiffs and the mighty of this world, and at the same time confess that he had not the strength for martyrdom. He feared that if put to the test he, like Peter, would deny Christ. Delineating the character of a man so complicated is no easy matter, and it is no wonder at all that even the experts make widely varying assessments of his person and work.

Four different views of Erasmus predominate in the great mountain of literature about the man. The first interpretation characterizes him as a man of weak character whose timidity and weak will kept him from the consequences of his own premises. He is portrayed as a little man fearful for his reputation, a trimmer who was Lutheran in his heart of hearts, but who conformed to Catholicism in the interest of his comfortable external circumstances.

The second interpretation represents him as a devotee of reason who followed this natural light through storm and stress to the very end. It represents him as a forerunner of the eighteenth-century Enlightenment whose ideas were only temporarily submerged by the medievalism of the Protestant movement and the Counter-Reformation before emerging again to make a world-historical impact.

A third interpretation portrays Erasmus as the forerunner of Luther, the John the Baptist of the evangelical revival. "Erasmus laid the egg and Luther hatched it" was a saying current during his own lifetime. According to this view Erasmus, with his criticism of the church, his emphasis on the original texts of the Scriptures, and his Christocentrism, took the first step toward the Reformation. Luther, with his Pauline Christology, took the second step and thereby left Erasmus a full stride behind. Erasmus pointed out where pruning needed to be done, commented the young humanist poet Eobanus Hessus, but Luther, a greater man because of him, took the axe and did the pruning.

Each of these three views contains a modicum of truth, and yet a fourth interpretation comes nearer to the heart of the matter and of the man. Erasmus was a man with his own positive reform program, in part critical, for the most part constructive. He had his own conception of which tools and materials would be most useful in building a new platform for reform, namely, the tools of scholarship and the materials provided by Christian antiquity. Philological accuracy, a historico-critical sense, and diligent labor would enable the grammarian to reveal the pure spiritual gold in the Scriptures and in the Church Fathers. The heavenly treasure of the philosophy of Christ would, when taught to the learned and brought to the simple, infuse new spiritual life into all Christendom. Erasmus clung doggedly and courageously to this program even after his early optimism was dashed to the ground by the wild winds of the Reformation. He was in his heart a loyal Catholic, even though cool and reserved compared with strong party men like Eck, Aleander, Latomus, or Edward Lee, and highly spiritual and liberal by post-Tridentine standards of orthodoxy. Erasmus commands our respect for his constancy and loyal devotion to this program, whatever its limitations may have been, no matter how fierce the assaults of opponents to the right or left of him became. Erasmus complained that he was "a heretic to both sides." He retained his poise, however, even when isolated by events, and he stood alone with spirit.

III

An essential preliminary to the realization of Erasmus' humanist reform program was clearing away the thickets of idle ceremonies, superstition, obscurantism and ignorance, the brambles of vice and corruption, and the strongholds of graft and religious tyranny. Only when the ground had been cleared of abuses and the soil well prepared could the good seed of the philosophy of Christ be planted and bear a full harvest. Erasmus' satirical writings were an important part of his total program. He was neither the first nor the only voice calling for reform. The *verus imperator* Innocent III had charged the Fourth Lateran Council in 1215 to undertake reforms. The Conciliarist William Durandus the Younger had coined the phrase *reformatio in capite et in membris,* reformation in head and in members. The general of the Augustinian order, Egidio da Viterbo, had pleaded with all the rhetorical power at his command that the Fifth Lateran Council (1512–17) should carry out a thorough reform. Shrill medieval preachers and suave humanist orators cried out for reform. But Erasmus, through his satirical writings, did more than any other man to express the popular feelings of impatience, amusement, anger, and disgust at the gross mischief and abysmal failings of men in all levels of society, but especially in the church. Many felt that his dry corrosive laugh damaged the medieval church more than did the loud cries of Luther.

The most famous biographer of Erasmus, Johan Huizinga, observed that Erasmus was his most brilliant and profound when he was being humorous in an ironic way. This dimension of his satirical works, quite as much as their wit and entertaining qualities, explains the fantastic popularity and impact of his *Praise of Folly* which has appeared in more than six hundred editions through the centuries, and the *Colloquies*, which have been published in more than three hundred editions down to the present time. In the *Praise of Folly*, which he composed while a houseguest of Sir Thomas More upon his return from Italy (hence, *Encomium Moriae*), he poked fun at the weaknesses and follies, the fetishes and vices of men in all walks of life — soldiers and merchants, priests and kings, and even scholars such as he. "We have praised Folly," he commented to More in the preface, "not quite foolishly!"

In the *Colloquies*, which he began originally as pedagogical dialogues for his pupils in Paris and supplemented with new material through the decades which followed, he mocked the powers attributed to relics, repetitious prayers, pilgrimages, social fopperies, and, above all, all monkish ignorance and superstition. Such was his reputation for clever satire that when the dialogue *Julius exclusus* appeared, in which Peter shuts the doors of heaven on the warrior pope Julius II, whom Erasmus had seen entering Bologna on a white horse wearing a full suit of armor, it was generally believed that Erasmus was its author. He stoutly denied having written it, but few believed him. Most scholars today suspect that it originated in the circle of antipapal French Humanists in Paris.

Erasmus reserved his greatest scorn for the monks and his deepest contempt for the scholastic doctors. The louse-bitten obscurantist monks opposed all good learning and paraded about as though there were no Christianity without a cowl. "Monasticism is not piety!" he wrote in the *Enchiridion*. Erasmus may have inherited a basic suspicion of scholastic theology from his nonspeculative *devotio moderna* educators and humanist friends and may have reacted negatively to the scholastic studies in Jean Standonck's Collège de Montaigu, but he certainly derived much of his deeply ingrained hostility to both of the scholastic *viae* from John Colet. "Twenty doctors expound one text in twenty days," Colet growled, "and with an antitheme of half an inch some of them draw a thread nine days long. They usually look on no more Scriptures than they find in their Duns [Scotus]."[3] On one occasion when Erasmus had praised Thomas Aquinas, Colet broke out like one possessed and exclaimed: "Why do you preach up that writer to me? For, without a full share of presumption, he never would have defined anything in that rash and overweening manner; and without something of a worldly spirit he would never have so tainted the whole doctrine of Christ with his profane philosophy."[4]

Erasmus did not have a metaphysical bone in his frail body and had no real feeling for the philosophical concerns of scholastic theology. To him they were quibblers and "word players," logic choppers, syllogism manipulators, and pedantic abusers of the Latin language. But his gravest charge against them was that they damaged true devotion and piety by their speculative methods and impractical theologizing. In the *Ratio verae theologiae* he wrote about the scholastics in a less than complimentary way:

> We may therefore philosophize upon the sacred writings
> in so far as our industry leads us to the conclusions which

---

[3] F. Seebohm, *The Oxford Reformers* (London, n.d.), pp. 17–18, cited in Frederick B. Artz, *Renaissance Humanism 1300–1500* (Kent, Ohio, 1966), p. 75.

[4] *Opus epistolarum*, IV, 520–23; *Opera* (10 vols.; Leiden, 1703–6), III, 458, F; also cited in Ernest Hunt, *Dean Colet and His Theology* (London, 1956), p. 9.

Paul has recorded. But those who have not fixed for themselves this limit but choose this profession in order that they
may bring forth any kind of paradoxes or novelties by
which they may win the admiration of the populace, who
are always ready to admire insipid things, are vanity-
mongers, not theologians. . . . Now into the sacred assem-
blies themselves this ostentation has penetrated. . . . I see
the simple multitude panting and hanging eagerly upon
the lips of the orator, expecting food for their souls, desiring
to learn how they may return better to their homes, and
there some theologaster . . . ventilates some frigid and
perplexing question from Scotus or Ockham.[5]

Erasmus had discovered a source of purer theology than that
of the scholastics— in the Scriptures and in the writings of those
prisco theologi, the theologians of old, the devout and learned
patristic writers. "I had rather be a pious theologian with Chrysostom," Erasmus confessed, "than an invincible one with Scotus!"[6]

IV

In his monarchic drive to conquer and restore Christian antiquity, Erasmus went far beyond the achievements of any Italian
Humanists and excelled all of his northern contemporaries. Here
was a field in which his agile and powerful intellect had a wide
range within which to maneuver. Here was material sufficiently
difficult to demand his best scholarly talents as he sought to pene-
trate to the inner core of the ancient oracles. "Scholars are the
heart and eyes of the world!" Emerson once pronounced. Erasmus
turned scholarship itself into an instrument of reform, an Archimedean lever with which the scholar, standing on a point outside
mundane affairs and earthly battles, could strive to move the
world.

He worked with an enthusiasm that was virtually a compulsion.
He wrote feverishly, "standing on one foot," as he once put it.

---

[5] *Opera,* V. 135-36, F and A. The text of the *Ratio verae theologiae* is
also to be found in Hajo and Annemarie Holborn (ed.), *Ausgewählte
Werke* (Munich, 1933), pp. 177-305.

[6] Ibid., 137, B.

"My mind is in such a glow over Jerome that I imagine myself to be actually inspired!" he exclaimed. He called his study in Basel a "mill" where he doggedly ground out prefaces, learned editions, translations, and commentaries for eight solid years in his period of peak productivity. "The eagerness for writing grows with writing," he expostulated. The texts he produced would themselves be powerful agents for reform by providing a new living theological essence and inspiration for the revitalization of religion. In his *Life of St. Jerome* Erasmus described his plan for restoring the ancient treasures to the church and expressed his faith in the inherent force and dynamism of truth itself. "Although the artisan can bring out the sparkle and luster of any jewel," he wrote, "no imitation ever comes to possess the inner quality of a jewel. Truth has its own energy which no artifice can equal!"[7]

Erasmus' major triumph as a textual scholar was the publication of the New Testament in 1516, a pioneer work based upon Greek manuscripts. The Complutensian Polyglot Bible produced at the same time under the sponsorship of Cardinal Ximenes in Spain was far more carefully done and was a superior publication. Erasmus was in a hurry as usual and was satisfied to base his text upon poor Greek manuscripts, a fourteenth-century one for the Gospels, two of the same vintage for the Book of Acts and the Epistles, and a poor eighth-century one for the Apocalypse. His Latin translation which he appended was no great improvement upon the Vulgate and he made some arbitrary changes without sufficient textual or contextual justification. Nevertheless, for all of its technical shortcomings, Erasmus' work gave evidence of a critical spirit not evident in Cardinal Ximenes' edition. Lorenzo Valla's influence made itself felt in Erasmus' treatment of the text and translation. He omitted, for example, the verse in I John [5:8] with the trinitarian formula because it was not to be found in the Greek manuscripts, though in later editions he included it

---

[7] Wallace K. Ferguson (ed.), *Opuscula* (Leiden, 1933), p. 136. Cited in Myron P. Gilmore, *Humanists and Jurists* (Cambridge, Mass., 1963), p. 107, slightly altered.

again under ecclesiastical pressure. He substituted the word *sermo* for *verbum* in order to bring out the full theological implications of the Greek vocable *logos,* the Word made flesh.

His critical spirit showed through in other aspects of his biblical studies. He was quite certain that Paul was not the author of the Epistle to the Hebrews and that John had not written the Apocalypse. He recognized that Dionysius the Areopagite, converted by Paul's sermon on Mars' Hill, was not the author of the Neoplatonic writings ascribed to him (but actually belonging to the fifth century). However, very close textual work was not Erasmus' forte. His true *métier* was a literary form which he devised for himself and perfected with practice, the paraphrase, which was midway between a loose translation and a running commentary. Between the years 1517 and 1524 he did a paraphrase of the entire New Testament, omitting only the Apocalypse, which he instinctively disliked and did not know how to handle. Protestant England required that the 1548 English translation of the *Paraphrases* be placed in every parish church in the realm, where many are still to be found on the book bench next to the Bible.

Erasmus' herculean labors on editions of the patristic writings will always remain a great monument to his dedication and perseverance. If the great edition of his own model and favorite Latin Father, Jerome, was his first and greatest success, like Michelangelo's David, he pressed on to make available to the learned world a major corpus of Latin and Greek writings. He followed up Jerome with the Latin Cyprian in 1520, the Pseudo-Arnobius in 1522, Hilary in 1523, Ambrose in 1527, and Augustine in 1528. Perhaps an even greater service to the Western learned world than editing the Latin Fathers, many of whose works were in circulation either as such or in *Sententiae* and in scholastic quotations, was his translating and editing of the Greek Fathers.

The Greek revival played an important role in the Italian Renaissance during the second half of the fifteenth century. Erasmus now undertook to complement the revival of the Platonic and Neoplatonic corpus through the efforts of Ficino, Pico and other Italian Humanists by producing scholarly texts of the Greek Christian authors. In 1526, he published Irenaeus in Latin. In 1530 he brought out Chrysostom in Latin, and in 1532 he edited Basil in Greek — the first Greek author, in fact, ever printed in the Empire. In 1536 he was working on Origen in Latin nearly to the time of his death. He also did various translations from Athanasius.

It was fairly easy for the pedantic Ciceronians to find egregious errors in the work of an editor as prolific as Erasmus. The supercilious Julius Caesar Scaliger sniffed that "Erasmus' Jerome is full of sorry blunders." But as a piece of scholarly engineering, Erasmus' editions of the patristic writings loom larger in mass and tower in significance above the writings of all of his harshest critics put together. Erasmus had his blind spots and strong prejudices unworthy of a man of scholarship and religion. He found Hebrew a primitive and uncultivated tongue and, because of a strong anti-Judaic predisposition, never cultivated a knowledge of Jewish letters or of cabalistic mysticism. But considering the broad scope of his learning and usual liberal spirit, his limitations should not be overemphasized. Goethe once observed that when we criticize a great man of history we should be sure to stand on our knees.

V

Erasmus' deft critical thrusts at follies and evils in society and in the church and his lifelong labors to make available the wisdom of Christian antiquity served the cause of his own positive efforts to promote the *philosophia Christi* as a powerful force for reform and renewal. The recovery of true theology required a return to the pure gospel, removing the triple palimpsest of glosses, traditions, and scholastic complications. Simplicity should replace subtlety, inwardness should supplant mere external conformity, spirituality should displace mechanical practices, and Christ and his teachings should become the central focus of the religious life. Erasmus never laid out his *philosophia Christi* in a major systematic work such as Melanchthon's *Loci* or Calvin's *Institutes*. But the writing which contains the most characteristic expression of his religious thought is the *Enchiridion militis Christiani,* the dagger or handbook of the Christian knight, written in 1501 and published in 1503 in the Netherlands. He wrote it for a hot-tempered and rowdy soldier named John at the request of the wife who was worried about her husband's soul and sought better counsel than the scholastic doctors offered. The emphasis of the *Enchiridion* is upon undogmatic ethical piety and genuine love, in contrast to ritual or the outward forms of religion and worthless practices such as fasting, pilgrimages, the invocation of saints, or purchase of indulgences. The *Enchiridion* was not popular at first, but soon enjoyed an enormous vogue from Germany to Spain. Antischolastic, antimonastic, and antiascetic in tone, it was highly moralistic in emphasis and drained Christianity of its apocalyptic and deeply mystical elements.

In the introduction to the New Testament entitled the *Paraclesis* he summarized briefly the main features of his christocentric moral philosophy, expanding this unsystematic statement into a work entitled *Ratio seu Methodus* ("The Method of Theology"). In the *Paraclesis* he described his philosophy of Christ in these words:

> This kind of philosophy is situated more truly in the emotions than in syllogisms, it is a life rather than a disputation, an afflatus rather than erudition, a transformation rather than reason. To be learned is the lot of only a few; but no one is unable to be a Christian, no one is unable to be pious, and I add this boldly, no one is unable to be a theologian. For that which is most of all in accordance with nature descends easily into the minds of all. But what else is the *philosophia Christi,* which he himself calls a rebirth, than the instauration of a well founded nature?[8]

Understanding the precise nature of Erasmus' christocentric

8 *Opera,* V, 141, F, The *Paraclesis.* Also in Hajo and Annemarie Holborn (ed.), *Ausgewählte Werke,* pp. 139–49. See the fine translation of the *Para-*

theology is crucial for an appreciation of the whole thrust of his life's work. Essentially three views of Christ's person and work are possible: the theological or religious belief which accepts the mystery of trinitarian dogma and high Christology; the basically moralistic emphasis upon Christ's example and teachings; and historico-philosophical interpretations deviating in varying degrees of radicality from the traditional ecclesiastical understanding of the nature of Christ and the meaning of his incarnation.

There can be little doubt that the center of gravity in Erasmus' philosophy of Christ is basically moralistic, although it in no way excludes elements of the first and third emphases. In conformity with the first view, Erasmus is impeccably correct in his orthodox dogmatic definitions; nevertheless he does not plumb the depths of Christology understood soteriologically in the manner of Paul, Augustine, Bernard, or even Colet. In relation to the third view, Erasmus does not venture far from the protecting shadow of the church. Nevertheless, he confesses in the *De libero arbitrio* that if it were not for the authoritative statements of the church he could be a skeptic on certain points of belief. He feels perfectly at home, however, with the moralistic emphasis and so defines the real theologian in the *Paraclesis*:

> In my eyes he is a true theologian who, not by syllogisms craftily turned, but in affection and in his very countenance and eyes and in his very life teaches that riches are to be scorned, ... that injuries must not be revenged, ... that death is even to be longed for by the devout as if it were nothing else than a passage to immortality. . . . If anyone displays these qualities in his moral conduct, he, in short, is a great doctor.[9]

The strong moralistic strain and the nonspeculative cast of his thought combined with a Platonic spiritualism to color Erasmus' entire reading of Paul. If one were to ask for a single clue to Erasmus' theology, the answer would clearly have to be the

---

clesis in John C. Olin (ed.), *Desiderius Erasmus: Christian Humanism and the Reformation* (New York, 1965), pp. 92–106.

[9] *Opera*, V, 140, E–F.

Pauline passage, "the written code kills, but the Spirit gives life." The basic formula in his system of piety is the upward ascent from things visible to things invisible. In the *Enchiridion* Erasmus advised: "Among the philosophers I would prefer you to follow the Platonists, for . . . in very many of their opinions and in their way of speaking they approach as closely as possible the prophetic and gospel pattern."[10] Erasmus was no Platonist and he abhored and ignored the fantastic speculative systems of the Neoplatonists. He was, nevertheless, influenced by the Platonic component in medieval theology and in the Latin classics, and in the Greek and Latin patristic writers with whom he spent his waking hours. The resultant consistent dualism between spirit and flesh, symbolized by his anthropological dichotomy of soul and body, which he at times refines into a trichotomy of spirit, soul, and body, affected his understanding of nearly all phases of theology.

His moralistic spiritualism was reflected in his exegetical exposition of the Scriptures. He stressed a spiritual interpretation as the religiously significant reading of the text rather than the historico-critical or the literal interpretation, even though he rejected the fourfold-interpretation of the Scriptures inherited by medieval tradition from sources as ancient as Origen and embalmed in Nicholas de Lyra's standard work on exegesis, the *Postillae*. His emphasis upon spirit over letter led him to favor a spiritualized view of the Lord's Supper, though he remained formally orthodox and subservient to the authoritative definitions of the church.

His moralistic spiritualism instilled in him that universalistic outlook which he found so highly developed in Greek Fathers such as Justin Martyr, Gregory Nazianzen, or Clement of Alexandria. The spermatic *logos* or the spirit of Christ, he ventured to hope in the colloquy *The Religious Banquet,* perhaps "diffuses itself farther than we imagine and there are more saints than we have in our catalogue." He sometimes found things in the ancients, in heathen authors and poets, so chaste, holy, and divine that he could not

---

[10] *Opera,* V, 7, F.

persuade himself but that "when they wrote them they were divinely inspired." Impressed by the wisdom of Cicero, Cato, and Plato, Erasmus has Nephalius say in the dialogue: "Indeed, it was a wonderful elevation of the mind in a man, who did not know Christ nor the Holy Scriptures: and therefore I can scarce forbear, when I read such things of such men, but cry out, *Sancte Socrates, ora pro nobis!*" To this, Erasmus has Chrysoglottus reply: "And I have much to do sometimes to keep myself from entertaining good hopes for the souls of Virgil and Horace."

Most crucial of all, however, both as the critical determinant of the heart of Erasmus' theology and as the factor which most precisely defines his place in the religious revolution of the day was the decisive influence of his moralistic spiritualism upon his understanding of Paul. After his early encounter with Colet's lectures on the Epistle to the Romans he might very well have developed into a Paulinist with a high Christology and strong soteriological emphasis, for Colet appreciated the stress of Paul upon the comprehensiveness of carnal man's envelopment in sin and his desperate need for God's forgiving grace. Erasmus developed instead an ethical Paulinism which skimmed over the agonizing depths of Paul's radical sin-grace theology.

If Paul used the term "flesh" to denote man in a lost state of estrangement from God and "spirit" to describe the whole man restored to his proper trusting relation to God, Erasmus gave a moralistic and spiritualistic interpretation to these words. When doing his paraphrases on such verses (so central for Reformation theology) as Rom. 1:17 or Rom. 3:21, he basically repeated Paul's terminology and his phrases could be understood in a Paulinist sense. But in reality he associated flesh with the downward sensuous drives of man and spirit with the Godward soul-uplifting aspects of man's being. Similarly he consistently interpreted Paul's antithesis of "law" and "gospel" as a contrast of "Jewish ceremonial law" and the new "spiritual law of Christ." His reading of Paul, then, was not the evangelical interpretation in depth which was to provide the revolutionary religious force of the century.

Erasmus was so hopeful that the pure and simple *philosophia Christi*, freed of all traditional encumbrances, would renew the world that he favored teaching it to the masses and instructing those in high places how they might apply it to their rule in society. In the *Paraclesis* Erasmus penned what may well be his most famous lines:

> I would to God that the plowman would sing a text of the Scripture at his plow and that the weaver would hum them to the tune of his shuttle. . . . I wish that the traveler would expel the weariness of his journey with this pastime. And, to be brief, I wish that all communication of the Christian would be of the Scriptures.[11]

In a surge of optimism Erasmus indulged in an ecstatic vision, hailing the dawn of a golden age. In the year 1516 he penned his *Institutio principis Christiani*, an instruction for young Prince Charles, soon to inherit the Hapsburg lands and to be crowned Emperor of the Holy Roman Empire. The best prince must emulate Christ in ruling in love for the highest good of his subjects. In the *Querela pacis*, or complaint of peace, he chided the Christian princes for their incessant warfare contrary to the commands of the Prince of Peace.

VI

Historical judgments on the impact of Erasmus' reform efforts have varied down to the present time nearly as much as have the estimates of his own person and writings. Perhaps, then, one more opinion can be tolerated which ventures to underline the tremendous significance of Erasmus for Western culture and his great importance for the Reformation. As a man of letters Erasmus is one northern Humanist who can stand shoulder to shoulder with the best intellects of the Italian Renaissance. As a figure and as a

---

[11] *Opera*, V, 140, C. Also in Hajo and Annemarie Holborn (ed.), *Ausgewählte Werke*, 139–49.

symbol Erasmus loomed large in the eyes of his contemporaries; he has retained his stature through the centuries as a cherished favorite of learned men everywhere. In many respects he fits in beautifully with the programs of Italian Humanism, cultivating the classics, showing civic concern, and being antimonastic in spirit. But with his enormous labors for the *Restitutio Christianismi* and the *Restauratio pietatis* ("Restoration of Piety") Erasmus became the great archetype of the dedicated Christian Humanist.

The assessments of Erasmus' relation to the old church and his effect upon Roman Catholicism have differed widely. Recent studies have tended to see him as basically a good Catholic, especially during his last years. He was fairly sincere in those long apologies in which he asserted that he had always been concerned for the welfare of the true faith and had always remained obedient to the teaching office and loyal to the church. Nevertheless, there is some justification for the conviction of the papal legate, Aleander, a onetime friend, that Erasmus with his keen wit and cultural religiosity was damaging the church more than Luther could hurt it. Ignatius Loyola related that he "nearly froze" when he read the *Enchiridion,* because it lacked the fervor of true devotion. In 1537 the Spanish Inquisition prohibited the reading of Erasmus' work in Castilian and expurgated his writings in Latin. The Council of Trent ordered his books to be carefully censored and some were proscribed by the Index. Some contemporary Catholic historians naively assume in retrospect that because he was an opponent of Luther he must be embraced as a defender of the faith. Others, such as the great Catholic ecumenicist Joseph Lortz, feel that Erasmus' philosophy of Christ as expressed in the *Enchiridion* lacked the churchly patina and that Erasmus, while correct, was cold in contrast to the prophetic evangelical Luther.

Erasmus was horrified at Luther, who could cite with gusto the words of II Cor. 6: 4–5, "Let us approve ourselves . . . in tumults!" Scholars like Erasmus have always been more inclined to take a position rather than a stand. He believed that due to the Evangelicals literature was "everywhere declining." Erasmus was jealous of Luther and for petty as well as conscientious reasons tried to keep Froben from printing Luther's works. But Erasmus only very reluctantly took up the pen and wrote against Luther in 1524. Luther congratulated him for selecting a central theme on free will in his *De libero arbitrio,* thus reaching for Luther's jugular vein! But perhaps the most serious blow that Erasmus delivered to Luther and Protestantism he landed indirectly through the person of Ulrich Zwingli. Zwingli was much influenced by "that other spirit" or "spiritualism" of Erasmus which was reflected in his sacramental theory and which made the breach with Luther unbridgeable at Marburg (1529).

Yet Erasmus' main contribution to the Protestant Reformation was positive, though not by intention. For just as in the twentieth century decades of intense preoccupation with textual and higher criticism in modern biblical scholarship have been followed by an emphasis upon biblical theology, so the textual and philological concerns of scholarship from Valla to Erasmus were followed by the biblical theology of the Magisterial Reformers. Luther's sermon was based upon Erasmus' text in Greek.

Erasmus should not be judged exclusively from a humanist or Catholic or Protestant perspective. History passed Erasmus by and played strange tricks on him in passing. Viewed solely in terms of his own vision of reform and his personal efforts to realize the high hopes he cherished, Erasmus' career as a reformer must be pronounced an idealistic and courageous endeavor worthy of mankind's eternal respect and gratitude.

BIBLIOGRAPHY

ERASMUS EDITIONS

Allen, P. S. (ed.). *Opus Epistolarum Desiderii Erasmi Roterodami.* 12 vols. Oxford, 1906–58.
Erasmus. *Opera.* Leclercg (ed.). 10 vols. Leiden, 1703–6.
Ferguson, Wallace K. (ed). *Opuscula.* Leiden, 1933.
Holborn, Hajo and Annemarie (eds.). *Desiderius Erasmus Roterodamus Ausgewählte Werke.* Munich, 1933.

Phillips, Margaret Mann (ed.). *The Adages of Erasmus*. Cambridge, 1964.

Reedijk, C. (ed.). *The Poems of Desiderius Erasmus*. Leiden, 1956.

Thompson, Craig (ed.). *Colloquies*. Chicago, 1965.

BIOGRAPHICAL STUDIES

Allen, P. S. *The Age of Erasmus*. Oxford, 1914.

Huizinga, Johan. *Erasmus*. New York, 1924.

————. *Erasmus and the Age of the Reformation*. (Paperback.) New York, 1957.

Hyma, Albert. *The Youth of Erasmus*. Ann Arbor, 1930.

Mestwerdt, Paul. *Die Anfänge des Erasmus*. Leipzig, 1917.

Smith, Preserved. *Erasmus: A Study of His Life, Ideals, and Place in History*. (Paperback.) New York, 1923.

————. *Erasmus*. New York, 1962.

SELECT SCHOLARLY MONOGRAPHS

Battaillon, Marcel. *Erasme en Espagne*. Paris, 1937.

Kaiser, Walter. *Praisers of Folly: Erasmus, Rabelais, Shakespeare*. Cambridge, Mass., 1963.

Kisch, Guido. *Erasmus und die Jurisprudenz seiner Zeit*. Basel, 1960.

Kohls, Ernst Wilhelm. *Die Theologie des Erasmus*. 2 vols. Basel, 1966.

Mann, Margaret. *Erasme et les débuts de la réforme française (1517–1536)*. Paris, 1934.

Nolhac, Pierre de. *Erasme en Italie*. Paris, 1888.

Phillips, Margaret Mann. *Erasmus and the Northern Renaissance*. New York, 1950.

Renaudet, Augustin. *Erasme et l'Italie*. Geneva, 1954.

————. *Erasme, sa pensée religieuse (1518–1521)*. Paris, 1926.

————. *Etudes Erasmiennes (1521–1529)*. Paris, 1939.

Ritter, Gerhard. *Erasmus und der deutsche Humanistenkreis am Oberrhein*. Freiburg im Breisgau, 1937.

Schätti, Karl. *Erasmus von Rotterdam und die Römische Kurie*. Basel, 1954.

Schottenloher, Otto. *Erasmus im Ringen um die humanistische Bildungsform*. Münster, 1933.

Stange, Carl. *Erasmus und Julius II. Eine Legende*. Berlin, 1939.

SELECT SCHOLARLY ARTICLES

Caspari, Fritz. "Erasmus on the Social Functions of Christian Humanism," *Journal of the History of Ideas*, VIII (1947), 78–106.

Ferguson, Wallace K. "Renaissance Tendencies in the Religious Thought of Erasmus," *Journal of the History of Ideas*, XV (1954), 499–508.

Gilmore, Myron P. "Erasmus and the Cause of Christian Humanism: The Last Years, 1529–1536," *Humanists and Jurists: Six Studies in the Renaissance*. Cambridge, Mass., 1963.

Gundersheimer, Werner L. "Erasmus, Humanism, and the Christian Cabala," *Journal of the Warburg and Courtauld Institutes*, XXVI (1963).

Rice, Eugene F., Jr. "Erasmus and the Religious Tradition," *Journal of the History of Ideas*, XI (1950), 387–411.

Thompson, Craig R. "Erasmus as Internationalist and Cosmopolitan," *Archiv für Reformationsgeschichte*, XLVI (1955), 167–95.

PART THREE

PROTESTANT REFORM

CHAPTER FOUR

MARTIN LUTHER

F. Edward Cranz

Martin Luther confronted and reformulated in an age of crisis the most profound possibilities of Western Christianity. If we are to understand him, we must first see his place within the general movement of Christianity in the late medieval period. What did Luther confront as an unquestioned Christian inheritance, and where did he find that choice and even innovation were thrust upon him?

I. LUTHER'S HISTORICAL CONTEXT

Luther's unquestioned inheritance consisted of the basic dogmas of the early church. A trinitarian God created all things out of nothing; God in the person of the Son became incarnate as Jesus Christ; through Christ, God's grace is given to sinful men, and through him they attain to salvation. In the interpretation and explanation of this inheritance, tensions and options had emerged during the long history of Christianity. Three areas of uncertainty and controversy were of particular importance for Luther's age.

In the first place, and of most significance for Luther's early development, there were the two opposing tendencies characterized as Augustinianism and Pelagianism. All Christians agreed that men needed God's grace if they were to be saved, but on the Augustinian side the part played by grace was maximized as against what could be done through human freedom and responsibility. In Pelagianism, human freedom and responsibility were of great importance, even in the area of grace and salvation.

86

Luther, in this disputed area, begins with a commitment to the Augustinian emphasis on the overriding importance of grace.

In the second place, there was the problem of the relation of what is specifically Christian in the life of man and in society to what is merely natural, secular, worldly. The best-known medieval answer was that of Thomas Aquinas. Man has a natural or worldly goal which he can reach by his natural abilities; man also has a higher, supernatural goal which he can reach only by supernatural grace. However, the natural and the supernatural aspects are never in opposition; together they constitute a Christian unity whether in one man or in a whole society. "Grace does not destroy nature but perfects it."[1] After Thomas this Christian unity of the natural and the supernatural came under many and varied attacks. There were those who would emphasize the Christian aspect and almost ignore the natural; there were those who would make the natural aspect self-sufficient and complete to the virtual exclusion of the Christian aspect. Luther's theological thinking started from the first option, and in his earliest writings the natural area has little positive importance in the life of a Christian.

Finally, there was the problem of the relation between Christianity and the thought-forms which the Christians had borrowed from the Greeks. For Luther's time this was the problem of scholastic theology, in which Aristotle dominated the natural area and in which he had great influence even within the specifically Christian domain of the supernatural. In the centuries after Thomas, there had been strong Christian opposition to this Greek influence. Nominalists like William Ockham denied many of the cosmic and universalist aspects of Thomistic scholasticism; Nicholas of Cusa tried to substitute new Christian thought-forms in place of the Greek. The dynamic of Luther's early thought was always on the side of eliminating any Greek intrusions into Christian theology.

From a broader perspective, these three pairs of opposing posi-

---

[1] Thomas Aquinas, *Summa Theologica,* I, q. 1, art. 8, ad. 2.

tions may be regarded as illustrations of a single, more basic, contrast. On one side, there was the Old Testament prophetic sense of creator and the Pauline analysis of the sinful creature; on the other side, there was the attempted adjustment of Christianity to other civilizations, in this case primarily the Greek. In his early theology, Luther's commitment was always to the prophetic and Pauline side.

In the Christianity of the Middle Ages, the essential assumption was that somehow these apparently opposed tendencies might be combined and reconciled within a Christian unity institutionally organized as the church or Christendom under the pope. One could be Augustinian without totally denying human freedom and responsibility; one could make the natural and secular area a part of a great all-embracing Christian society; and one could somehow combine Aristotle and the Bible in a great *Summa theologica.*

We have seen that Luther's commitments in his early thought always lay on the side of the prophetic and Pauline emphases. The crucial point, however, is that as we follow the development of his thinking we encounter one of the great mutations of Christian thought, comparable to those of Augustine or Thomas. A new center emerged out of a welter of conflicting tendencies; Luther found an Archimedean place-to-stand from which the whole of the old world could be moved. Much was preserved, for Luther was one of the great conservatives; and yet, more important, all was new.

Our problem now is to see how Luther's particular and unique development took its course against this general background. The story falls into two main parts. The first period, through about 1521, was one of development; Luther started from the old world and its tensions but he went on to find his new center which placed him forever outside that world. The second period, from about 1521 on, was one of reconstruction. Luther now had his new starting point, which he would never doubt, but through laborious and creative years he must try to discover all that this meant for the Christian church, for the Christian world, and for the whole life and thought of the Christian.

II. LUTHER'S DEVELOPMENT

Luther's birth and upbringing placed him squarely within a strict, late-medieval piety. Man lived within the all-embracing context of a Christian civilization; this whole civilization was for its members a temporal stage on the way to eternal salvation or eternal damnation. The goal of heaven could be reached only after God's final judgment, and for those who were serious about religion, all of life must be a preparation for this judgment. For help, one had in the first place the means of grace offered by the church in its sacraments, and one could hope for intercession by the saints, the Virgin, and even Christ himself. For an elite, the monastery was the place where one could prepare for the judgment under especially favorable conditions, but this did not mean that the struggle ever became easy. Luther later recalled the impression made on him by Prince William of Anhalt, who had become a begging friar. "I saw him with my own eyes, when I was fourteen years old in Magdeburg. . . . I saw him carrying the sack like a donkey. . . . He had so worn himself out by fasting, vigil, and asceticism that he looked like a death's head, mere skin and bones. . . . No one could look upon him without being ashamed of his own life."[2]

Luther's family came of peasant stock, but his father had turned to mining and achieved a moderate prosperity. Hans Luther planned better things for his son and intended him to become a lawyer. Accordingly in 1501 Martin entered the University at Erfurt. He took the traditional Arts course as a preparation for later professional study, and in 1505 he became a Master of Arts. The next step should have been the study of law, but in July, on the way back to school, Luther was caught in a sudden thunder-

---

[2] *Verantwortung der aufgelegten Aufruhr von Herzog Georg* ("Justification of the Tumult Imposed by Duke George"), 1533, *Luthers Werke* (Weimar, 1883——), 38, 105. (Hereafter cited as *WA*. Where the source is available in translation, the English title is cited.).

storm near Stotternheim. In terror he cried out to St. Anne that he would become a monk if his life were spared. Despite the opposition of his father, Luther two weeks later began his novitiate at the strict Augustinian monastery at Erfurt. In the context of the time, there was nothing extraordinary about the decision, which seems to have been preceded by a period of heightened religious tension. Its basis may be found most simply in Luther's later statement that he intended "to escape hell by becoming a monk,"[3] or when he tells us, "I was acting in deepest seriousness; I was one who terribly feared the last judgment and who nevertheless with all my heart wished to be saved."[4]

Luther's career as a monk may first be described in terms of his external progress. In 1507 he was ordained as a priest and celebrated his first mass. In 1512 he won his doctorate in theology and began to lecture on the Bible. We have for the next years manuscripts of his lectures on the Psalms (1513–15) and Romans (1515–16) and student notes of his lectures on Galatians (1516–17) and Hebrews (1517–18). Meanwhile, Luther had begun to take an increasingly active part in the affairs of his order. In 1510 he went to Rome with another monk to plead the case of seven of the Augustinian monasteries. In 1511 he was elected subprior of the Wittenberg Monastery, and in 1515 he became district vicar with responsibility for some ten monasteries. In terms of his position within the order, Luther was more than the "obscure monk" of popular fancy. He had at an early age undertaken important teaching assignments, and he had been entrusted with administrative duties of some weight.

But Luther found no Christian peace in the monastery. He made every effort to do so, and there seems no reason to doubt his later statement: "It is true that I was a pious monk. I followed the rule of my order so strictly that I may say: if ever a monk could have gained heaven through monasticism, I should have done so. All my

---

[3] *Predigt* ("Sermon"), 1538, *WA* 47, 90.
[4] *Preface to the Completed Edition of Luther's Latin Writings*, 1545, *WA* 54, 179.

brothers in the monastery will bear witness to this."[5] Nevertheless, in ways finally beyond the grasp of the historian, not clear to Luther at the time and probably oversimplified and stylized by him later, a new destiny emerged.

The monastic assumption was that the monk was free from the dangers of the world, that he had all the help of the sacraments and prayer, and that he could devote himself completely to sustained self-discipline. In consequence the good monk would gain sufficient merit so that he might face God's final judgment hopeful that God in his great mercy would accept him and grant him salvation. In Luther's case, the quest led to the opposite result; the higher he pitched his endeavor, and the more zealous his good works, the more disastrous were the consequences. In a later recollection, Luther speaks of the total frustration of his monastic hope. "In the monastery . . . I was often frightened by the name of Jesus, and when I saw him hanging on the cross, I fancied that he seemed like lightning. When I heard his name mentioned, I would rather have heard the name of the devil, for I thought that I had to perform good works until at the last through them Jesus would become a friend and gracious unto me."[6] And in a work of 1518, Luther seems to speak autobiographically as he describes the agony of the soul confronted with God's wrath. "At such times God appears to a man as terrifyingly enraged, and with him the whole creation. At such times, there is no flight, no comfort within or without but all things accuse him. . . . All that remains is the stark-naked desire for help, and a terrible groaning, but the soul does not know where to turn for help . . . every corner of the soul is filled with the greatest bitterness, dread, trembling, and sorrow, and all of these in their eternal forms."[7]

Thus Luther's later recollections reveal that his monastic zeal

---

[5] *Die kleine Antwort auf Herzog Georgs nächstes Buch* ("A Brief Reply to Duke George's Most Recent Book"), 1533, *WA* 38, 143.

[6] *Predigt* ("Sermon"), 1539, *WA* 47, 590.

[7] *Resolutiones disputationum de indulgentiarium virtute* ("Resolutions on the Dispute Concerning the Value of Indulgences"), 1518, *WA* 1, 557.

had simply led to a confrontation with the God of justice and of wrath, the God who always condemns a man and who condemns him more the harder the man strives — even with the help of grace — for merit and a justice of his own. Like Augustine in his *Confessions,* Luther in his recollections doubtless made use of later insights in assessing the significance of his earlier life. Nonetheless, these recollections are essential to our understanding of what "happened" in the monastery.

A different kind of evidence is found in writings Luther produced while in the monastery, primarily biblical lectures. Here we see less of the final failure of Luther's monastic efforts, and much more of the movement of his theological thought away from the earlier tradition toward his new starting point.

On the negative side, we find in Luther's thought an early and persistent denial of anything Pelagian or Aristotelian in theology. He sums up his rejection of both in his *Disputation against Scholastic Theology* of 1517. "1. To say that Augustine spoke immoderately against heretics is to say that Augustine is almost everywhere a liar. 2. And this is to give the Pelagians and all heretics an occasion for triumph, nay it is to give them victory. . . . 43. It is an error to say 'Without Aristotle one does not become a theologian.' 44. Indeed, one does not become a theologian unless without Aristotle."[8]

On the positive side, we find in Luther's early writings a steady transformation and eventual transmutation of the theological positions from which he had started.

Thus, for example, one of the earliest motifs of Luther's thought was what may be called an image-exemplar theology. All things temporal are images of what is eternal and divine; the temporal Law of the Old Testament is a figure or image of the spiritual Law of the New Testament; the tropological, or moral, interpretation of the Bible shows how all Christians through grace should become like Christ. But as time went on, the fundamental tendencies of

---

[8] *Disputation Against Scholastic Theology,* 1517, *WA* 1, 224, 226.

Luther's Christian experience, his sense of the nothingness of the creature in the presence of the creator, worked against the implications of such an image-exemplar doctrine. Luther did not immediately abandon the inherited position, but gradually gave it a more extreme, even distorted, form. Thus in the *Commentary on Romans,* Luther argues that all revelation takes place under opposite images; only in this way can he make it plain that continued grace is necessary for our grasping of God's message. "Our good is hidden and it is hidden so profoundly that it lies under its opposite. Thus our life is under death, love of ourselves under hate of ourselves ... justice under sin ... and universally every one of our affirmations under its negation, so that faith may have its place in God."[9] In the *Heidelberg Disputation* of 1518, Luther develops this doctrine of opposite images systematically into a "theology of the cross" as against a false "theology of glory." "For since man abused the knowledge of God to be gained from [his] works, God in turn wished to be known through [his] passions and to reprove the wisdom of things invisible by the wisdom of things visible, so that those who did not worship God manifest in [his] acts, should worship him hidden in [his] sufferings."[10]

A second main motif of Luther's early theology concerns Christian righteousness or justice. From the start Luther insisted that saving righteousness comes only through grace; he would have nothing of any Pelagianism or Aristotelianism. But in his earliest writings, righteousness fits into the image-exemplar theology, and it is a positive quality of the Christian. Once again, however, the deepest drives of Luther's thought worked against the position which he had inherited. He defined righteousness less and less in terms of likeness; less and less was it anything which the Christian could possess, even by grace. In the *Commentary on Romans,* righteousness takes on a paradoxical form comparable to that of the opposite images of the *Heidelberg Disputation.* The righteous-

---

[9] *Lectures on Romans,* 1515–16, *WA* 56, 392.
[10] *Heidelberg Disputation,* 1518, *WA* 1, 362.

ness of the Christian through grace is simply his acceptance of God's condemnation of him as a sinner; his only justice is the confession of his own injustice. God is marvelous in his saints, "for he has so hidden them that while they are holy [*sancti*], they seem to themselves to be nothing but unholy [*profani*]."[11]

In the writings of the early period, the problem of righteousness became more and more dominant, and it was at this point that Luther moved forward to his fundamental transmutation of Christian theology. In a famous and disputed passage of the *Preface* to the 1545 edition of his collected works, Luther tells us how this happened. Perhaps he has telescoped the stages somehow; the *Preface* still remains Luther's basic statement of how God finally revealed to him the true meaning of the "righteousness of God."

In the *Preface* Luther tells us that he had long been troubled by the meaning of the "righteousness of God" and particularly by Paul's statement that the righteousness of God is revealed in the gospel (Rom. 1:17). Luther had understood this as the formal or active righteousness "by which God is just and in accord with which he punishes sinners and the unjust.[12] As a result Luther, as we have already seen, found himself at a total impasse in the monastic life. "Though I lived as a monk without reproach, I felt that before God I was a sinner with a most unquiet conscience, and I could not believe that he was placated by my works of satisfaction. I did not love, nay I hated that God who was just and punished sinners. In secret, if not blasphemously at least with great grumbling, I was angry with God."[13] But Luther continued to search out the meaning of Rom. 1:17. "At last by the mercy of

> God, in daily and nightly meditation, I noted the connection of the words, namely, "In it [the gospel] the righteousness of God is revealed, as it is written 'The righteous

---

11 *Lectures on Romans*, 1515–16, *WA* 56, 290.
12 *Preface to the Complete Edition of Luther's Latin Writings*, 1545, *WA* 54, 185.
13 *Ibid.*

man lives out of faith.' " There I began to understand the righteousness of God as that by which the righteous man lives by a gift of God, that is to say, out of faith. And this is the meaning of the passage [in Paul]: the righteousness of God is revealed in the gospel, namely the passive righteousness, by which a merciful God justifies us through faith, as it has been written, "The righteous man lives out of faith." Here I felt that I was altogether reborn and had entered through open gates into Paradise itself. There a totally different countenance of the whole Bible showed itself to me. I then ran through the Scriptures from memory, and I found that there was an analogy in other words as well, such as the work of God, which God works in us. . . . And I extolled my sweetest word with a love as great as the hatred with which I had formerly hated that word, "the righteousness of God."[14]

Scholars may disagree about the dating of this so-called "Tower Experience,"[15] but there can be no doubt that Luther is here speaking about the most basic reorientation and the most profound mutation in his thinking. It is never easy to give a simple description of such a change. One whole language of thought has suddenly, as it were, changed into a different one; neither the earlier language nor the later one can state both the "before" and the "after" of the reorientation.

Perhaps we come closest to the heart of the matter when we see that the whole *direction* of Luther's thinking about salvation has been reversed. In his early period, however much he may have maximized and radicalized the need for God's grace, Luther still thought *forward* to a future salvation. The Christian sinner,

---

14 *Ibid.*, p. 186.
15 The majority of Luther scholars favor a dating at the time of the *Commentary on Romans* (1515–16). For a statement of this position, see Heinrich Bornkamm, "Zur Frage der Iustitia Dei beim jungen Luther," *Archiv für Reformationsgeschichte*, LII (1961), 16–29 and LIII (1962), 1–60. The present author favors a later dating in 1518–19. For a defense of this dating, from different standpoints, see U. Saarnivaara, *Luther Discovers the Gospel* (Saint Louis, 1951); Ernst Bizer, *Fides ex auditu* (3rd. ed.; Neukirchen, 1966); Kurt Aland, *Der Weg zur Reformation (Theologische Existenz Heute,* N.F. 123), München, 1965.

through God's grace and through his own works, achieves some measure of righteousness and because of this he looks forward to God's acceptance of him. After the Tower Experience Luther lived *out of* a righteousness which he already possessed in heaven through faith. And he was careful to deny that one might ever return to the old direction of thought and think forward from the Christian here and now toward his heavenly salvation. All the works of the Christian, even those done in grace, are valueless in God's final judgment. "Even just and pious men, whose justice might be found pure outside God's judgment in the realm of mercy, are in his judgment not at all helped by this justice, but are like the last and most vile of sinners."[16] Not even faith may ever be regarded as a *cause* of salvation. The Christians "are safe under Christ's grace, not because they believe and have faith and his gift, but because they have these in his grace."[17] The Christian's heavenly righteousness is already complete; it is not given "piecemeal."[18] "Therefore the whole life of a good believing Christian after baptism is nothing more than awaiting the revelation of a holiness which he already has. He surely has it whole, though it is still hidden in faith."[19]

By this reversal of the direction of his thought about Christian righteousness and salvation, Luther transcended the medieval options which constituted the dynamics of his early theology. This was notably true in the case of the Augustinianism which had been central for him. Luther began and continued with an Augustinian emphasis on grace in contrast to man's own abilities, and in Augustine grace constitutes a miraculous transformation of man by God; through this transformation man is justified and made worthy of a future salvation. Luther gradually modified the form of his inherited Augustinianism to the extreme position of the *Commentary on Romans,* in which he asserts that the righteousness conferred by

---

16 *Against Latomus* (1521), *WA* 8, 67.
17 *Ibid.,* p. 114.
18 *Kirchenpostille* ("Church Postil"), 1522, *WA* 10^{I,1} 344.
19 *Ibid.,* p. 108.

grace is merely the recognition of one's own sinfulness. But it is only with the Tower Experience that he leaped to a fundamentally new position, holding that Christian righteousness is given by God all at once and that man henceforth lives out of this righteousness. On the level of the Christian's heavenly righteousness, Pelagianism has not simply been minimized; it has disappeared. On the level of the Christian's life in the world, the older Augustinianism has no more relevance. But, more important, the way of thinking, the form or direction of thought common to both Augustinianism and Pelagianism has been reversed.

Similarly, Luther is no longer concerned with the problem of how to combine the supernatural and the natural within an all-embracing Christian unity; the Christian's hidden righteousness in heaven is totally independent of his life on earth. Finally, Luther is no longer forced to construct a unity out of Greek thought-forms and the Christian message. Within the area of Christian experience, a historic act of God's grace has completely supplanted the Greek movement of thought toward a universal, timeless ideal; within the "world," as we shall see, the Christian knows no more of ethics and politics than does the non-Christian.

By 1518–19 at the latest Luther reached his new starting point, the place where he could stand and move the world. But meanwhile, in a connected but separate development, Luther came to realize that the movement of his thought must eventually involve a break with the established order of church and empire. As Luther later insisted, such a revolution was far from his intention; in the beginning he was a fervent papist and long continued so.[20] Nevertheless, from 1517, when Luther published his *Ninety-five Theses*, it became steadily clearer that the only alternatives open to him were either the abandonment of his emerging theological insights or rebellion.

---

[20] *Preface to the Complete Edition of Luther's Latin Writings, WA* 54, 179. The position of the present author is that Luther's trouble over indulgences stemmed from his early "Augustinianism," but that he might eventually have yielded to "Catholic" criticism if he had not found a more fundamental base in a new theology.

In the *Ninety-five Theses* themselves, Luther attempted to limit some of the practical abuses connected with the sale of indulgences and to give a more precise definition of the doctrine itself. His main concern, however, was with the crucial importance of a continuing and inward penance. "1. Our Lord and Master Jesus Christ, when he said 'Repent' (Matt. 4:17) meant that the whole life of believers should be one of penitence."[21]

To Luther's amazement, the *Theses* attracted wide popular attention. They posed a threat to the official church and in particular to Archbishop Albrecht of Mainz, for whose benefit the indulgences in question were being sold. Legal action was begun in Germany and in Rome against Luther, and one would have expected a speedy settlement of the case by Luther's submission or by his execution. However, the procedures against Luther became involved with the long and tortuous negotiations over the election of a new German emperor. Luther's protector, the Elector of Saxony, was important to the papacy in these negotiations, and therefore no quick action could be taken against the elector's will. Luther was given time to think, and his opponents, notably John Eck, made it plain to him that if he maintained his position on indulgences and the theology which supported that position, he would have to go against both papal and conciliar decrees. Eventually, in the Leipzig Disputation of 1519, Luther burnt the final bridge. The papacy itself, he declared, was in its present form a merely human institution, devoid of divine right; even the councils had erred.

Once the election of Charles V as emperor made further papal maneuvering in Germany unnecessary, Pope Leo X issued a bull (*Exsurge Domine*, June 15, 1520) threatening excommunication unless Luther submitted within sixty days. Luther responded with a sharp attack on the bull; when his own books were burned, he retaliated by burning both the bull and the canon law at Wittenberg in December, 1520. The last act was the hearing before the

---

[21] *The Ninety-five Theses, WA* 1, 233.

emperor at the Diet of Worms in April of 1521. Both in preliminary hearings and finally before the entire Diet, Luther refused to
recant unless convinced of error by Holy Scripture or by clear
arguments of reason. According to the traditional account he con-
concluded, "Here I stand; I cannot do otherwise."[22] Emperor
Charles V took his stand too. "A single monk, led astray by private
judgment, has set himself against the faith held by all Christians
for a thousand years or more, and impudently concluded that all
Christians up till now have erred. I have therefore resolved to
stake upon this cause all my dominions, my friends, my body and
my blood, my life, and soul."[23] In May, the emperor issued the
Edict of Worms, which declared Luther an outlaw of the Empire.

III. LUTHER'S WORK OF RECONSTRUCTION

By 1521 Luther, because of his pursuit of a true theology, had
been outlawed by the Empire and excommunicated by the church.
Further, it had been clear for several years that he did not stand
alone; thousands of Germans who looked to him for guidance
were prepared to stand with him.

It is important to remember how much hard thinking remained
to be done. If Luther had simply attacked abuses, whether moral
or ecclesiastical, the task would have been clear — to purge the
body ecclesiastic and the body politic of these abuses and to carry
on. But the implications of Luther's new experience of Christian
righteousness went deeper than the eradication of abuses, and
they could not be defined by reference to a pre-existent standard.
More important, while the Tower Experience cut the ground from
under the old view of the church, of government, and of the
Christian life in general, it did not immediately provide the proper

---

[22] For the manuscript evidence, see A. Wrede (ed.), *Deutsche Reich-
stagsakten, Jüngere Reihe* (1893–95), II, 555.
[23] *Ibid.*, p. 595.

alternatives. Hence the years following Luther's breakthrough to his new starting point were slow and difficult years of working out new answers to new problems. In some cases Luther solved these problems by the natural development of his own thought; more frequently he did so in response to attack and to what he regarded as error.

The first step, one which was somehow achieved during the tumultuous years before 1521, was to translate the theological discovery of the Tower Experience into religious terms as a pattern for the Christian life. The classic statement is probably that of the *Freedom of a Christian,* published in 1520 and sent to Pope Leo X. Here, in contrast to his exegetical or controversial works, Luther is able to make his own choice of what is essential to Christianity, and he emerges with what he calls "the whole of Christian life in a brief form."[24] His contemporaries found in this his most important introduction to Christian piety; we of a later age find it perhaps the statement least bound up with his own age and the most "catholic." It is nevertheless clear that the Tower Experience, with its reversal of the direction of thought about Christian righteousness, furnishes the basic framework for the *Freedom of a Christian.* Because of his heavenly righteousness, the Christian is free of all possible worldly limitations; out of his heavenly righteousness, he moves into the world in love and service of his neighbor.

In the *Freedom of a Christian* Luther speaks in terms of hallowed New Testament contrasts. On one side, there is man's spiritual nature; in terms of it we find the spiritual, new, and inner man. On the other hand, there is his bodily nature; in terms of it we find the carnal, old, and outer man. Luther then uses this terminology to formulate his two main theses: (1) A Christian is a perfectly free lord of all, subject to none. (2) A Christian is a perfectly dutiful servant of all, subject to all.

---

[24] *Ein Sendbrief an den Papst Leo X* ("Open Letter to Pope Leo X"), 1520. *WA* 7, 11.

The exposition of the first thesis tells how man lives out of the heavenly righteousness which he already possesses through faith. The Christian is righteous, free, and pious as a spiritual, new, and inner man. This has nothing to do with any works of the body or with anything bodily at all. The one thing which the soul needs is the word of God, the gospel of Christ, the righteousness which is revealed in the gospel. "One thing, and only one thing, is necessary for Christian life, righteousness, and freedom. That one thing is the most holy word of God, the gospel of Christ, as Christ says in John 11:25, 'I am the resurrection and the life; he who believes in me shall never die.' "[25] And the only way of receiving and cherishing the word is through faith, as in Rom. 1:17.

Through faith, the Christian's soul is united with God's word and honors God. It becomes the bride of Christ and is united with him. Thus all the grace, salvation and life of Christ belong to the soul; all the sins and weaknesses of the soul are taken over by Christ. "The believing soul by means of the pledge of its faith is free in Christ its bridegroom, free from all sins, secure against death and hell, and endowed with the eternal righteousness, life, and salvation of its bridegroom."[26] Finally, through Christ, the Christian in his spiritual aspect becomes king, lord over all things, and a priest "worthy to appear before God to pray for others and to teach one another divine things."[27]

If the first thesis is the explanation of the glory of the Christian as he lives out of his heavenly righteousness in Christ, the second thesis explains the very different way in which the believer lives into the world of his fellowmen. Man is a believer, righteous in Christ, and "yet he remains in this mortal life on earth. In this life he must control his body and have dealings with men."[28] Since

---

[25] *The Freedom of a Christian*, 1520, *WA* 7, 50. This and the following quotations are taken from the Latin original and not from the German translation.

[26] *Ibid.*, p. 55.

[27] *Ibid.*, p. 57.

[28] *Ibid.*, p. 60.

by faith he is created in the image of God, since he is both joyful and full of thanks because of Christ, "therefore it is his one occupation to serve God joyfully, without thought of gain, in love that is not constrained."[29] Hence he will first of all discipline his body so that he may better serve God and others. "Behold from faith thus flow forth love and joy in the Lord, and from love a joyful, willing, and free mind that serves one's neighbor willingly and takes no account of gratitude or ingratitude, of praise or blame, of gain or loss."[30] And Luther concludes, "Who can comprehend the riches and glory of the Christian life? It can do all things and has all things and lacks nothing. It is lord over sin, death, and hell, yet at the same time it serves, ministers to, and benefits all men."[31]

One might wonder why Luther as a theologian could not stop with such works as the *Freedom of a Christian*. The main reason was that a Christian theology may not stop when it has described the specifically Christian aspects of a believer's life; it must go on to describe the non-Christian aspects as well. Augustine's theory must include the earthly as well as the heavenly city; Thomas must clarify what is natural as well as what is supernatural. And if Luther's theology starts with his "Let God be God!" it must always continue with "Let the world be the world!"

It is this problem of the relation between the Christian and the worldly which is fundamental in Luther's work of reconstruction. Here again we find him working with the fundamental categories of the Tower Experience, as he tries to explain how a man lives out of his heavenly and Christian righteousness into the "world" of his fellowmen and fellow creatures.

In analyzing Luther's work of reconstruction, one must start from the position which he confronted. This was the great synthesis of medieval Christianity, the unity of a Christian civilization with its harmonious ordering of the natural and the supernatural

---

29 *Ibid.*
30 *Ibid.*, p. 66.
31 *Ibid.*

within a single society. Within this society there were the spiritual estates of the clergy and the secular estates of the laity; the monks played a special role as they performed certain religious functions for the whole society and were in turn supported by the lay members of that society. The whole society was, finally, the church under one pope, and, in the words of *Unam Sanctam,* subjection to the papacy was necessary for salvation. From the presuppositions of this society Luther could be convinced of error in the peripheral doctrine of indulgences; all the more could he be convinced of error in his fundamental reinterpretation of the Christian life.

Contrariwise, as Luther thought about this society from his own starting point, it would gradually disintegrate and a new order must be established. Again, it must be noted that such disintegration and reconstruction was in no sense Luther's prime motive. He wanted a gracious God and a sound theology, but the theology through which his gracious God could be described implied a whole new universe of thought. On the basis of his Tower Experience Luther had to attack the view that men live in a society which is a mixture of the worldly and the Christian and that through this society they move toward salvation. Luther had to defend a position which permits the assertion of an already achieved righteousness in heaven, out of which we live into a world which is disproportionate to heaven and salvation.

On the pressing question of the church, Luther, as we have seen, had declared as early as 1519 that the papacy was a human institution and a historical growth, devoid of divine right. Further, in his treatise of 1520, the *Babylonian Captivity of the Church,* Luther had denied that the sacraments were a means of grace on the way to salvation; they must be given another explanation to make faith in them primary. Luther made a crucial practical decision when he returned to Wittenberg to put a stop to Karlstadt's program of radical destruction and innovation. Henceforth Luther favored organic and cautious change; in the case of the order of service, for example, he gradually worked out new forms which eliminated those features inconsistent with his new doctrine of righteousness but which otherwise made large use of traditional material.

˙ Luther went on from his new doctrine of righteousness to deny the medieval doctrine of the church as the legal and governmental form of Western Christendom. The true church consists of those whose righteousness is hidden in heaven; it is the invisible communion of the saints which cannot be made into a legal organization of this world. But, as regularly in Luther's thought, this rigorous disjunction of heaven and earth must somehow be combined with their conjunction; in the terminology of John 17, what is not "of the world" must be "sent into the world". "The church is in the flesh and appears as visible; it is in the world and appears in the world. Nevertheless it is not the world nor in the world, and no one sees it."[32] The invisible church, Luther goes on to say, is present in the world wherever its signs, and notably the preaching of the word, are present.

With such general presuppositions, it is clear that Luther was in no position to proceed systematically in organizing a new church. His influence lay rather in having set up a general principle which must be maintained at all costs, and then in favoring one or another of the possible solutions consistent with that principle. Thus we have seen that in 1521 Luther threw his weight on the side of organic growth as against revolutionary innovation. In a second series of choices, Luther favored a public Christianity in which only one form of Christian worship would be accepted within a single political unity; the Lutheran development does not lead to sects or congregations. Finally, without much enthusiasm, Luther consented to the development which put the territorial princes in administrative charge of the new churches, although he always insisted that they had this right only as leading members of the Christian assembly. The only essential point was that true doctrine be preached, that the Christians could hear the word of Christ's saving righteousness.

---

[32] *Disputationes* ("Disputations") 1542, *WA* 39[II], 149.

As Luther had separated the "church" from the "world," so he found it necessary to attack the traditional description of society as consisting of the spiritual estates of the clergy and the secular estates of the laity. In the case of the spiritual estates, to make something spiritual a part of the society of this world represented the "mixing" of the heavenly and the earthly which Luther attacked. All Christians, not just the clergy, have their spiritual estate in heaven, but this spiritual estate cannot be made into a worldly order. In the case of the laity, Luther reformulated their position in the world through his new doctrine of "callings." Previously the concept of calling had been restricted to the clergy. Luther extended it to all professions and duties, from the lowest to the highest. Men are not saved through these worldly callings, but in them they recognize God's voice; through acceptance of the calling, men serve their neighbors in love. Here again Luther has preserved in a new context his fundamental pattern of a life which is lived out of heavenly righteousness into the world. "Our spiritual calling is that we are all called through the gospel to baptism and the Christian faith. . . . Therefore let everyone attend to that to which his heavenly and Christian order through baptism calls him. Afterwards let him look to his outward estate, and he will so live rightly."[33] Or in somewhat different language, two "persons" are borne by each Christian, the "world-person" and the "Christian-person." "Every Christian must be some sort of world-person, since he is at least in body and goods subject to the emperor. But for his own person in his Christian life, he is all alone under Christ."[34]

Finally, Luther must give an account of secular government itself. His first steps in this direction were designed to limit the power of the secular ruler over religion. In the treatise *Secular Authority: To What Extent It Should Be Obeyed* (1523), Luther first demands that Christians acknowledge secular government as an ordinance of God; secondly, he insists that the Christian must

---

[33] *Predigt* ("Sermon"), 1531, *WA* 34[II], 300, 308.
[34] *Wochenpredigt über Matth. 5–7* ("Weekday Sermon on Matt. 5–7"), 1532, *WA* 32, 390.

always refuse to obey the government when its demands are contrary to the word of God. Luther gradually makes this doctrine more explicit in terms of the two governments of God. There is his spiritual government, which consists in the gospel and in the granting of heavenly righteousness; there is his worldly government, by which he maintains civil justice and punishes the wicked. Ministers of this gospel share in God's spiritual government but they have no coercive power; the power of kings is a part of God's worldly government, but it is out of relation to salvation.

From one standpoint this doctrine was developed against the medieval position which would place the royal and the papal powers as two legal authorities within the unity of a Christian society. From another standpoint Luther was reacting against the demands of the peasants, who would deduce worldly consequences from the Christian's heavenly righteousness: because the Christian man is free, there should be no more serfdom on earth. Luther was inclined to agree with the peasants on the basis of natural right, but to translate heavenly and hidden realities into earthly terms would have made a mockery of all his theology. He attacked the peasants violently for their faulty theology and for their rebellion against duly constituted authority.

The tendency seen in the claims of the peasants appeared more generally in the ideas of the Enthusiasts and the Antinomians, who argued that because the Christian in his heavenly righteousness is free of the Law and of all men, therefore Christians need no further proclamation of the Law and are under no obligation to worldly government. In his earliest writings after the Tower Experience, Luther had confronted a mixing of heaven and earth on the basis of medieval theology; in the peasants and in the Antinomians, he confronted a mixing which started from new Lutheran ideas of heavenly righteousness. But in Luther's experience heaven and the world were disproportionate, and he would allow the second form of mixing no more than the first. Luther accordingly worked out a more careful statement of the place of the Law in the life of the Christian.

God uses the Law in two ways, theologically and civilly. The theological use of the Law is an essential part of the religious life of the Christian. In this use, God shows the Christian that all men, even those with grace, are sinners when they stand before God and his Law without Christ. Hence, there can never be any return to the old direction of thought. But God also uses the law civilly, as part of his worldly government; through it he prevents anarchy and disorder. No man is saved by it, but all men, including the Christians, are subject to it in this world.

Luther had worked out many of these ideas separately, though all are ultimately based on the new view of salvation and the world implied by his Tower Experience. In the great *Commentary on Galatians* (Lectures of 1531; printed, with Luther's approval, from student notes in 1535) and in the *Disputations* of the 1530's and 1540's, Luther comes closest to giving a systematic theological statement of his position. He begins with the basic contrast between two kinds of righteousness or justice. "There is a righteousness wherein we act ourselves, whether this is done through our pure natural abilities or through God's gift. . . . Christian righteousness, however, is quite the opposite, a merely passive righteousness, which we only receive, where we do not act at all, but where we suffer another, God, to act in us."[35] Christian righteousness is the righteousness of Rom. 1:17 and of the Tower Experience, the righteousness out of which the Christian lives. In sharpest contrast to it there is the active or civil righteousness of the Christian in the world.

As God separated the heavens and the earth, so we should separate these two justices or righteousnesses, for any "mixture" leads to the ruin of all theology. "Whoever knows these distinctions well, let him give thanks to God and know himself a theologian, as he puts the gospel in heaven and understands it as a heavenly righteousness, and as he puts the Law on earth. . . . Just as God carefully separated heaven and earth, so we should carefully sep-

---

[35] *Commentary on Galatians*, 1531, WA 40^I, 40.

arate these two righteousnesses."[36] The failure to preserve these distinctions had been the fundamental error of the medieval Catholics on one side and of the Enthusiasts and Antinomians on the other. As to what happens if one mixes the Law and the gospel, there is Luther's well-known exclamation "If I have Christ as *legislator,* then I am indeed damned."[37]

Not only are the two justices separate, but also each is supreme in its realm. "The highest art of the Christian is to know nothing of active righteousness and to ignore the Law. . . . Contrariwise, in the world, I should so urge and emphasize the Law as if there were no grace."[38] As a final assertion of the independence of the "world" as one aspect of the Christian's experience, Luther argues that there is no specifically Christian law or morality or worldly order. In the world, the Christian constantly confronts God's masks as they appear in the various forms of authority, but God remains hidden behind the masks. If we want to learn the content of ethics or politics, there are no better guides than Aristotle or Cicero. "The Christian so uses the world and all the creatures that there is no difference between him and the non-Christian."[39] Even charity is not a specifically Christian precept but a part of God's law of nature; it is the error of the "papists" that they make of the gospel a Law of charity."[40]

Thus Luther, who had learned in his Tower Experience to "let God be God," had now taken the main steps toward working out a theology which would also "let the world be the world." The Christian is the man who lives out of his heavenly righteousness into the world where God is always masked. The Christian alone is free in the world, because he alone has his heavenly righteousness outside the world. "Hence our theology is certain because it places us outside ourselves."[41] The Christian does not enter the

---

36 *Ibid.,* p. 207.
37 *Ibid.,* p. 50.
38 *Ibid.,* p. 43.
39 *Ibid.,* p. 289.
40 *Ibid.,* p. 141.
41 *Ibid.,* p. 589.

world with special formal qualities provided by grace. "In order better to understand these questions, I am in the habit of thinking this way: there is in my heart no quality of any kind that could be called faith or love. In their stead I put Jesus Christ and say: There is my righteousness. He is in fact what this quality and this so-called formal righteousness are supposed to be. . . . It is within me that he must be, stay, live, speak . . . so that we are the right-eousness of God in Christ and not in love or in the gifts which follow."[42] Luther therefore had this *one* center, this ground of heavenly righteousness, and from it he lived with complete joy and freedom in the world of God's masks. "Therefore the way to heaven is the line of an indivisible point, the conscience."[43] Here the harsh contrasts of Luther's mature theology eventually find their unity. "There is one simple justice of faith and works, just as God and man are one person, and the body and the soul, one man."[44]

In conclusion one must emphasize the complete harmony be-tween the simple statement of Christian piety in the *Freedom of a Christian* and the almost demonic disjunction of such works as the *Commentary on Galatians* of 1531. One can translate the Tower Experience into a Christian life; one can attempt to state it with theological precision against the background of the whole intellectual tradition of the West. The heart of the matter remains the same.

IV. LUTHER'S SIGNIFICANCE

In evaluating Luther's significance, we do well to begin with his own estimate of his work. On one hand, he contemptuously referred to himself as an insignificant "bag of worms" and re-gretted that any Christians should call themselves "Lutherans."[45]

---

[42] *WA*, Br, 7, 100–1 (No. 1818).

[43] *Commentary on Galatians*, 1531, *WA* 40^{I}, 21.

[44] *De loco justificationis* ("On the Place of Justification"), 1530, *WA* 30^{III}, 659. See *WA*, TR, 2, 247 (Nos. 1886–87).

[45] *Eine treue Vermahnung* ("A Faithful Admonition"), 1522, *WA* 7^{I}, 685.

It will be remembered that Luther never occupied any high official position in the new Christian society but throughout his later years remained simply the professor and preacher at Wittenberg. Nevertheless he had a high sense of the dignity and responsibility of the professorial office. "I did not wish to win profit from the world through my professorship. Indeed I should finally have given up and despaired in the great and heavy tasks imposed on me, if I had entered upon it by stealth without vocation or command. But now God and all the world must testify to it, that in my office as professor and preacher, I began under public auspices and I have so carried it further with God's grace and help."[46] Luther always insisted that what he had accomplished lay in the area of doctrine and not in that of moral reformation. "Doctrine and life are to be distinguished. Our lives are just as bad as those of the papists; therefore we are not fighting about how we live nor condemning our opponents in this respect. . . . But no one previously attacked doctrine; that is my vocation."[47] But even in the special area of his vocation, Luther did not think that men by themselves could do much; his basic attitude may be seen in some advice he intended for Melanchthon: "continue to admonish Philip in my name that he should fight against the longing for divinity that is inborn in us and planted in our hearts by the devil. . . . We must be men and not God. This is the sum of it all. It cannot be otherwise; if it were, only unceasing restlessness and sorrow would be our reward."[48] The last written words we have from Luther conclude, "We are beggars. That is indeed true."[49]

The historian can agree, in his own terminology, with much of Luther's self-judgment. Luther appeared at a time when the Christian West was in a singular state of religious and intellectual uncertainty. Quite apart from Luther, many men found that their

---

[46] *Predigt* ("Sermon"),1532, *WA* 30^{III}, 522.
[47] *WA*, TR, 1, 294 (No. 624). See *WA*, TR, 1, 439 (No. 880).
[48] *WA*, Br, 5, 415 (No. 1612). See also *Commentary on Galatians* (1531), *WA* 40^{I}, 225, 229.
[49] *Letzte Aufzeichnung Luthers* ("Luther's Last Written Statement"), Feb. 16, 1546, *WA* 48, 241. See *WA*, TR 5, 318 (No. 5677)

ultimate commitments, their deepest religious insights were more and more losing contact with the traditional intellectual and institutional forms of Christianity. It was given to Luther to find one way out of this uncertainty and irrelevance. Many of his contemporaries greeted Luther's solution as the one for which they too had been searching. It is foolish to assert that if Luther had not appeared, some other man would have reached the same solution; it is rash to maintain that if Luther had been killed by the lightning near Stotternheim in 1505, everything would have been different.

The center of Luther's achievement was clearly religious, and so was his influence, although he also left his mark on German society, the German family, and the German language. Against the immediate medieval tradition of Christianity, Luther gave a fundamentally new statement of the Christian's relation to Christ and to salvation; this was the change in doctrine which was his "vocation." If one asks how far Luther's theology represented a break with tradition and how far it preserved continuity, the historian hesitates to answer. Luther himself seems to have thought in 1545 that had Archbishop Albrecht of Mainz and Pope Leo X acted otherwise some agreement might have been reached;[50] in this case there might have been a new "doctrine," but no "Reformation." Christianity by its very nature requires, one might say, a new theology for every new age. It might even be argued that the intellectual change from Anselm of Canterbury through Thomas is greater than that from Thomas through Luther. Yet whereas Thomas was touched only incidentally and temporarily by the condemnations of 1277, Luther's new doctrine for a new age led to his expulsion from the old church and the consequent fragmentation of Western Christendom.

One must be equally tentative in wondering whether there were other possibilities for the West, unrealized because of Luther. First of all, it does not seem that anything less fundamental than

---

[50] *Preface to the Complete Edition of Luther's Latin Writings,* 1545, *WA* 54, 185.

Luther's theological reorientation could have broken the unity of Christian civilization in the West as a "church." To use Luther's metaphor, it was he who broke the walls; once the walls had fallen, the way was open to all, including many whose purposes were quite opposed to Luther's.

Secondly, it does seem that Luther was of crucial significance in setting up a rigorous dichotomy between Christianity and a total "world" as one of the key categories of the West. Such a dichotomy, although its roots lie far back in Christian history, was largely recessive in the medieval tradition. Further, Erasmus' "reform" worked in a quite different direction, toward a more natural and even a more "worldy" Christianity. But Luther powerfully reasserted the dichotomy, and it has not since disappeared from the dynamics of Western thought. It is true that in the post-Lutheran centuries this most often took the form of a world or of a secularism which claimed totality *against* Christianity. Nevertheless, without Luther, it seems that in the context either of medieval sacramentalism or of Erasmian reform, both Christianity and the "world" might have developed very differently.

For all his crucial historical significance, Luther has not become one of the permanent voices of Western thought, particularly outside Germany. We know of Thomas and we know of Descartes; Luther's power and scope were surely equal to theirs. And in our present historical context, he has a particular relevance. For the Christian, he is the thinker who can probably best suggest that there are Christian reasons for the total "world" within which men now find themselves; this situation may be a crisis for contemporary Christianity, but it is far from being alien to the Christian tradition and in its historical origins it derives from that tradition. For the non-Christian, at a time when the meaninglessness of the world in itself is constantly asserted, Luther can suggest, historically at least, what forces created that world and how it was justified and glorified as the mask of transcendent yet historical God. We too are beggars, and we would do well to seek more help from that greatest and most generous of beggars, Martin Luther.

BIBLIOGRAPHY

EDITIONS OF LUTHER'S WRITINGS

D. Martin Luthers Werke. Kritische Gesamtausgabe. Weimar, 1883——. The nearly complete edition of all of Luther's writings. It contains four parts: (1) The writings; (2) The letters; (3) The table-talk; (4) The German Bible.

Luthers Werke in Auswahl. Ed. O. Clemen. Bonn, 1912–33, and later reprints. A convenient selection which includes no biblical commentaries, except for the period before 1518. Vols. I–IV contain the writings 1517–45; V, The young Luther; VI, Letters; VII, Sermons; VIII, Table-talk.

Kurt Aland, *Hilfsbuch zum Lutherstudium.* Gütersloh, 1957. A very useful guide through the labyrinth of the various editions.

TRANSLATIONS

American Edition of *Luther's Works.* Ed. Helmut T. Lehmann and Jaroslav Pelikan. Philadelphia and St. Louis, 1955——. This edition will contain 55 volumes. Vols. 1–30 contain selected biblical commentaries, and Vols. 31–55 contain the Reformation writings and other occasional pieces.)

The *Library of Christian Classics* (Philadelphia, 1953——) is to devote four volumes to Luther, three of which have already appeared.

 Vol. 15. *Lectures on Romans.* Trans. Wilhelm Pauck. 1961.

 Vol. 16. *Early Theological Works.* Trans. James Atkinson. 1962.

 Vol. 18. *Letters of Spiritual Counsel.* Trans. Theodore G. Tappert. 1955.

 Vol. 17. *Luther and Erasmus on Free Will.* Trans. E. Gordon Rupp and Philip S. Watson.

The Bondage of the Will. Trans. James I. Packer and O. R. Johnston. London, 1957.

Martin Luther, Selections from his Writings. Ed. John Dillenberger. New York, 1961. Excellent selections, in paperback.

The Reformation Writings of Martin Luther. Ed. Bertram Lee Woolf. 2 vols. London, 1952–56. Mainly the early works.

Selected Writings of Martin Luther. Ed. Theodore G. Tappert. 4 vols. (Paperback). Philadelphia, 1967.

BIOGRAPHIES AND GENERAL INTRODUCTIONS

Bainton, Roland H. *Here I Stand.* New York, 1950.

Bornkamm, Heinrich. *Luther's World of Thought.* St. Louis, 1958.

Ebeling, Gerhard. *Luther. Einführung in sein Denken.* Tübingen, 1964.
Erikson, E. *Young Man Luther.* New York, 1958.
Lau, Franz. *Luther.* Philadelphia, 1963.
Mackinnon, James. *Luther and the Reformation.* 4 vols. London, 1925–30.
Pauck, Wilhelm. *The Heritage of the Reformation.* Glencoe, 1950.
Schwiebert, E. G. *Luther and His Times.* St. Louis, 1950.
Watson, Philip S. *Let God be God!* London, 1948.

THE EARLY LUTHER

Boehmer, Heinrich. *Road to Reformation: Martin Luther to the Year 1521.* Philadelphia, 1946.
Fife, R. H. *The Revolt of Martin Luther.* New York, 1957.
Rupp, E. Gordon. *Luther's Progress to the Diet of Worms.* London, 1951.

SPECIAL TOPICS

Bornkamm, Heinrich. *Luther im Spiegel der deutschen Geistesgeschichte.* Heidelberg, 1955.
Cranz, F. Edward. *An Essay on the Development of Luther's Thought on Justice, Law, and Society.* Cambridge, Mass., 1959.
Forell, George W. *Faith Active in Love.* New York, 1954.
Gerrish, B. A. *Grace and Reason: A Study in the Theology of Luther.* Oxford, 1962.
Pelikan, Jaroslav. *Luther the Expositor.* St. Louis, 1959.
Prenter, Regin. *Spiritus Creator.* Philadelphia, 1953.
Rupp, E. Gordon. *The Righteousness of God.* London, 1953.
Wingren, Gustav. *Luther on Vocation.* Philadelphia, 1957.
Zeeden, E. W. *The Legacy of Luther.* Westminster, Md., 1954.

CHAPTER FIVE

ULRICH ZWINGLI
BARD THOMPSON

I

Ulrich Zwingli was born on January 1, 1484, seven weeks after the birth of Luther, in the Alpine village of Wildhaus, some forty miles southeast of Zurich. He was the third child of Uly and Margaretha (née Bruggmann) Zwingli, who tended flocks on the steep slopes and reared a large family in frugality and conventional piety. Compared to Luther's youth, Zwingli's was uneventful. He got by on two inspirations. One was the Alpine grandeur which supplied him with many theological illustrations, as well as a curious translation of the Twenty-third psalm, *In schöner Alp weidet er mich*.[1] The other was Swiss patriotism, instilled in him at the family hearth, which left him an ardent nationalist.

At five, Zwingli was turned over to his uncle Bartholomäus, Dean at Wesen, who gave him the rudiments of Latin, upon which all scholarship was based; but seeing that the boy was precocious, Bartholomäus sent him off to the primary school in Basel when he was ten. There, under the pedagogy of Gregory Bünzli, young Zwingli attained proficiency in Latin. About 1496, he was transferred to yet another school, in Bern, where he attended the instruction of the celebrated Heinrich Wölflin (Lupulus) who first set the classics before him — a circumstance of no small importance, as it was from Humanism that Zwingli came to the Reformation. By this time, he had also become a promising musician. He had such an excellent voice that the Dominicans of Bern would gladly have enrolled him, had not his father and his uncle put a stop to their designs. In October, 1498, having been intellectually

---

[1] "He makes me graze in a beautiful mountain meadow."

prepared for university study, Zwingli ventured to Vienna to take the baccalaureate degree. But his name on the university register carries the notation, *exclusus:* he was dismissed for some reason now obscure to us, but perhaps on account of his over-ardent patriotism. The matter could not have been serious, however, for Zwingli re-enrolled for the summer semester of 1500 and pursued his study there until 1502.

Early in 1502, Zwingli returned to Switzerland and entered the university at Basel which had been founded at the middle of the fifteenth century by scholars and churchmen devoted to the Renaissance. Basel was the intellectual capital of the Swiss confederacy. With its splendid university and its burgeoning printing industry, the city attracted Humanists of the first rank, including the prince of Humanists, Erasmus of Rotterdam, who resided periodically in Basel, where his greatest works, the Greek New Testament (1516) and the polemic against Luther, *On Free Will* (1524), were published by the famous Basel printer, John Froben.

The Christian Humanists assumed, so far as they thought alike, that the reform of the church, which they all anticipated, was an intellectual and ethical problem. For them reform involved merely the riddance of medieval dogmatism and superstition and the moral rejuvenation of Christianity. Fundamental to this program was the recall of the church to the legitimate Christian sources, the Bible and the Fathers. The Humanists were excedingly zealous both to uncover and to communicate the biblical faith — an enterprise which could not be managed, however, without concern for the texts and skill in language. While Reuchlin labored to supply the lexical tools needed for the Hebrew Bible, Erasmus lavished his energies on the Greek New Testament. The Humanists did not take kindly to the medieval doctors whom they blamed for the burial of the Bible beneath layers of human commentary. The humanistic problem was precisely to break through this dogmatic encrustation and, by using text and language, to reveal again the very sources of the faith.

In this vital environment Zwingli matured as a scholar. He took his Bachelor of Arts degree from the university in 1502, his Master of Arts degree in 1506. Walther Köhler has shown that Zwingli, as a candidate for holy orders, was given very thorough training in the medieval theologians, and that he acquired a particular competence in Thomas and in the Aristotelian world of thought, Myconius, who was Zwingli's contemporary and first biographer, left the contrary impression that Zwingli was quite torn asunder by his intellectual experience, and could not seem to reconcile his theological side and his humanistic side. It was Myconius who had Zwingli speak disparagingly of the work of the schoolmen as "the folly of the Sophists" and who declared that when Zwingli attended lectures in theology he felt "like a spy in the enemy camp." There were, at any rate, two eminent Basel Humanists who enabled Zwingli to overcome — eventually — any disjuncture he may have felt between Christian Humanism and Christian theology. One was Thomas Wyttenbach, who probably came to Basel in November, 1505, in which case his unusual style of theology could scarcely have escaped Zwingli's notice. In his exegetical lectures, especially those on Romans, in which the skills of Humanism were bent to uncover the biblical word, Wyttenbach pronounced indulgences "a cheat and delusion" and professed, in Paul's name, a doctrine of justification by grace through faith. There are some scholars who defer Wyttenbach's arrival until 1515, long after Zwingli's tenure in the university. In any case, Zwingli reckoned Wyttenbach a precursor of evangelical theology, and did not hesitate to call him "my master and esteemed and faithful teacher."

The other Baseler who appreciated the importance of Humanism for theology was Johann Ulrich Surgant, who since 1490 had been pastor of St. Theodore's Church and sometime lecturer in *pastoralia* in the university. To him Christian Humanism, with its compelling interest in the Christian sources, meant the revival of preaching, so that the biblical word might resound in the congregations to their edification. When Surgant referred to the "reviving word" he meant the preached word. As a supplement to the mass he actually proposed a vernacular preaching office in his book, *Manuale Curatorum* ("Manual for Pastors," 1502), which Julius Schweizer has shown to be the basis of Zwingli's own Sunday service of preaching, introduced at Zurich in 1525.

In the autumn of 1506, Zwingli was appointed vicar at Glarus. On September 29, he celebrated his first mass in the church of his childhood, having been newly ordained to the priesthood by Bishop Hugo of Constance. Zwingli was a conventional priest. When the parishioners of Glarus complained of wet weather, he paraded the host through the streets of the village on behalf of sunshine. The medieval church in whose structures he served had become inefficient and demoralized in Switzerland, without a real champion either of learning or of moral influence. Zwingli himself suffered his most profound failure in the matter of personal morality. Unable to cope with his own virility, he broke the vow of chastity on more than one occasion. He himself spoke of the shame which overshadowed his life. It is a mistake to suppose that he did not suffer some of the spiritual anguish that beset Luther or share Luther's quest for a gracious God.

But the greater part of Zwingli's evangelical awakening was intellectual. The priest of Glarus administered his parish from the first floor of the vicarage, while on the second floor he sequestered his books. His two-storied universe was typical also of his person: he was part pastor, part Humanist. He had not learned well enough the lessons of Wyttenbach and Surgant. Erasmus was the teacher who proved to be decisive for Zwingli. When Erasmus took up residence in Basel in 1514, the hitherto impersonal attachment which Zwingli had felt toward him became both personal and fervent. Erasmus persuaded Zwingli to jettison the medieval doctors once for all, to put aside even the classics in which he honestly delighted, and to commit himself profoundly to the Christian sources, namely, the New Testament and its earliest interpreters, the Fathers. It was this reverence for the sources, this rigorous intellectual discipline in uncovering them, this passion to learn the biblical languages, that Zwingli owed to Erasmus. But

Zwingli overstated his debt to the prince of Humanists when he declared in *Auslegen und Bergründen der Schlussreden* ("Expositions and Proof of the [Sixty-seven] Articles," 1523) that already in 1514–15 Erasmus had unveiled to him that Reformation theology. Erasmus harbored no such theology, and as there was actually no basic alliance between them, their friendship eventually collapsed, and turned to enmity. But in the education of Ulrich Zwingli as an evangelical man, Erasmus was nevertheless decisive.

Zwingli was turned out of Glarus, not on account of his moral lapses or his theological irregularity, but on account of his opposition to the Swiss mercenary system. Popes and kings vied with each other to obtain the services of those strong and wily warriors from the Alps. As often as not, Swiss youth found themselves at spearpoint with each other, fighting in opposing armies, without much thought of right and wrong, or much consideration for life itself. The immorality implicit in the mercenary system filtered down into every level of society and cheapened Swiss life. At least twice Zwingli went to battle in Italy as a chaplain to Swiss mercenaries. After the murderous battle of Marignano (1515) in which Swiss dead were strewn over the field, Zwingli wrote an allegorical poem, *The Labyrinth*, to denounce the mercenary system as a potential destroyer of the nation. His stout hostility to that traditional and lucrative system cost him his place at Glarus in 1516.

He repaired to Einsiedeln which in his era, as in ours, was one of the famous Roman Catholic shrines in Switzerland, the site of a chapel which had been dedicated by angels, of a statue of the Black Virgin which had drawn the veneration of pious folk for many years, of a Benedictine abbey so exclusive that no aspirant was admitted unless he could show so many quarterings of his coat of arms. Pilgrims from all Switzerland and south Germany swarmed over these holy premises seeking indulgences. The sign over the entrance promised "full remission of all sins."

At Einsiedeln Zwingli was employed by the Benedictines as chaplain to the pilgrims. At first, however, he seemed oddly preoccupied with his own interior development, and his labors were directed largely to his own good. In 1516 occurred one of the momentous events in the history of Christian scholarship — the appearance of Erasmus' Greek New Testament. With that choice volume propped up before him, Zwingli passed his days and nights in the abbey library, searching the depths of Paul, whose epistles he copied out word for word in Greek, and annotated according to the commentaries of Origen, Jerome, and Ambrose.

II

It was in Einsiedeln that Zwingli began to be an evangelical theologian. He commenced to preach the word of God, the word that is broken out of Scripture, the word that awakens faith in men by which they are united to Christ and receive in him the forgiveness of sin. "I began to preach the Gospel of Christ," wrote Zwingli in *Auslegen und Begründen der Schlussreden,* "in the year 1516, before any man in our region had so much as heard the name Luther; and I never left the pulpit that I did not take the words of the Gospel, as read in the mass of the day, and expound them by means of the Scriptures alone."

In this way Zwingli became a celebrity. To the pilgrims who came to Einsiedeln, he preached in love against the piety that had brought them. To the prelates who visited the shrine — for it was, in fact, an ecclesiastical spa — he gave warning of grave doctrinal errors practiced by the church, and prophesied a "great upheaval" if amendments were not made. In August of 1518 the Franciscan, Bernard Samson, arrived in the vicinity selling indulgences by license of Leo X. His slogans and promises were scarcely less extravagant than those of John Tetzel, who had recently worked havoc in Germany. Zwingli used his pulpit to denounce this huckster, and with such success that Samson fled.

When the office of people's priest at the Great Minster of Zurich fell vacant in October, 1518, the celebrated Zwingli of Einsiedeln was immediately considered for the post. (His indiscretions were not overlooked; but his chief rival, the father of six, suffered by comparison.) Zwingli was formally inducted into this eminent post on January 1, 1519, his thirty-fifth birthday. The next day, which was Sunday, he mounted his pulpit to commence a splendid innovation: he would abandon the lectionary of appointed lessons (which he believed to limit the free course of God's word) and would preach a continuous exposition of the New Testament starting with Matthew; and he would preach the word out of the word itself without reference to traditional commentary (which he called *Zwang*, human contrivance and constriction of God's word). As he said in one of his more memorable utterances: "The Word of God will take its course as surely as does the Rhine."

In the course of six years Zwingli's preaching ranged over the whole New Testament; and by the power of that preaching — for he had no other status in civic Zurich — the Reformation came to the small city on the Limmat. Lutheran ideas were also in the air. The books of the German Reformer reached Basel in December, 1518, and caused an immediate sensation. Zwingli's correspondence of 1519 was full of Luther, this "Elijah" whom he could not but admire. But he would not be called a Lutheran. "Why don't you call me a Paulinian since I am preaching as St. Paul preached .... If Luther preaches Christ, he does just what I do." If there was anything that gave depth to Zwingli's preaching in these early years at Zurich, it was the plague of 1519 that swept away nearly a third of the 7000 townsmen and brought Zwingli himself to the last boundary of man's threatened existence.

In his sermons of 1520–21, Zwingli declared that certain aspects of conventional piety — fasting, for example — had no basis in Scripture and ought to be curtailed. Opposition to such pronouncements came from three communities of friars in the city. In December, 1520 (if the date can be trusted), the Zurich magistrates intervened on Zwingli's behalf. Their quaint mandate guaranteed freedom to preach "the holy gospels and epistles of the apostles," but counseled preachers to "say nothing about other accidental innovations and rules."

Conscience-stricken by Zwingli's sermons, some Zurichers

decided to break the Lenten fast in 1522. On Ash Wednesday, according to one eyewitness, the printer Froschauer flouted the fast by cutting up two dried sausages and serving nibbles to certain brazen men, among them Zwingli himself. Zwingli, however, taking heed of Paul's admonition against scandalizing one's neighbor, refrained from eating. Soon the issue spilled out into the streets where men argued and brawled over the Lenten fast. Zwingli defended those who had eaten meat, in a sermon *On the Choice and Free Use of Foods,* which was written with the same evangelical ardor that one finds in Luther's treatise *Freedom of a Christian.* The Christian, Zwingli said, must be given freedom to live by his conscience as informed by the word of God. Alarmed at these developments, the Bishop of Constance, in whose jurisdiction Zurich lay, sent commissioners to Zurich to counsel obedience toward ecclesiastical laws. Despite this episcopal intervention, the magistrates resolved to do no more than bid the people keep the Lenten fast, until further "elucidation" could be brought to the issue.

One thing led to another. On July 2, 1522, eleven priests met in Einsiedeln, where on their behalf Zwingli drafted a petition to the Bishop of Constance: "Petition To Allow Priests To Marry, or at Least Wink at Their Marriage." The signers of this curious piece declared that chastity is a gift of God given to a few. Alas, they confessed, "this gift has been refused to us." Therefore they invoked their scriptural right to marry, in order to be rid of the intolerable burden imposed on their conscience by the tyranny of Rome. Bishop Hugo, already beset by the improprieties of some of his priests, did not find it appropriate to answer. But priests made bold to marry; and Zwingli himself entered into wedlock with the widow Anna Reinhart.

At midsummer of that memorable year, a third issue was provoked by Francis Lambert of Avignon, a Franciscan of some prominence, who was traveling from one Reformation city to another. In Zurich he was drawn into debate with Zwingli on the intercession of saints, but as the basis of argument was declared to be the Bible, Francis was left speechless. He mounted his donkey and rode off to Basel.

At Francis' departure, the local friars took up the cudgels against Zwingli, who had been making sport of their ignorance and sloth. Owing to these trifles of the year 1522, Zurich had been thrown into a crisis over the issue of scriptural authority. When the friars ventured to test this sensitive point, the Zurich Council reacted in Zwingli's favor and resolved to follow the Scriptures in doctrine and worship "to the exclusion of Scotus, Thomas, and suchlike." Now even the convents were thrown open, by the order of the magistrates, to evangelical preaching. Zwingli took this occasion to deliver an important sermon, *On the Clarity and Certainty of the Word of God,* to the nuns of the Oetenbach cloister.

The word of God, said he, is characterized by its "clarity" and "certainty." It is *clear,* not because it is written lucidly or spoken articulately, but because the Holy Spirit makes it clear by inward understanding. And it is *certain* in the sense that God in his word accomplishes what he purposes and promises. Zwingli's sermon is ultimately a sermon about the nature of preaching. True preaching is God speaking. Through the work of the Holy Spirit, the esoteric Scriptures and the human discourse of the preacher spring alive in the believer and are heard by him as the real, immediate, and effective word of God.

As 1523 opened, it was imperative to consolidate religious opinion in Zurich and to bring the other cantons abreast of events there. The council therefore scheduled a public disputation in the Town Hall, to which both friends and foes of reform were invited. As the basis for argument, Zwingli prepared *Sixty-seven Articles,* the first confessional document of the Swiss Reformation. The first sixteen articles were positive in nature; they insisted upon salvation by grace alone and upon the full and final authority of Scripture. Thesis 17 commenced a relentless series of "noes" in which the structure of medieval religion was dismantled, including the pope, the mass, good works, monastic orders, celibate clergy, penance, and purgatory. Priests and layfolk crowded the hall on January 29 to hear Zwingli defend the *Articles*. But Johannes Faber, who represented the Bishop of Constance, was reluctant to engage in debate, for he insisted that the meeting was no proper church council. The disputation was nonetheless deemed a victory for Zwingli, whose doctrines met no serious contradictions. The magistrates now issued a mandate, more decisive than the the others, declaring that the clergy of the canton should "preach nothing but that which can be proved by the Holy Gospel, and the pure Holy Scriptures." The disputation had the effect of committing Zurich more firmly to Zwingli while weakening the ties of the city to its Roman Catholic bishop.

The tempo of reform now increased. Zwingli found the time propitious to address himself to theological questions. Three of his longer treatises appeared in the months succeeding the January disputation. In *De Canone Missae Epichiresis*, he subjected the canon of the mass to exhaustive scrutiny. Aside from his humanistic impatience with its literary imperfections, he was distressed by its bad theology, namely its doctrine of the sacrifice which confounded the one all-sufficient offering of Christ on Calvary. He presumed to write four eucharistic prayers to replace the Roman canon which illustrate, if nothing else, that his eucharistic theology was still tentative.

In *Auslegen und Begründen der Schlussreden*, he expounded the skeleton theology of the *Sixty-seven Articles*, and demonstrated his own creativity and integrity as a Reformation thinker, Luther notwithstanding. Scarcely had he finished that work than he dispatched to the printer a sermon *On Divine and Human Justice*, in which his views of church and state are expressed. In Zurich he envisaged a Christian state, the *corpus Christianum*, a single, unified, Christian society in which church and state owe one another a reciprocal relationship of trust, assistance, and freedom. In the Christian state both the minister and the magistrate hold "spiritual offices." The magistrate is invested by God with the ministry of the sword; it is his function to execute human justice, even as Christ himself counseled and practiced obedience to civil authority. But social tranquility is no end in itself. What is really to be sought is a situation in which human justice will guarantee the preaching of the gospel to maximum effect, a situation devoid of tyranny and tumult in which all members of society are led by preaching to hear and receive God's gracious word of forgiveness.

III

But not all of the new believers saw things exactly as Zwingli did. Following the January disputation, a small party of radical reformers arose, dedicated to a more precipitate reformation than Zwingli preferred. They were the nucleus of the Swiss (Anabaptist) Brethren. Incited by Zwingli's own courage, as the champion of *sola scriptura,* these men saw no reason to temporize, no conceivable justification for delay. Let the "idols"[2] be removed at once. No one contributed to the excitement more than Zwingli's own colleague, Leo Jud, pastor of St. Peter's Church, who on September 1 used his pulpit to denounce pictorial Christianity and to demand the prompt removal of all scenic apparatus from the churches. Iconoclasm ensued. Hottinger the bootmaker led a contingent of overzealous souls in pulling down a great wooden crucifix at which the pious had made devotions for many years.

Iconoclasm prompted the magistrates to sponsor a second Zurich disputation, devoted to the issues of images and the mass. The problem of the first disputation had been to reconcile old believers and new. The current problem was to discover the proper way between Catholic conservatism on one extreme, and Anabaptist radicalism on the other. The leaders of the Anabaptists appeared for the first time at the second disputation. First among them was Conrad Grebel, who publicly deplored Zwingli's caution

---

[2] A word which meant all unscriptural things and usages in the church, but especially physical and pictorial things.

in the course of that debate. His closest colleagues were Felix Manz and Louis Haetzer, the author of a recent attack against pictorial Christianity. Associated with these men was the well-known pastor at Waldshut, Balthasar Hubmaier, who claimed to have challenged Zwingli on the subject of infant baptism as early as 1523.

The second disputation opened on October 26 in the presence of some five hundred priests. The bishops, to whom urgent invitations had been sent, were conspicuously absent. In three days of debate it was resolved that images were unscriptural and should be abolished, and that the mass was not a sacrifice, but a memorial of Christ's one, all-sufficient offering, and should be reconstructed as such. But, despite the strenuous objections of the radical theologians, the Zurich Council deferred the execution of these decisions until an orderly program of reform could be worked out, and until preachers had ranged over the canton, edifying the people as to the meaning of these changes.

The second disputation was crucial for the Anabaptists. Zwingli, for both theological and tactical reasons, proposed to temporize until the people had been sufficiently taught by God's word so that the changes would be received with unanimity and peace. But in order to gain time he insisted upon the competence of the state, as God's own agency for the well-being of society, to delay the demands of Scripture. In the eyes of the radical theologians, it appeared that Zwingli had thereby raised a second norm alongside that of Scripture. He was merely a pretender of *sola scriptura.* They commenced to distrust the idea of a *corpus Christianum,* and to doubt the integrity of the so-called Magisterial Reformation, in which the magistrates played a decisive part. It now occurred to them that all those who were seriously committed to the New Testament standards would have to be drawn out of society into gathered communities of the saints.

In the course of the second disputation, Zwingli had occasion to preach a sermon on the Christian ministry entitled "The Pastor." The church, he said, exists among those who adhere to God's word and confess Christ according to that word; so the ministry, which is responsible for the publication of that word, pertains to the *esse* of the church; and those who hold that high office must take the utmost care that they proclaim only the word, to the exclusion of all human doctrines. Zwingli was not content simply to use the word "minister"; the clergyman is also an "overseer," for surveillance is part of the pastoral office. In addition to preaching, the pastor must watch over the moral and spiritual integrity of the flock by exercising discipline in the parish.

The purification of the cultus, which the second disputation had anticipated, commenced in the summer of 1524. In one sweeping action, clergy and craftsmen entered the parish churches; they removed the relics and images, whitewashed the paintings and decorations, carted away the utensils, and nailed the organs shut in token that no music would resound in the churches again. To Zwingli these were strokes against ambiguity and superstition; they were strokes on behalf of simplicity and clarity. It seems inappropriate to define Zwingli's idea of authority as biblical legalism. His policy was really shaped by the seriousness with which he took symbolism. In the church, where man's salvation hangs in the balance, one must say exactly what one means, whether by word or by physical symbol. Remnants of the old cultus which are ambiguous or superstitious or sentimental must be rigorously cast aside, and forms must be found which express the New Testament gospel with simple clarity and power.

By Christmas, 1524, only one vestige of medieval religion survived — the mass. Shortly that liturgy itself came under a sharp, final attack in *Commentary on True and False Religion* (March, 1525), Zwingli's major effort at systematic theology, in which his doctrine of the eucharist first appeared in a definitive form. Zwingli and his colleagues supported this literary assault on the mass by vigorous representations to the town council that the Roman rite be abolished. The council acceded to their demands on April 12 — Wednesday in Holy Week. On Maundy Thursday, 1525, the Zurich rite was inaugurated.

Nearly every liturgical decision that Zwingli made depended upon his eucharistic theology. He insisted that faith, which constitutes the new relationship between the believer and God, is not fed by external things, and surely not by anything so crass as the eating of flesh and blood. It was typical of him to say, "None but the Holy Spirit gives faith, which is trust in God, and no external thing gives it." Moreover, an antagonism between spirit and body loomed in his thought. He could not see how material things could participate in the holy, or convey grace. They stood, in fact, in contradiction to one another. "Spirit and flesh contradict each other," Zwingli had told Luther at Marburg. His foremost pericope on the eucharist was John 6 which included the decisive verse (63), "It is the spirit that quickeneth; the flesh profiteth nothing." In any case, Zwingli supposed the glorified body of Christ to be locally resident at the right hand of the Father in heaven. So it is "wrong by the whole width of heaven" to imagine that his body is available on Christian altars so that communicants can feed on him. Zwingli ruled out entirely the possibility that Christians could participate in the substance of Christ's body.

If it was neither possible nor profitable to feed on the body of Christ in the Lord's Supper, it did not strike Zwingli as an enormity if one were to reinterpret "This is my body" to mean "This signifies my body." At that redefinition, the Lord's Supper became a "commemoration of the death of Christ," a memorial of our redemption on Calvary. Thus the bread and wine were *reminders* of a grace already received rather than *vehicles* of a present sacramental grace.

As Zwingli conceived it, the eucharist is the contemplation of the mystery of Calvary. This is no bare memorialism. *Contemplatio* is the critical word. The Supper is an occasion of profound, almost mystical contemplation of the mystery of man's deliverance on Calvary, a contemplation so powerful that the worshiper could "grasp the thing itself." The bread and wine serve as powerful stimulants to the communicant, reminding him of the body broken and the blood shed on his behalf, and enabling him to fix his mind in contemplation more quickly and effectively. In this contemplative sense, Zwingli was even prepared to say, "We have the Lord's Supper distinguished by the presence of Christ." But however ecstatic the Supper might be, it did not include our being nourished by the substance of Christ's body.

Zwingli saw no reason to observe the eucharist every Sunday. It did not convey grace, or mediate the divine life, or remit sin — as these benefits had been traditionally understood. Preaching was the proper center of an evangelical cultus, for it was normally by preaching that men were brought to faith and sustained in faith. The eucharist as a contemplative event might even suffer loss of effectiveness by too frequent occurrence. Zwingli decided upon a quarterly celebration of the Lord's Supper — a momentous decision which meant the disconnection of the eucharist from the normal Sunday service and which sundered the unity of word and sacrament that had prevailed in the West since Justin Martyr. Zwingli's decision committed him to the creation of a new type of Sunday service which would feature the sermon. For this use, he borrowed the preaching office that Surgant of Basel had designed in 1502 to accommodate the "reviving word." So, the worship of the Lord's Day came to be called, not inappropriately, "the sermon," and the eucharist retired from weekly prominence to become an occasional event.

Zwingli also proceeded to create a liturgy of the Lord's Supper which was used for the Easter celebration in 1525. Brilioth seems to test our credulity when he asks us to believe that this mean and radical liturgy is a "liturgical masterpiece" of "dogmatic expression." But he is precisely right. Zwingli resolved to create a liturgy which would accommodate his idea of *contemplatio*. What were chiefly required were stillness and repose, so that the worshiper need suffer no distraction but could fix his mind in the contemplation of Calvary, to which all Chrisian faith referred. Thus, there was no music,[3] no speech except the reading of Scripture. Instead of going forward to the altar to communicate, the people did not

---

[3] In other parts of this service, Zwingli arranged congregational recitations as a substitute for the congregational singing of hymns, but the magistrates refused to allow the recitations to be performed.

stir from their seats. The elements were brought down from the table in wooden plates and cups and delivered to the people where they sat. Each communicated and passed the elements to his neighbor. No one stirred; no one disturbed the monumental stillness of the Zwinglian eucharist.

The last phase of evangelical reconstruction pertained to the training of ministers. For this purpose Zwingli inaugurated what he called prophecy,[4] a daily period of rigorous Bible study which commenced in June of 1525. Its whole intent was to train theological students and retrain the priests. (And, by comparison, the Anabaptists might soon appear to be *false* prophets — untrained and irresponsible interpreters of the Scriptures.) In daily sessions at the Great Minster, the scholars dealt with the Old Testament chapter by chapter (and, after Zwingli's lifetime, with the New Testament as well). The first reader read the appointed chapter from the Vulgate. He was succeeded by the professor of Hebrew who read and expounded the passage from the Hebrew text. The professor of Greek proposed still other nuances from the Greek Septuagint. The fourth scholar, speaking in Latin, summarized all the insights and suggested how they could be used in preaching. Meanwhile the laymen had congregated. In their presence, Zwingli (or another) took to the pulpit and preached on the passage under discussion. Not only was the Zurich prophecy the means of training evangelical clergy; it also stimulated the production of early Protestant commentaries, to say nothing of the Zurich Bible of 1529. Some scholars see in this institution the origin of Reformed seminaries.

IV

A short excursion into the thought of this courageous and unfettered Reformer is appropriate here. Out of convenience we will confine ourselves to the *Commentary on True and False Religion,*

[4] See I Cor. 14:29–32.

his longest and most systematic work. At the outset, Zwingli agrees with Cicero that "religion (from *relego,* "to bring together") refers to "the *whole* piety of Christians," including doctrine, discipline, and worship. True religion is that which springs from the font of God's word, while false religion is responsive to human tradition and speculation. Zwingli proceeds immediately to the doctrine of God. He concedes that the existence of God is knowable by human reason, as the ancient philosophers bear witness. But to the pagan world, this partial knowledge is entirely without spiritual profit. The difference between the pagan and the Christian believer is that the latter knows God not merely by rational thought, but in faith; he has been taught by God himself.

But how does God teach us? We might expect the answer to be: through the preaching of the gospel, or, by the Holy Scriptures. Indeed, Zwingli does direct us to the "divine oracles" (the preaching and reading from the Bible), but what he really intends has a slightly different accent. It is the Holy Spirit who teaches. Did not Paul say plainly that all are ignorant of the things of God except his own Spirit? It is thus rash to expect knowledge of God from any other source. Normally the Spirit teaches us as we listen to the preaching of the Scriptures. But there are places in his theology where Zwingli ventures to say that the Holy Spirit may bring men to faith without any external means at all. Preaching itself is no prerequisite to the Spirit.

Having been directed to the "divine oracles," let us ask what the Scriptures say of God. They say: (1) "that he alone is the *being* (*esse*) of all things"; (2) that he is the "source and fountain of all *good*"; (3) "that as God is being and existence to all things, so he is the *life and motion* of all things that live and move"; (4) that in God is *prudentia* by which creation is purposefully ordered; "his wisdom knows all things even before they exist, his knowledge comprehends all things, his foresight regulates all things"; (5) that he is *love,* whose love is freely given apart from any human claim, and is most clearly seen in the delivery of Christ his son to the cross for our sins. These, however, are not the affirmations of a philosopher; they are the affirmations of God revealed in his word, and acceptable only as God himself gives men faith to understand them.

Whenever the doctrine of man is proposed for discussion, men naturally count themselves experts. Zwingli considers this a serious mistake, indeed! For a man to comprehend the nature of man is as unlikely as trying to seize a squid, which emits a cloud of inky fluid to hide itself. Man's camouflage is pride and feigned innocence. To learn of ourselves, we must resort again to Scripture. The God who built man knows the secrets of the human heart.

Zwingli proceeds to discuss the Fall, which he atributes ultimately to self-love, epitomized in man's absurd pretension of having equal status with God. "The death that is sin . . . consists in man's unceasingly loving himself, pleasing himself, trusting himself, crediting everything to himself, thinking he sees what is straight and what is crooked, and believing that what he approves, everyone ought to approve, even his Creator." The discourse on anthropology closes on a sombre note: "It has now been quite sufficiently shown that man does everything from self-love, and, unless he undergoes a change, will always do so."

In a chapter simply styled "Religion," Zwingli teaches man to distrust his works and to seek his whole help from God. "Religion," he observes, "took its rise when God called runaway man back to himself, when otherwise he would have been a deserter forever." In that very transaction man was shown the deplorable state of his affairs as well as the loyal devotion of this heavenly Father. Piety, then, consists in the despair of oneself, coupled with faith in the generosity of God. "This clinging to God, therefore, with an unshakable trust in him as the only good — this is piety, this is religion." But piety does not stop at that. Having been brought to faith, the Christian is eager to perform God's will; with a devotion like that of a man for his spouse, he is persuaded by no speech except that of God alone.

The next chapter, called "the Christian Religion," establishes the whole of Zwingli's theology upon Christ. But to make his point, he found it necessary to begin by testing the assumptions of works-righteousness, with predictable results. Good works are shown to be vitiated by pride. Pious service is exposed as self-service. The justice of God, which must indeed be satisfied, cannot be satisfied by human merit. It is satisfied by God himself in Christ:

> Wishing . . . to help this desperate plight of ours, our Creator sent one to satisfy his justice by offering himself for us, not an angel or a man, but his own Son, and clothed in flesh in order that neither his majesty might deter us from communion with him, nor his lowliness deprive us of hope. . . . For what can't he do, or what can't he have, who is God? Moreover, being man, he promises friendship and intimacy, indeed kinship and community. What can he refuse who is a brother and shareholder of our weakness?[5]

Zwingli regarded the virgin birth to be of critical importance in the economy of redemption. Only through that could it be said that deity took flesh without imperfection. Only in that way could the sacrifice for man's atonement be unblemished. Zwingli asserted the perpetual virginity of Mary, so that it could be said that virginity was her "quality." His delicate Mariology was expressed in an early sermon *On the Perpetual Virginity of Mary* (1522), and came to light in the Zurich liturgy which retained the *Ave Maria*, just before the sermon, as a hymn to the incarnation of Christ.

The gospel, which occupies Zwingli's next chapter, is something to be preached. It is the news "that sins are remitted in the name of Christ." When this announcement is truly preached and truly heard, a set of saving events occur in the life of man. Preaching first elicits repentance. In despair over himself, the Christian casts himself on God's mercy, which preaching has held out to him. Yet the prospect of God's justice still frightens him, for he knows that he is without any justice in the presence of God. Preaching, how-

---

[5] *The Latin Works of Huldreich Zwingli*, III (Philadelphia, 1929), 106; translation adjusted according to the Latin text in *Huldreich Zwinglis Sämtliche Werke*, III (*Corpus Reformatorum*, XC; Leipzig, 1914), 681.

ever, also brings Christ who has satisfied the divine justice. When the Christian, by faith, finds himself in solidarity with Christ, he knows that he is forgiven and indeed "just"; and he begins to live in newness of life. But is there a possibility that this theology of the gospel leads to antinomianism? It is an unlikely prospect, according to Zwingli. No man who has felt the terrible disease of sin and the marvelous health of forgiveness will resort willingly to the disease again. The man newly recovered from a broken limb does not say, "I have found a splendid physician; I must break my leg again."

In the succeeding chapters (on "Repentance" and on "Law"), Zwingli conceives of the Christian life as properly double-sided; it is a life of peace and war, of joy and sorrow; it is unremitting struggle against the weakness of the flesh and the ravages of self-love, broken now and then by the satisfaction of having loved God and done his will. Zwingli's point is that both sides pertain to the believer. It is the Christian's reasonable expectation to undergo both the comfort and the struggle that the gospel entails.

Zwingli's doctrine of election establishes a secondary line of development in his thought that includes the doctrines of the church, the ministry, and the sacraments. Election is most fully treated in the sixth chapter of the Reformer's treatise *On the Providence of God* (1530). It is immediately apparent that he will not allow us to pull apart God's justice and God's mercy, as if to assign election to one and reprobation to the other. Election is rather to be seen as the expression of God's undivided justice and mercy; the accent in Zwingli's thought falls on God's disposition to gather mankind into the church. He elects in order to save. "Election," wrote Zwingli, "is the free disposition of the divine will in regard to those that are to be blessed."

If election is the sole ground of our salvation, how can the structures of grace in the visible church make any conceivable difference? Calvin found a plausible way of dealing with that dilemma so that he could affirm the "treasures of grace" in the visible church. But Zwingli was far more apt to depreciate the traditional structures:

Since faith is a gift of the Holy Spirit, it is clear that the Spirit operated before the external symbols were introduced.[6]

For if the celebration [of the eucharist] could do anything of this kind, [that is, convey grace] Judas would have returned to his senses. . . .[7]

Election precedes faith, and faith follows election as a sign of it. For Zwingli, faith is a state of being which is created in us by the Holy Spirit; it is a new relationship between man and God; it is the "light and security of the soul," by which we are delivered from anxiety and defended against adversity; and it involves a spiritual union with Christ, although that union is not so clearly defined as the *mystica unio*[8] of Calvin. When Zwingli says that election precedes faith, he is tempted again to minimize the structures of the visible church. Infants and sundry pagans are chosen by God quite irrespective of those structures, "for His election is free." Thus, Zwingli is sure that Socrates and Seneca will be among the saved.

In Zwinglian thought, the term "church" is used in two ways. In the first instance, it applies to the whole company of the elect, which, because its constituency is known only to God, is properly called the invisible church. But the term "church" also pertains to the visible institution which includes all who are rated as Christians, all who are enrolled in the name of Christ and who participate in parish activities. This church is visible because its constituency is recognizable. But how can we be sure that the visible church is a true church of God? Melanchthon and Calvin refer to the marks of the true church, according to which such a determination can be made. Where the word is preached and the dominical sacraments are administered according to Christ's intention, one may speak confidently about the church. Instead of marks, Zwingli foresees certain indications that the saving work of God is being done in the congregation. Where the people are gathered around the word of God, where discipline is practiced, where the

---

[6] *The Latin Works,* II (Philadelphia, 1922), 190.
[7] *Ibid.*
[8] "Mystical union" or "spiritual union." See Calvin's *Institutes,* III.xi.10.

sacraments are correctly celebrated, where Christ is confessed, there are trustworthy indications that the will of God is being served. In these instances the visible church somehow transcends its empirical existence, its sociological reality, and participates in the *una sancta*.

V

In the course of 1525, the Anabaptist problem became acute in Zurich. In their letter of the previous year to Thomas Muentzer, Conrad Grebel and his colleagues had said that "infant baptism is a senseless, blasphemous abomination, contrary to Scripture." Zwingli, for his part, had now taken a firm stand on behalf of the baptism of infants. In his newly published disquisition *On Baptism* (1525), he declared that children of Christian parents are born within the sphere of the church; they are accounted heirs of the covenant through the faith of their parents; and the covenantal promises which God holds out to these children of the church ought to be established to them by the sacrament of baptism as a sign of the covenant. But the Anabaptists refused to practice this vestige of medieval life. Baptism, as they understood it, was a sacrament of commitment of one's whole life to Christ, which could not possibly be made except out of a genuine conversion that far exceeds the religious capacity of even the most precocious child.

The year of the impasse over infant baptism (1525) saw the first rebaptisms and the actual "gathering" of the Anabaptist communities. It was in January, apparently, at the home of Felix Manz, that the ex-priest Blaurock, who had had sacramental hands laid upon his head at least three times as a Catholic, demanded to be rebaptized "upon his faith and knowledge." The deed was done by the layman Conrad Grebel, and the event marks, as well as any other, the advent of sectarian Protestantism. In March of the succeeding year (1526), after protracted negotiations, the Zurich government delivered a decisive stroke to the Anabaptists: ". . . If anyone hereafter shall baptize another, he will be seized by our [magistrates] and, according to the decree now set forth, will be drowned without mercy." Thus, on January 5, 1527, Felix Manz was rowed to the middle of the Limmat and, trussed hand and foot, was cast into the deep. In such severity did Anabaptist martyrdom begin.

As early as 1524, the Forest Cantons of Switzerland — rural, conservative, and Roman Catholic — struck up an informal alliance to forestall the Reformation. A Protestant organization, the Christian Civic Alliance, was shortly called into being to offset the Roman Catholic power; by 1530 the Civic Alliance included the urban cantons of Zurich, Bern, and Basel, as well as certain lesser cantons and cities. Thus threatened, the Roman Catholics translated their informal alliance into the Christian Union, which sought and received the support of Roman Catholic Austria. By 1529, the Swiss confederacy was torn asunder over the Reformation. In that year, the First War of Cappel occurred; one cannot say that it was fought, for a negotiated settlement was reached prior to actual battle, in which it was agreed that neither side would persecute the other for the sake of religion, and that the treaty with perfidious Austria would be dissolved. The Roman Catholics came slowly to believe that this settlement, which implied the parity of the religions, was to their disadvantage, and they waited an opportunity to win a better decision.

Meanwhile, Philip of Hesse, the leader of the German Lutheran princes, conceived of an international Protestant alliance as a means of extending the Reformation. The inclusion of the Swiss seemed the proper first step. But their participation was made extremely difficult by Luther's undisguised contempt for Zwingli, whose monstrous doctrine of the Lord's Supper exhausted the Saxon's large vocabulary of abuse. It occurred to Philip of Hesse, nevertheless, to attempt a reconciliation of the Reformers. In April, 1529, he invited them to confer at his Marburg castle in the autumn forthcoming. The Marburg Colloquy convened on October

1, with Luther and Melanchthon in attendance on the Lutheran side, Zwingli and Oecolampadius representing the Swiss. Other divines were also present, notably Martin Bucer of Strassburg, who, as an advocate of the "true presence,"[9] fancied himself a mediator between the schools.

On the first day of the colloquy, wide areas of agreement were found to exist between the parties with respect to the chief articles of religion. But conflict arose on the morning of October 2, when the discussion was directed to the eucharist. Luther attributed Zwingli's error to a caprice in his use of the Bible. He therefore insisted upon the literal words of institution, "This is my body," which in fact he had scribbled in chalk on the surface of the great conference table. These words, he said, deserve to be received with wonder, with amazement, but certainly not with a giddy propensity to interpret them symbolically.

Oecolampadius, the venerable Reformer of Basel, responded from the Swiss side. He proposed the classic Zwinglian pericope from John 6:63, "the flesh profiteth nothing"; and he ventured to suggest that that verse cast a different light on the words of institution and made allowance for their symbolical interpretation. But the question which Oecolampadius pressed upon Luther was the most profound of all questions from the Swiss standpoint: "Since we have a spiritual eating, what need is there of a bodily one?" If, in other words, our relationship to God is by faith (as evangelical theology declares) and if that relationship is a spiritual one, begun and sustained in us by the Holy Spirit, then why do we need to communicate in the substance of Christ's body? According to some versions of the colloquy, Luther gave a spirited reply: "I don't care what need there is; I am a prisoner of the word of Christ. If Christ should command me to eat dung, I would do it, knowing that it would be good for me." The inelegance of Luther's remark does not detract from the seriousness of his intent. By insisting upon the integrity of the biblical words, he sought to

---

[9] Bucer soon began to teach the doctrine of the Spiritual Real Presence which was also typical of Calvin.

protect the sacramental dimension of Christianity, which Zwingli seemed to jeopardize.

Zwingli himself now interposed the critical text from John, "the flesh profiteth nothing," and insisted that it must be considered very seriously in the way the eucharist is explained. The words of institution, "This is my body," mean "this signifies my body" — an interpretation no more outrageous than countless examples of metaphorical speech in Scripture. The Lord's Supper is a memorial meal in which Christian people bear witness to the death of Christ as the *sole* source of their salvation, and contemplate this high mystery of their deliverance.

To this line of argument, Luther replied bitterly. "The words *hoc est corpus meum*," said he, "are not our words but Christ's. The devil himself cannot make it otherwise. I ask you therefore to leave off tampering with the word of God." Zwingli was now infuriated by this persistent appeal to the literalism of the words. Said he: "I remain firm at this text, 'the flesh profiteth nothing.' I shall oblige you to return to it. You will have to sing a different tune with me." Said Luther: "You speak in hatred." Replied Zwingli: "Then declare at last whether or not you will allow John 6 to stand?" Said Luther: "You are trying to overwork it. . . ." Replied Zwingli: "No, no, it is just that text that will break your neck." Said Luther: "Don't be too sure of yourself. . . . Our necks don't break as easily as that."

On October 2–3, the issue turned upon another prickly question — whether as the Zwinglians said, the body of Christ is "in one place," at the right hand of the Father in heaven, so that it "does not come down into the bread of the Lord's Supper," or whether, according to Luther's doctrine of ubiquity, the body of Christ is everywhere present and thus accessible in the sacrament of the altar.

Always Luther came back to the Scripture: "The Word, the Word, the Word, the Word, do you hear, that is the decisive factor." Under that sort of battering, the Swiss slowly retired into silence. Zwingli even wept under Luther's abuse, and the colloquy became a shambles. The ecumenical debacle at Marburg displayed the Lord's Supper as a major point of Protestant contention. The Marburg Colloquy defeated the politics of Philip of Hesse and left the Swiss evangelicals at the mercy of their Catholic foes.

In the course of 1530, the political crisis increased in Switzerland as both religious parties anticipated resumption of the war. The canton of Bern, reluctant to let blood, proposed to bring the Catholic cantons to terms by an embargo on essential supplies. "If you have the right to starve the cantons to death," said Zwingli in a curious Whitsunday sermon (1531), "you have a right to attack them in open war. They will now attack you with the courage of desperation." It was a fair prediction. In the Second War of Cappel, on October 11, 1531, the army of Zurich was routed, and Zwingli, struck down by the blows of outraged Catholics, died on the field in his forty-eighth year.

The word "Zwinglian" in theological parlance is often used imprecisely and pejoratively. On both counts, the word may be unfair to the Reformer of Zurich. We should see him properly as one of the eminent Reformed theologians, the first of that tradition. His reliance upon the word of God in Scripture as the sole ground of theology, his circumspect use of biblical authority to repair and regulate all parts of ecclesiastical life, his unmistakable accent upon the work of the Holy Spirit, his idea of preaching as the possibility of hearing the divine word, his ruthless purge of ambiguous, weak, and distracting symbols, his interest in discipline as an indispensable part of parish ministry — all of these put Zwingli in the mainstream of Reformed theology. Some of the newer interpreters of the Swiss Reformer are not content at that; they suggest that we must also pay our respect to Zwingli for the unfettered courage of his thought. In his idea of symbolism, in his radical doctrine of the Lord's Supper, in his reordering of the Christian cultus, we see Zwingli's resolve to be responsible to the Bible, to be consistent with his own theology, and to be led by both to the utmost limits of their suggestion.

BIBLIOGRAPHY

Many of the writings pertinent to Zwingli which appeared between 1918 and 1950 are listed in Bard Thompson, "Zwingli Study Since 1918," *Church History,* 29 (June, 1950), 116–128.

BIOGRAPHIES

There are three English biographies of Zwingli, none of which is entirely satisfactory. Samuel Macauley Jackson's *Huldreich Zwingli* (New York, 1901) is dated. Oskar Farner's *Zwingli the Reformer* (New York, 1952) is popular. Jean Rilliet's *Zwingli, Third Man of the Reformation* (Philadelphia, 1959) lacks theological perception. There are, however, major biographical works in German: Oskar Farner's *Huldrych Zwingli* in four volumes (Zurich, 1945–60); Walther Köhler's *Huldrych Zwingli* (Leipzig, 1943), which is perhaps the most useful of that distinguished scholar's writings on the Reformer of Zurich.

INTERPRETATIONS

Two excellent interpretations of Zwingli's thought have appeared in recent years: Jaques Courvoisier, *Zwingli, A Reformed Theologian* (Richmond, 1963); Gottfried Locher, *Die Theologie Huldrych Zwinglis im Lichte seiner Christologie,* Vol. I (Zurich, 1952).

Zwingli's sacramental theology and liturgical policies have been studied in a number of excellent books and manuscripts, among which are: Gottfried Locher, *Im Geist und in der Wahrheit: Die reformatorische I Wendung im Gottesdienst zu Zürich* (Neukirchen Kreis Moers, 1956); Cyril C. Richardson, *Zwingli and Cranmer on the Eucharist* (Evanston, Ill., 1949); Julius Schweizer, *Reformierte Abendmahlsgestaltung in der Schau Zwinglis* (Basel, n.d.) and Fritz Schmidt-Clausing, *Zwingli als Liturgiker* (Göttingen, 1952).

ZWINGLI'S WORKS IN ENGLISH

There are only two English editions of Zwingli's works. One of these is the very selective volume (XXIV) in the *Library of Christian Classics,* entitled *Zwingli and Bullinger* (Philadelphia, 1943). The standard English edition, the translations of which are never very felicitous, is now out of print and extremely rare: *The Latin Works and the Correspondence of Huldreich Zwingli . . . Together with Selections from His German Works,* in three volumes (New York, 1912; Philadelphia, 1922, 1929).

CHAPTER SIX

JOHN CALVIN

B. A. Gerrish

Few leading figures in the church's long history have suffered more than John Calvin from partisan interpretations, so that any serious account of him is almost obliged to become polemical. Diametrically opposed judgments on both the man and his thought can readily be drawn from the secondary literature. And it may be that the secret of his personality and the key to his thinking have, so far, eluded us. Calvin has been portrayed as narrow dogmatist and as ecumenical churchman, as ruthless inquisitor and as solicitous pastor, as inhuman authoritarian and as humanistic social thinker. Likewise, contradictory judgments can be found concerning the man's thought: some hold that he was a mere organizer who contributed no new ideas, and others believe that even the doctrine of the Holy Trinity remained incomplete until he completed it; some hold that the center of his theology was predestination, others that the center was forgiveness, and still others that his theology had no center.

Not all of these interpretations can be right. This much is obvious, even if we allow the possibility that John Calvin may have been a man of contradictory traits and a theologian of inconsistent ideas. (Here, too, one runs into difficulties. While some interpreters have viewed Calvin as a dialectical theologian, whose ideas lie together in sharp tension, the prevailing impression is that in Calvin's theology cool Gallic logic has harnessed and organized the impetuous Teutonic spirit.) Some of the contradictions can be attributed to overhasty historical construction. For example, it is obvious that many have formed their impression of Calvin's personality by elevating and isolating his role as the accuser of Michael Servetus (1553). Calvin is then deplored as the grand inquisitor of Protestantism who silenced freedom of thought with the stake and the faggots. Why Calvin should thus be singled out for reprobation remains a mystery. In France, not one, but a multitude of Protestants paid for their faith with their lives. In England, Protestants or Catholics (depending on which party was currently in power) were executed by hundreds during the sixteenth century. And in Saxony, Melanchthon prepared, and Luther signed, a document (1536) demanding the death penalty for denial of any article in the Apostles' Creed or even for the refusal to serve as a magistrate.

Similarly, a historical understanding of Calvin's thought has been hampered by the persistent tendency to read him through the spectacles of later Calvinistic (or supposedly Calvinistic) developments. Hence it is commonly supposed that a Calvinist is a man who is fascinated by the evidences of his own growth in grace and who applies them to his frantic quest for assurance of being predestined. One can only say that such "Calvinism" reverts to the kind of religion against which Calvin himself directed his keenest shafts. Assurance, for him, was a part of the meaning of faith. Hence he who has faith in Christ already knows himself elect. But if the Christian looks to his own "works," and not to Christ, he can find in himself nothing but cause for doubt and fear. Incipient doubt and immature faith are remedied, not by seeking an impossible assurance in oneself, but by turning back again to Christ, "the mirror of our adoption."[1]

Our own profile of John Calvin — the man, the theologian, and the reformer — takes no further account of the controversies in the secondary literature. It presents simply one man's sketch for the

---

[1] See, for example, *Institutes* (hereafter *Inst.*), III.xxiv.5. References are to the 1559 edition (cited by Book, chapter, and section). The Latin text will be found in *Johannis Calvini Opera Selecta* (hereafter *OS*), ed. Peter Barth and Wilhelm Niesel (5 vols.; Munich 1926–36), Vols. 3–4. See also *Corpus Reformatorum. Johannis Calvini Opera quae supersunt omnia* (hereafter *CO*), ed. G. Baum *et al.* (59 vols.; Brunswick, 1863–1900), 7, 464, 479 (on the Decrees of Trent); 8, 114 ("congregation" on election); 49, 312 (commentary on I Cor. 1:9). Translations from the sources are by the author of the present essay.

Calvin gallery. No doubt, like all historical portraiture, its style is impressionistic. But the intention, at least, is to permit the sources to make their own impressions. An important clue — though not the only one — to the personality of Calvin is found in his vocational struggle. And although Christology may not be the structural center of Calvin's "system," the attempt is made to display "Christocentrism" as at least a characteristic habit of Calvin's thought — a habit which determined both his theology and his conception of reform.

I

John Calvin was born on July 10, 1509, in Noyon. His father, Gérard, was a lawyer associated with the cathedral chapter. His mother died when he was still a child. Brought up in the shadow of the great cathedral, John was early marked for a career in the service of the church. Aided by the income from a benefice without pastoral obligations, he set out for Paris in 1523, at the age of fourteen, in quest of an education. He completed his general studies at the Collège de la Marche and moved on for his theological studies to the Collège de Montaigu, where Erasmus had preceded him and Loyola was to succeed him. If we believe his friend and biographer, Theodore Beza, Calvin was already remarkably religious and strict in censuring all the vices of his companions.[2] (Unwittingly, Beza lends some credibility to the legend that Calvin was nicknamed "the accusative case.")

Partly for financial reasons, and partly because of a quarrel with the clergy at Noyon, Calvin's father changed his plans for the youth and directed him into the study of law. Calvin moved from Paris to Orleans (1528), and devoted his energies to his new subject. Beza represents him as a diligent and successful student who kept his lamp burning till midnight and occasionally stood

---

[2] The biographies of Calvin by his two friends, Beza and Colladon, are both in CO, Vol. 21. A further major source for Calvin's life is his voluminous correspondence: CO, Vols. 10–20.

in for his professors. True, he did like to lie in bed a while in the mornings, but this, Beza explains, was in order to think over what he had been reading the night before. The next year (1529) Calvin continued his studies at Bourges, and there began to find time for the ancient classics as well as for law. Indeed, when his father died two years later (1531), Calvin made it plain that his pursuit of legal studies had become only a matter of filial obedience, for he promptly abandoned law, returned to Paris, and embarked on a literary career. In 1532 his first book was published, a learned commentary on Seneca's treatise *De clementia* ("On Clemency"). Calvin was immensely proud of his first book, in which he dared even to correct the great Erasmus. He boldly commended his labors to his friends and to professors who might be induced to use *De clementia* in their classes. But the scholarly world was not interested.

It has been supposed that Calvin's choice of *De clementia* for his first efforts as a commentator was an indication of his conversion to Protestantism. As Seneca wrote to instruct the Roman Emperor Nero, so, it is suggested, Calvin wrote his commentary as a plea to King Francis I of France to show clemency toward the Evangelicals. But there is no solid reason to accept this speculation, since Calvin's commentary was not dedicated to the king. By 1534, however, Calvin had penned his first statement of Protestant belief: a preface to a French translation of the New Testament by his cousin, Olivétan. Sometime between 1532 and 1534 he exchanged the classics for the Scriptures as his main love. And we know that during the year 1533 he was somehow implicated in the arrests which followed an allegedly Protestant address by Nicholas Cop, Rector of the University of Paris. Calvin himself, in a rare autobiographical passage which he prefixed to his *Commentary on the Psalms* (1557), tells of a "sudden conversion." "I was utterly amazed that, before the year was past, all who had some desire for pure doctrine began to come to me for instruction, although I myself was a mere novice." He assigns to the incident no particular date, but 1533 seems a reasonable choice. The significance of the conversion is explained largely in vocational terms, so to speak. Although Calvin did not drop his other studies, his enthusiasm was turned to the pursuit of evangelical theology. In his *Reply to Sadoleto* (1539), however, Calvin gives an evangelical testimony which conforms closely to the "Lutheran" pattern. He tells of a struggle with legalistic piety and a stern picture of God, resolved by instruction in the true message of the gospel. Although Calvin does not himself say so, it is commonly assumed that the testimony is drawn from his own experience of the bruised conscience and the comfort of free forgiveness.

Calvin's conversion did not, however, awaken in him any ambition to become a reformer. As he said to Sadoleto, the summit of his desires was the enjoyment of literary ease. In other words, he still thought of himself as a writer, though now his gifts of authorship were to be devoted to true religion. Hence in 1534 he wrote a preface to the New Testament and a treatise against the Anabaptists (not published until 1542); and by the summer of 1535, at the age of twenty-six, Calvin handed the first edition of his *Institutes* to a printer in Basel. Early in 1536 he traveled to Italy, the cradle of the Renaissance; returned to Basel, where the *Institutes* had now been published; and paid a visit to France under the terms of an edict which granted amnesty to the Protestants. With his brother, Antoine, and half sister, Marie, he then set out for Strassburg, which he apparently had chosen as the headquarters for his "literary ease." The three travelers found the road barred by imperial troops because Emperor Charles V was at war with France, and they determined to make a long detour which brought them to Geneva. It was one of those apparently trivial decisions by which a whole lifetime is determined. The young convert's presence in Geneva was made known to William Farel, the reformer, who begged him to stay and aid in the task of reforming the city. Calvin refused. He was, he said, a scholar, not an administrator; and in any case he did not have the right temperament, being by nature rather reserved. Farel, in a white heat of anger, warned Calvin that he was merely indulging his own desires and that God

would curse his quiet, scholarly life if he refused the Lord's
assignment for him in Geneva. Overawed, Calvin yielded, and so
began his lifelong association with the Swiss city.

Calvin heartily detested the labors that had been thrust upon
him. "This I can honestly testify: not a day passed in which I did
not long for death ten times." And yet the thought of deserting his
post never entered his head. His official appointment was as
"reader in Holy Scripture." So little known was Calvin at this time
that when the authorities approved the appointment, the secretary
missed his name and wrote simply, "that Frenchman." As it happened, the first attempts of Calvin to reform the Genevans ended
in failure. It was axiomatic to Calvin that the worship and discipline of the church ought to be in the hands of the church's own
officers, not of the politicians. But this the civil authorities refused
to grant. The crisis came in 1538, when the ministers were
instructed to administer communion according to the practice of
the church in Bern. Neither Calvin nor Farel cared deeply about
the "Bernese rites" (which required the use of unleavened bread
in the Supper), but they could not concede to the civil authorities
the right to dictate in ecclesiastical affairs. On Easter Sunday,
Calvin made his way to St. Pierre and Farel to St. Gervais, as
usual. They preached their sermons, then proceeded to excom-
municate their entire congregations in a body. The response was
fearful; swords were unsheathed, and the ministers had to escape
amidst the uproar. They were promptly relieved of their appoint-
ments, and Calvin set out for Basel to resume his interrupted
career of scholarship.

But Farel was not the only one who knew how to intimidate
the reserved young scholar by the threat of divine anger. This time
the call — and the threats — came from Martin Bucer, reformer of
Strassburg. And again Calvin reluctantly packed his belongings.
In actual fact, the years at Strassburg (1538–41) were among
the happiest and most productive in his life. Calvin was pastor to
the French congregation and lecturer in the academy. For his congregation of refugees he compiled a book of Psalms in French

(1539) and a simple liturgy (1540). A new edition of the *Institutes* appeared in 1539; the first of Calvin's great series of commentaries, on Romans, was published in 1540; and his admirable *Short Treatise on the Lord's Supper* followed in 1541. It was also at Strassburg that Calvin, on the recommendation of his friends, began to look for a wife. Not being, he said, one of those mad lovers who fall in love with a fine figure at first sight, he specified a woman who should be modest, thrifty, and likely to be careful of his health. He found a suitable match in a widow named Idelette de Bure, whom he judged a model of womanhood. (Farel, who noticed such things more than Calvin, mentions that she was also beautiful.)

But Calvin was not left at Strassburg in peace. The situation at Geneva had become critical after the dismissal of Calvin and Farel. The distinguished Roman prelate, Cardinal Sadoleto, had advised the Genevans that they should return to the Roman fold, in which their salvation would be secure. Embarrassed, the Genevan magistrates wrote to Calvin and asked the man they had summarily dismissed to respond to Sadoleto on their behalf. This Calvin did in one of the best evangelical apologies to come from his pen. Among other points, he professed astonishment and regret that the cardinal should have appealed to such an inferior motive as the desire for salvation. Shortly afterwards, the Genevans began pleading with Calvin — though not with Farel — to return and resume the work of reform. Calvin responded that he would rather die a hundred times than go back to Geneva. He had, in any case, plenty to do at Strassburg, and was now actively engaged in the Protestant-Roman conferences arranged under the patronage of the emperor. And once again it required the voice of Farel and the final sanction of God's wrath before Calvin would yield. The Strassburgers granted him a temporary leave. But the secretary who recorded his arrival at Geneva in September, 1541 rightly put down that he was "to be forever the servant of Geneva."

Calvin's reformatory goals were laid down in the celebrated *Ecclesiastical Ordinances* (1541), in which the "right order" of the church is explained from the word of God. Four types of ecclesiastical officers are described: pastors, to minister in word and sacrament; doctors, to instruct the faithful in sound doctrine; elders, to assist the pastors in the discipline of the church; and deacons, to manage the church's finances or to minister to the sick and the poor. The pastors were to meet each week in open sessions (later called "congregations") for exposition of the Scriptures, and each quarter for fraternal admonition (the "venerable company"). Discipline was placed in the hands of a "consistory," composed of the pastors and elders, which was to assemble once a week. Further, prescriptions were laid down for the church's worship. The draft of the *Ordinances*, made by Calvin (still a young man of 32) in consultation with the other ministers and a group of elected councilors, did not entirely commend itself to the civil authorities, who were determined to retain control over ecclesiastical affairs. They ensured, for instance, that the election of all four types of ecclesiastical officers should be either directly in their hands (the elders and deacons) or subject to their supervision (the pastors and doctors).

Equipped with the machinery of reform, the Genevan authorities set out to transform the moral and spiritual condition of the Genevans. Severe measures were taken against swearing, drunkenness, gambling, wife-beating, adultery, blasphemy, and absence from church or misconduct during church. Eating, drinking, dancing, clothing, all came within the purview of the Genevan reformation. A sample problem concerned the taverns. One section of Geneva had roughly one tavern to every three houses. An attempt was made to replace them by community centers, the proprietors of which were strictly charged to watch for excessive drinking, obscene songs, and gambling. No food was to be served to anyone who omitted to say grace. And, to foster edifying conversation, copies of the Bible in French were placed at the tables. The experiment, however, proved a failure. The community centers attracted few customers, and the proprietors reported anxiously to the authorities. The taverns were reluctantly reopened, and the people flocked back rejoicing. All of this may strike the modern man as a futile experiment in the infringement of personal liberties. Yet, as T. M. Lindsay observed: "Every instance quoted by modern historians to prove . . . Calvin's despotic interference with the details of private life can be paralleled by references to the police books of medieval towns of the fifteenth and sixteenth centuries."[3]

The moral recalcitrance of the people was not the only obstacle to Calvin's program of reform. He also encountered theological and political opposition. As Erasmus had chosen to attack Luther on the evangelical doctrine of human bondage, driving the German Reformer to take his stand upon the doctrine of predestination, so Calvin's chief critics, Jérôme Bolsec and Jean Trolliet, chose the same ground of controversy. More serious, however, was the political opposition which organized itself around the families of François Favre, Ami Perrin, and Philibert Berthelier. Even the young son of François Favre played his modest role in the opposition by bouncing tennis balls against the wall of St. Gervais while Calvin was trying to lecture inside. The most formidable opponent was perhaps Favre's daughter, Madame Perrin, whom Calvin nicknamed "Penthesilea, Queen of the Amazons." The political struggles demanded great personal courage on Calvin's part. Once he threw himself in the path of a mob which was demonstrating on Perrin's behalf and had forced entry into the council chamber. Calvin shouted that if the mob was bent on shedding blood they could begin with his. The crowd wavered, and Calvin launched into a long speech, by the end of which tempers had cooled.

In the Servetus trial of 1553 the political opposition lent assistance to the accused, no doubt foreseeing a chance to make trouble for Calvin. They made a fearful blunder. Servetus had denied the Trinity and rejected the practice of infant baptism, yet "a fatal fascination drew him to Geneva, like a moth to the candle flame."[4]

---

[3] *A History of the Reformation* (New York, 1907), II, 108.
[4] John T. McNeill, *The History and Character of Calvinism* (New York, 1954), p. 174.

He was apprehended, tried (with Calvin as his accuser), and sentenced to death by the authorities. And so Geneva, the haven for persecuted refugees, became a persecuting city. Calvin himself approved the sentence of death, though he objected to the method, death by burning. "We are today horrified," remarks Roland Bainton, "that Geneva should have burned a man for the glory of God, yet we incinerate whole cities for the saving of democracy."[5]

Calvin had entered the Servetus trial certain that his work in Geneva was finished. So intense was the political opposition that he even preached a farewell sermon. But he emerged from the incident strengthened, his opponents discredited. In the eyes of his contemporaries — with a few exceptions like Sebastian Castellio — Calvin had done well. The triumph of Calvin's reformatory program in the 1550's was sealed in 1559 by the foundation of the Genevan Academy and the final admission of Calvin to Genevan citizenship. That same year the definitive edition of the *Institutes* was published. It had now grown from a small manual of six chapters into a massive treatise in four books and eighty chapters. But Calvin's days were numbered; he had contracted tuberculosis. He drove himself to continue his duties, still preaching in St. Pierre when he could no longer walk but had to be carried there by his friends. He died on May 27, 1564, at the age of fifty-four, and on his own instructions was laid in an unmarked grave.

Calvin's history is the story of a man forced into work for which he had no taste. Best fitted, in his own judgment, for the life of scholarship, he was obliged to become pastor, teacher, preacher, and reformer. He was, besides, constantly troubled with demands that had no connection with his official duties. Calvin described his own story in a few simple words:

> Being of a rather unsociable and shy disposition, I have always loved retirement and peace. So I began to look for some hideout where I could escape from people. . . . My aim was always to live in private without being known. But God has so moved and turned me around with all kinds of

---

[5] *The Travail of Religious Liberty* (Philadelphia, 1951), p. 94.

changes that he has never let me rest anywhere. In spite of
my disposition he has brought me into the light and made
me get involved, as they say.[6]

As E. Harris Harbison put it, Calvin thought of himself as a "God-
frustrated scholar."[7] And as John T. McNeill suggested, he was
one of those persons who become assertive in overcoming the
inclination to retirement.[8]

If his labors were not to his liking, they were made all the more
burdensome as his almost unbelievable list of physical ailments
grew in number and intensity. He was tortured by asthma, catarrh,
indigestion, migraine, quartan fever, arthritis, ulcerous hemor-
rhoids, calculus, pleurisy, and tuberculosis. As his friend Colladon
testified, the burden of excessive work and constant illness contributed to make Calvin "irritable and difficult." But he was also,
it seems, sharp-tongued and short-tempered by nature. And he
knew it. Violent fits of anger were followed by intense remorse,
occasionally even by uncontrolled tears. But his friends, who were
ready to overlook his faults, testified to the deep affection and
unfailing concern which he showed toward them and to any who
turned to him for help.

II

The preface to Olivétan's New Testament (first published in
1535) was Calvin's first confession of evangelical faith. It contains
the fundamental ideas which never ceased to determine his conception of the Christian religion. From a sketch of the history of
salvation Calvin moves to a long, almost lyrical passage in praise
of the gospel and of Jesus Christ, whom the gospel presents. God
fashioned man in his own image and likeness for a parent's delight
in his child. But man's well-being depended upon his acknowledging God alone as the source of all good. Instead, he sought his

---

[6] *CO* 31, 22 (Preface to the *Commentary on Psalms*).

[7] *The Christian Scholar in the Age of the Reformation* (New York, 1956), p. 144.

[8] *Op. cit.*, p. 230.

dignity in himself, and through ingratitude defaced the divine image. But God continued to love those who deserved no love, surrounding his entire creation with tokens of his presence, revealing himself to his chosen people in word and action and, finally, offering man the new covenant of the gospel. This "joyful news" is the word of life and truth, the key to the knowledge of God, because it presents Jesus Christ. Faith, the one way to life and salvation, is given by hearing this word. Here, already, are some of the determinative ideas of Calvin's theology: man's blessedness is acknowledging God as the source of good; the heart of Scripture is Jesus Christ; and the gospel is the word of God which confers faith. These were the leading themes of Calvin's theology right up to the final edition of his *Institutes*.

1. *Religion as Thankfulness*

In his *Catechism* of 1537 Calvin explains that the essence of piety is not a fear which shrinks from the judgment of God, but rather a zeal which loves God wholeheartedly as Father and reveres him as Lord. The truly pious person therefore embraces God's justice and would rather die than offend him. In the *Institutes* (1559) Calvin maintains that piety in this sense is not merely the heart of religion, but an essential ingredient in the task of theology. Strictly speaking, God is not known where there is no piety (I.ii.1). The knowledge of God with which the theologian concerns himself is not academic nor disinterested, but embraces the knower and his knowledge of himself. Moreover, it is the awareness of God's benefits that induces piety. Only as men recognize that they owe everything to God — that they are nourished by his fatherly care, that he is the author of their every good — will they yield him their willing service. God, for Calvin, is the "fountain of all good"; "piety" is the acknowledgment that this is so.

Man was made for piety. God placed within him an awareness of deity and surrounded him with tokens of divine presence. Had man remained whole, the very order of nature would have led him to the knowledge of God; he would have lived in thankfulness, as

one who *knowingly* received his life from God. This, Calvin
believed, was the meaning of man's creation in the image of God.
The entire created order reflects God's glory as in a mirror; in this
sense all creation images God.[9] But man is set apart from the mute
creation by his ability to reflect God's glory in a conscious response
of thankfulness. It is this, in particular, which sets him apart from
the brute beasts, who likewise owe their existence to God and
reflect his glory, but do not know it. Man is endowed with a soul
by which he can consciously recognize God as the fountain of
good. The soul is not itself the image, but rather the mirror in
which the image is reflected. We can properly speak of man as
bearing the divine image only when he truly refers his excellence
to the exceptional gifts bestowed upon him by his maker (I.xv.3).
It is *in* man's faculties that the image is reflected (I.xv.4). Man is
the apex of God's creation in the sense that the entire creation has
its *raison d'être* in the praise which man alone, of all the earthly
creatures, can return to God. The creation of the world would
have been in vain if at any time there had been no people to call
upon God.[10]

Yet there would be none to praise or call upon God were it not
for the fact of redemption. Man is fallen man, who can possess the
divine image (in the uniquely human sense) only as it is restored
to him through Christ. The image in fallen man is not totally
annihilated, but it is fearfully deformed, and we can best recognize
the intention of God for man by viewing the New Man, the
"Second Adam," Jesus Christ (I.xv.4).

The nature and consequences of man's fall occupy Calvin
in Book II, chapters i–v, of the *Institutes*. The discussion
presupposes, of course, that Adam was the first parent of the
human race in the strictly historical sense. But it is plain that
Calvin's primary interest is not to account for the origin of sin but
to describe mankind as fallen. He wants to assert that all men are
one with Adam in his sin; the way in which Adam's sin is trans-

---

[9] For the image of God in all creation see *CO* 55, 145 (on Heb. 11:3).
Cf. also *Inst.*, I.vi.3, where, however, the Latin word is *effigies*, not *imago*.
[10] *CO* 32, 192 (on Ps. 115:17).

mitted he leaves somewhat obscure. (He expressly denies that each of us inherits sin by simple genetic laws.)[11] Original sin is "hereditary," so it seems, in the sense that all the children of Adam are tainted by it. But heredity is not in itself an explanation of how the taint of sin is transmitted. In any case, the chapters on sin belong under the rubric of "Redemption in Christ," and find their point in chapter vi: "Fallen man should seek redemption in Christ." Apart from this point of reference, Calvin's anthropology is by no means gloomy. The fallen man is the one who has turned away from God; refusing to respond in faith to the voice of God (he is *verbo incredulus*), he spurns God's bounty by his ingratitude and opens himself to the sins of carnal self-indulgence (II.i.4). From *this* viewpoint, man is wholly devoid of good (II.ii.9). But Calvin finds ample good in man viewed as a social animal, and he is eloquent in his praise of human science and virtue — for these, too, are the gifts of God's grace and occasions of gratitude. The point is, however, that even man's highest good is sin as long as its source in the bounty of the one true God is not acknowledged and as long as its motive is something other than the praise of God (II.iii.4).

Calvin's entire discussion, then, is from a strictly theological standpoint; it points forward to his treatment of redemption. Indeed, one must add that all is already seen from the vantage point of the redeemed man. Calvin's order of treatment is not experiential, but quasi-historical; he presents his material as the story of the race, not of the individual. But it is solely as an individual redeemed in Christ that he can discuss his themes at all. In the order of individual experience, knowing God as redeemer *precedes* knowing him as creator. Only as man's eyes are opened by the word and the Spirit — therefore, only as he is redeemed — can he recognize the true God in the created order. It is *by faith* that we understand the world to have been created by the word of God (Heb. 11:3). But Calvin has won an important advantage by

---

[11] *CO* 47, 57 (on John 3:6).

not following the order of individual experience; he has been able to show redemption, not as a merely negative removal of sin, but as a positive restoration to the state of true piety. The redeemed man is not merely the forgiven man, but the man whose eyes have been opened to the glory of God in the works of creation and providence; and he knows him truly as the triune God — Father, Son, and Spirit. These are the themes of Book I after Calvin has established the necessity and nature of revelation.

2. Christ as the Object of Faith

The entire argument of Book I and Book II, chapters i–v, of the *Institutes* has served to justify the christological claims of Book II, chapter vi. Calvin has kept a firm hand on the intricate and devious turns of the argument, and now brings the reader to the words of Paul: "Since, in the wisdom of God, the world did not know God through wisdom, it pleased God through the folly of preaching to save those who believe" (I Cor. 1:21).

> Therefore, although the preaching of the cross does not agree with human thinking, if we desire to return to God our author and maker, from whom we have been estranged, that he may again begin to be our Father, we ought nevertheless to embrace it humbly (II.vi.1).

The only course for fallen man leads to the cross and faith in Christ. To believe in God is to believe in Christ. As Calvin sees it, this holds as much for the faith of the Old Testament patriarchs as for the faith of the New Testament saints. For Christ is the "end" of the Mosaic Law — that is, the goal to which it points (Bk.II, chap. vii) [12] — and the mediator of both Testaments (Bk.II, chap. ix).

The true object of faith is our Lord Jesus Christ, or more precisely, "Christ clothed with his gospel" (III.ii.6). [13] But this does not mean that faith is a mere assent to the information conveyed in Christian preaching. Rather, Christ is really present in the act of believing. "Faith does not just contemplate Christ as though he

---

[12] Cf. *CO* 51, 427 (on Eph. 2:19–22).
[13] Cf. *CO* 46, 496 (*Harmony of the Gospels,* Sermon 40).

were far removed, but embraces him that he may become ours and dwell in us. It makes us grow together into his body, have life in common with him."[14] Faith, in fact, effects a hidden communion of the believer with Christ. This "matter of great importance" is the subject of a letter Calvin wrote to Peter Martyr (August 8, 1555).[15] It is something *subsequent* to the communion which we already have with Christ by virtue of the incarnation and *antecedent* to the communication of Christ's benefits.

> For the discussion concerns only the communion which flows from his heavenly virtue and breathes life into us and causes us to grow together in one body with him. I say that in the moment when we receive Christ by faith as he offers himself in the gospel, we become truly members of his body and life flows into us from him as from the head. For in no other way does he reconcile us to God by the sacrifice of his death than because he is ours and we are one with him. . . .
> How this happens, I confess is something far above the measure of my intelligence. Hence I adore this mystery rather than labor to understand it — save that I acknowledge that the life is transmitted from heaven to earth by the divine virtue of the Spirit. . . . It is therefore the Spirit who brings it about that Christ dwells in us, sustains us, gives us life, and fulfills all the functions of the head.

Redemption, then, as Calvin understands it, is placed in the "mystical union" of the believer with Christ. Properly speaking, this is the theme of Book III of the *Institutes*. But the same theme reaches back into the second book and forward into the fourth. Already in Book II Calvin describes the incarnation as a union of humanity with the Son of God. He became Emmanuel, God with us, in such fashion that his divinity and our humanity might grow together by mutual connection (II.xii.1). He took what was ours — not only our nature, but also our sin and our death — to impart to us by grace what was his by nature, his life and righteousness (II.xii.2–3, xvi.6). He achieved this for us by the whole course of his obedience (II.xvi.5) — a statement which Calvin demonstrates

---

[14] *CO* 47, 145 (on John 6:35).
[15] *CO* 15, 722–25.

in detail by surveying the events of the gospel narrative as summarized in the Creed.

Although a union of Christ and mankind is already effected by the incarnation itself, still, if what he did and suffered for *mankind* is to benefit *us,* we must be united with him by faith. This is the theme of Book III. Like Luther in his *Treatise on Liberty*, Calvin speaks of a "sacred marriage" of the believer and Christ, by which the possessions of Christ become ours (III.i.3). Or again he uses the expressions "wondrous communion" (ii. 24) and "mystical union" (xi.10). From this union we receive a twofold gift: first, we are reconciled to God and have him as our indulgent Father instead of as Judge; second, we are sanctified by Christ's spirit and cultivate integrity and purity of life (I.xi.1). All our good — summarized under the two graces of reconciliation (or justification) and sanctification — is therefore to be sought in Christ alone. The whole third book of the *Institutes* is but a commentary on the vision which inspired Calvin at the beginning of his career and which he presents in his preface to Olivétan's New Testament. Every good thing we could think or desire is to be found in Jesus Christ alone.[16]

The doctrine of election, far from being the first principle of Calvin's theology, is rather its final consequence. And Calvin expressed his intention well in the 1559 edition of the *Institutes* by placing the discussion of election *after* the chapters on the twofold gift of Christ: there it functions as a kind of appendix to the affirmation of his central theme, "by Christ alone." Even the decision of some (and not others) to respond in faith to the call of God must itself be included in the decision God made in Christ. The question why some accept the proffered grace, and others do not, cannot be answered in such a way as to negate the entire preceding argument, according to which all is of God through Christ. But it cannot be answered at all, save as a retrospective confession of faith on the part of those who do believe. Election precedes faith and is the cause of faith in the order of reality; but

---

[16] *CO* 9, 813. It is noteworthy that when Calvin revised the preface in 1543 the christological content of Scripture was still further emphasized (*CO* 9, 815).

faith precedes election in the order of knowing. Hence election plays no part in the Christian proclamation, but is a confession of those who believe and who must explain the fact that they have faith in a manner consistent with the content of faith itself (III. xxi.1, xxiii.14).

3. The Efficacious Word

Only as Jesus Christ becomes the object of highest loyalty is the image of God restored in fallen man. For faith in Christ is precisely living as one who receives in thankfulness (III.xi.7,xiii.1), and this is what it means to be made in the image of God. Faith, however, is not something a man acquires for himself, but a gift conveyed to him by the object of faith. It is "born from the word."[17] Or, since faith is the principal work of the Spirit, we may say that the Holy Spirit is the bond by which Christ effectually unites us to himself (III.i.1,4). These are not two different explanations of how the Christian is united with Christ, since Calvin has already affirmed that word and Spirit are joined together by an indissoluble bond (I.ix.1). The word is to be understood as the Spirit's instrument. It can be said, then, that the word is the means by which Christ is communicated to the believer.

> Now, all of Scripture tells us that the spiritual bread by which our souls are maintained is the same word by which the Lord has regenerated us. But it sometimes adds the reason: because in it Jesus Christ, our only life, is given and administered to us. For we must not suppose that there is life anywhere else than in God. But just as God has embodied all fullness of life in Jesus, in order to communicate it to us by means of him, so he has ordained his word as the instrument through which Jesus Christ, with all his graces, may be dispensed to us.[18]

Calvin immediately adds that "what is said of the word applies also to the sacrament of the Supper." He has, in fact, three "instruments" by which the Living Christ is communicated, since baptism must also be added.

---

[17] CO 45, 413 (on Luke 16:30). Cf. 49, 372 (on I Cor. 4:15), where the word or gospel is said to be the means by which we ourselves are born, "as Peter teaches from Isaiah."

[18] OS 1, 504–5 (Short Treatise on the Lord's Supper).

The sacraments, in Calvin's thinking, are not different in kind from the preached word. Indeed, they are simply visible words, graphic forms of the gospel, which make God's promises visible to the eye (IV.xiv.6). Hence what is offered in the sacraments is identical with what is offered in the word: not "secret powers of some kind," but Christ himself, who is the true "matter" or "substance" of the sacraments (xiv.14,16,17). For this reason the sacraments, like the proclaimed word, are not to be considered efficacious unless or until they evoke faith, which is the only way of receiving Christ. In the word and the sacraments, as in the incarnation itself, grace is offered to all, but not received by all (xiv.7). Each of the sacraments represents symbolically the benefits obtained from communion with Christ: baptism signifies cleansing through Christ (IV.xv.2); the Supper, nourishment from Christ (xvii.1). In both sacraments the thing signified is given through the sign, since this, according to Calvin, is the nature of signs: the reality is always joined with them, and it is precisely the function of a sign to pledge the presence of the reality. Sign and reality are to be distinguished, but not divided, like the two natures of the Incarnate Word.[19] Hence it is certain that forgiveness and new life are received in baptism (though not necessarily at the moment of administration), and in the eucharist a real communion with Christ's body takes place.[20] The eucharist is a witness to that "wondrous exchange" of which Calvin has already spoken in discussing the theme of Christ's work (IV.xvii.2), and it is also a liturgical representation of the Christian's entire life as a sacrifice of thanksgiving (xviii.16,17).

It is, of course, particularly in connection with the means of grace that Calvin's staunch churchmanship is most clear. (The fourth book of the *Institutes,* which deals with the church, is the longest.) The gospel and faith are not features of some private transaction between Christ and the individual. On the contrary, the gospel is a treasure deposited in the church (IV.i.1). Reconcili-

---

[19] Cf., for example, *ibid.,* p. 509, where the Chalcedonian formula seems to be in Calvin's mind.
[20] *OS* 2, 134, 138 (*Geneva Catechism*).

ation and regeneration have an ecclesiological aspect. The visible church — the only aspect Calvin chooses to discuss at length in the *Institutes* — is the mother of the faithful. "There is no other entrance into life unless she conceive us in her womb, give us birth, nourish us at her breast, and preserve us under her care and guidance. . . . Out of her bosom there is no hope for forgiveness of sins and no salvation" (i.4). But what is the church? Calvin answers that it is the communion of saints — that is, the community of Christ, in which all the members share their spiritual benefits (i.3). It is this fellowship that is the mother of the faithful. Since the church is the body of Christ, the idea of communion with Christ furnishes Calvin with the link between the individual and the corporate aspects of redemption: "ingrafting into Christ" and "reception into the church" are synonymous expressions, as is clear in Calvin's discussion of baptism (IV.xv.1).

III

What, then, according to Calvin, is the meaning of "reformation"? He answers the question expressly in his treatise *On the Necessity for Reforming the Church* (1543). Here Martin Luther is portrayed as a prophet whose voice was raised in protest against apostasy. Calvin indentifies himself with this prophetic protest because nothing less than the gospel is at stake. Against the charge of disturbing the church he replies in the words of Elijah to Ahab: "I have not troubled Israel, but thou and thy father's house in that ye have forsaken the commandments of the Lord." The Reformers have only obeyed their commission: to preach the gospel. "Reformation," then, means taking a stand for the gospel and leaving the consequences to God. But how has the gospel been forsaken? Among the themes of Calvin's treatise one stands out prominently: the glory of Christ has been impaired.[21] His prerogatives as mediator have been parceled out among the saints; men are enjoined to have more regard for their own works than for Christ;

---

[21] Calvin presented his treatise to the Diet of Spires (1544) "in the name of all who wish Christ to reign": *CO* 6, 452.

in baptism more attention is given to the outward sign than to Christ as the reality of the sacrament; in the mass he is robbed of his unique priesthood. These errors are opposed by the Reformers in the name of the catholic church. For it is the gospel which constitutes the church, and not the church that determines the gospel. There is no apostolic succession where the apostolic gospel has not been preserved.

Four years after the treatise *On the Necessity for Reforming the Church* Calvin gave his judgment that the Council of Trent had failed to correct misapprehensions of the gospel. Though he pronounced his willing "Amen" in response to much that the Tridentine Fathers affirmed, his *Antidote* (1547) to the decree on justification repeated the earlier accusations that the unique prerogatives of God were being shared by man. Faith, for Calvin, was *wholly* a matter of fixing the attention upon Christ.[22] But he saw the Tridentine Fathers as inviting the Christian to turn his attention also to his own activity. The singleness of vision is thereby impaired: alongside of *Christi intuitus* (the gaze fixed solely on Christ) there is placed also an *operum intuitus* (an interest in the "works" of the believer). In this way not only is the "glory of righteousness" shared between God and man, but the Christian is robbed of his assurance. Of course, the Christian is required to make progress in good works. But these can never merit an increase of righteousness; on the contrary, they are accepted as "good" only by the grace of God. "By faith alone are both our persons and our works justified."[23] Just how far Calvin understood the Tridentine Decrees remains open to question. But it is clear that his judgments are consistent with his fundamental position. He who lives by faith has no life in himself. The faithful live outside of themselves — that is, in Christ.[24]

---

[22] "... *fidem debere in Christi intuitu prorsus esse defixam*": *CO* 48, 464 (on Acts 20:21).

[23] *CO* 7, 472; 7, 458 (cf. 481).

[24] *CO* 43, 529 (on Hab. 2:4); 50, 199 (on Gal. 2:20). In his *Commentary on Hebrews* (Heb. 13:9) Calvin expressly asserts that all corruptions in religion arise from not abiding in Christ alone: *CO* 55, 190.

BIBLIOGRAPHY

Four volumes of the *Library of Christian Classics* (Philadelphia, 1953———), Vols. XX–XXIII, are devoted to Calvin. Vols. XX and XXI contain the best English version of the 1559 *Institutes* (trans. Ford Lewis Battles and ed. John T. McNeill). But a beginner would do better to sample some of Calvin's shorter works first: the Preface to Olivétan's New Testament and the autobiographical foreword to the *Commentary on the Psalms* are in Vol. XXIII; the *Reply to Sadoleto,* the *Short Treatise on the Lord's Supper, Draft Ecclesiastical Ordinances, The Necessity of Reforming the Church* and *The Cate-chism of The Church of Geneva* are in Vol. XXII. The 1537 *Cate-chism* has been translated by Paul T. Fuhrmann under the title *Instruction in Faith* (Philadelphia, 1949). A fresh translation of the New Testament commentaries is currently being edited by D. W. and T. F. Torrance.

Biographical studies of Calvin (in English) have been written by Williston Walker *(John Calvin, the Organiser of Reformed Protest-antism, 1509–1564* [New York, 1906]), R. N. Carew Hunt (*Calvin* [London, 1933]), James Mackinnon (*Calvin and the Reformation* [London, 1936]). T. H. L. Parker's brief *Portrait of Calvin* (London, 1954) is also worthy of mention. Two recent volumes of essays cover a wide range of Calvin themes: Jacob T. Hoogstra (ed.), *John Calvin: Contemporary Prophet* (Grand Rapids, 1959); and G. E. Duffield (ed.), *John Calvin* (Grand Rapids, 1966). Another sym-posium has a chapter by John T. McNeill on Calvin's political theories: George L. Hunt (ed.), *Calvinism and the Political Order* (Philadelphia, 1965).

The best general discussions of Calvin's theology available in Eng-lish (one by a Frenchman, the other by a German) are: François Wendel, *Calvin: The Origins and Development of his Religious Thought* (Eng. trans.; London, 1963); and Wilhelm Niesel, *The Theology of Calvin* (Eng. trans.; Philadelphia, 1956). Further help on the themes discussed in the present essay will be found in T. F. Tor-rance, *Calvin's Doctrine of Man* (London, 1949); R. S. Wallace, *Calvin's Doctrine of the Word and Sacrament* (Edinburgh, 1953) and *Calvin's Doctrine of the Christian Life* (Edinburgh, 1959). The best study of Calvin's ideas on communion with Christ is unfortun-ately not translated: W. Kolfhaus, *Christusgemeinschaft bei Johannes Calvin* (Neukirchen, 1939).

Other recent monographs in English are: Edward A. Dowey, Jr.,

The Knowledge of God in Calvin's Theology (New York, 1952; rev. ed. 1966); H. Jackson Forstman, *Word and Spirit: Calvin's Doctrine of Biblical Authority* (Stanford, 1962); J. F. Jansen, *Calvin's Doctrine of the Work of Christ* (London, 1956); T. H. L. Parker, *The Oracles of God: An Introduction to the Preaching of John Calvin* (London, 1947); and Paul van Buren, *Christ in Our Place: The Substitutionary Character of Calvin's Doctrine of Reconciliation* (Edinburgh, 1957).

CHAPTER SEVEN

THOMAS CRANMER

GEOFFREY W. BROMILEY

I. THE SCHOLAR

To look at Cranmer is to see first the face of a scholar. Even chronologically he began his work in the schools. But for an unexpected turn of events he would probably have ended it there. By endowment, opportunity and temperament he was more suited to the academic life than to the ecclesiastical. He was to look back to it later with nostalgia.

The beginning was none too auspicious. Cranmer was born at Aslockton, Nottinghamshire in 1489. The second son of a squireling, he had few prospects except in holy orders. He learned his first letters with a "rude parish clerk in that barbarous age,"[1] and he fared just as badly at grammar school under a "marvellous severe and cruel schoolmaster."[2] Through the latter he supposedly "lost much of that benefit of memory and audacity in youth that by nature was given to him."[3] Though this perhaps accounted for his later timidity, he remained a fearless horseman who could "ride the roughest horses that came into his stable. Which he would do very comely."[4]

After the rudiments at grammar school Cranmer took up real learning when he matriculated at Cambridge in 1503 or 1504. He apparently studied at Jesus College, a new foundation which as yet had no great fame but which offered good opportunities in divinity. But first he had to plod through the unreconstructed medieval curriculum: "He was nozzled in the grossest kind of sophistry,

---

[1] *Narratives of the Reformation,* ed. Camden Society (1859), pp. 238 ff. Hereafter cited as *NR.*
[2] *Ibid.*
[3] *Ibid.*
[4] *Ibid.*

logic, philosophy, moral and natural . . . chiefly in the dark riddles of Duns and other subtle questionists."[5] Cranmer himself had no very high opinion of at least one tutor: "When he came to any hard chapter which he well understood not, he would find some pretty toy to shift it off, and to skip over to another chapter, which he could better skill of."[6] He learned enough to satisfy the examiners, and graduated in 1511.

Indeed, he did sufficiently well to be elected to a fellowship at Jesus College. This was interrupted by an obscure episode: "it chanced him to marry a wife,"[7] the famous Black or Brown Joan. The rule of celibacy forced him to resign, but soon afterwards the young wife died in childbirth and he was promptly re-elected to the fellowship. He then remained at the college until translated to other spheres.

At this time he began to amass the collection of books and papers which at his death was to be larger than the university library of his student days. Prominent on the shelves were Hebrew and Greek Bibles, sets of the important Greek and Latin Fathers, the schoolmen, and the best contemporary authors. Equally significant was his growing collection of commonplace books. A slow and methodical student, Cranmer "seldom read without pen in hand, and whatsoever made either for the one part or the other of things being in controversy, he wrote it out if it were short, or at least, noted the author and the place, that he might find it and write it out by leisure."[8] He thus more than compensated for the weakened memory.

He earned his doctorate in divinity in 1526; even earlier he had been chosen as a university preacher — he was by then in orders. Cardinal Wolsey had marked him out as one of the coming Cambridge men and tried to tempt him to Cardinal's College in Oxford,

---

5 *Ibid.,* p. 219.

6 Thomas Cranmer, *Works,* ed. Parker Society (2 vols.; 1844 and 1846), I, 305. Hereafter cited as *PS.*

7 *NR,* p. 269.

8 *Ibid.,* p. 219.

but Cranmer declined the invitation. His inclinations were already in the direction of renaissance and reformation. In 1516–17, confronted by the acute controversies in the church, he "bent himself to try out the truth herein: and, forasmuch as he perceived that he could not judge indifferently in so weighty matters without the knowledge of the Holy Scriptures (before he were infected with any man's opinions or errors), he applied his whole study three years to the said Scriptures."[9] This had an uncomfortable result for the students, for when he became a university examiner in theology "doctor Cranmer . . . would never let any to proceed in divinity, unless they were substantially seen in the story of the Bible."[10]

Formally, Cranmer's removal to the king's service, and later to the archbishopric of Canterbury, interrupted his life of scholarship. But scholarly habits, once acquired, do not die easily. Indeed, in some ways Cranmer enjoyed new advantages when he became archbishop. He could expand his library more rapidly. He had secretarial help for his commonplace books. He "associated with learned men" — younger scholars like Ridley and Bradford, and, later, European exiles like Bucer and Peter Martyr — "for the sifting and boulting out one matter or another."[11] He was inevitably involved in important liturgical and theological tasks. The scholar could hardly be engulfed by the ecclesiastic.

Of the material achievements in this field there will be occasion to speak later. It may be said at once, however, that though traditionalists on the one hand and hotheads on the other minimized his scholarship, its solidity found general recognition. Henry VIII, whose theology was better than his ethics, knew where to turn when he wanted guidance. He would consult Cranmer, "and by the next day the King should have in writing brief notes of the doctors' minds, with a conclusion of his own mind, which he could never get in such readiness of none, no, not of all his clergy

---

9 *Ibid.*
10 *PS*, I, viii.
11 *Ibid.*, p. xi.

and chaplains about him, in so short a time."[12] After one discussion, when Henry and Stephen Gardiner had tried to argue a point against Cranmer, the king confessed: "My Lord of Canterbury is too old a truant for us twain."[13] Peter Martyr paid similar tributes in his letters: "He has shown himself so mighty a theologian against them as they would rather not have proof of, and they are compelled . . . to acknowledge his learning, and power and dexterity in debate."[14] Even the radical Ab Ulmis, once a severe critic, confessed that Cranmer (when espousing the same cause as he himself) "delivered his opinion upon this subject learnedly, correctly, orderly, and clearly."[15] The astonishing deployment of learning in the *Answer* to Stephen Gardiner bears out these judgments.

Cranmer the scholar is distinguished by four main characteristics: (1) He took Holy Scripture as his ultimate norm. (2) Taking Scripture as his raw material, he expounded it literally, according to the original. Though not an outstanding linguist or exegete, he adopted the Renaissance methodology and handled it with competence. (3) He saw the value of secondary authorities, especially the Fathers. This explains his diligence in collecting opinions from ancient, medieval, and contemporary authors. (4) He gave weight, in the best scholastic tradition, to both sides of disputed issues. This could be a disadvantage when decisive statement was needed, for he always had an awareness of what could be said to the contrary. But it also provided a guarantee against bigotry and superficiality. When he could not be dogmatic, Cranmer displayed not indecision, but humility and honesty. When he achieved and expressed a firm opinion, it had the force of solid learning and ripe deliberation.

---

[12] *NR*, p. 249.

[13] *Ibid.*

[14] *Original Letters*, ed. Parker Society (2 vols.; 1846 and 1847), II, 479. Hereafter cited as *OL*.

[15] *Ibid.*, p. 388.

II. THE ECCLESIASTIC

In the summer of 1528 a chance encounter with Henry VIII ended the halcyon days and made of Cranmer an ecclesiastic. He was doing some private tutoring when the plague struck Cambridge, and he retired with his pupils to their house at Waltham, Essex. While they were there the king, engaged in a royal progress, visited the manor. Henry had just had a series of vexatious blows: the postponement of his nullity suit against Catherine of Aragon; the defeat of France; and the enforced alliance between pope and emperor. Hope of ending his matrimonial problems seemed to have been quenched.

Cranmer of course did not meet Henry directly. But he spoke with Fox and Gardiner, university friends who were now the king's advisers. To them he made the suggestion that the matter should be taken right out of the papal courts and settled according to a majority judgment of the European faculties of canon law. When Henry heard this, he "swore by his wonted oath, Mother of God, that man hath the right sow by the ear."[16] "And so, by and by being sent for, he came to the king's presence at Greenwich."[17]

This was not in fact until the end of the year. He then took up as his first task the advancement of the king's suit in the schools. He "penned his mind and opinion concerning the said cause,"[18] and later replied in particular to the witty and eloquent treatise of the king's cousin, Reginald Pole, which he feared might have a damaging effect. He also spent some time in Cambridge arguing his point of view. With the later aid of judicious gifts this helped to turn the scale in the faculty. By 1530 Cranmer had moved abroad. He was attached to the papal and imperial embassies with a view to winning over Italian and German opinion. Although generously received, he cut no very eminent figure as a diplomat.

---

[16] John Foxe, *Acts and Monuments*, ed. G. Townsend (8 vols.; 1843–49), VIII, 8.
[17] *NR*, p. 242.
[18] *Ibid.*

Successes were achieved on the marriage question, but Cranmer ran into difficulties of his own. His earlier convictions seem to have been somewhat shaken by counter-arguments, perhaps especially on the Lutheran side. He also contracted a hazardous marriage of his own with the niece of the Lutheran reformer Andrew Osiander. Since he was now in orders and shortly to be an archbishop, this was to be a source of great embarrassment. Though he had come to see — and he never went back on this — that clerical marriage is biblically legitimate, it was inevitable that until canon law was altered concealment and temporary periods of exile would be his spouse's lot.

His diplomatic career ended inopportunely with Warham's death and Cranmer's own elevation to Archbishop of Canterbury. The appointment was apparently a surprise. His contemporaries thought so, and Cranmer evidently neither expected it nor wanted it: "There was never a man that came more unwillingly to a bishoprick than I did to that."[19] There were probably two main reasons for Henry's choice. First, he knew he could count on Cranmer in the marriage question, and secondly, he found it more suitable, as the church's declared head, to have an archbishop who could concentrate on pastoral matters while a vicegerent dealt with matters of ecclesiastical policy. A more able man like Gardiner could still serve the king and have less opportunity of meddling if he remained in the diocese to which he had recently been appointed.

As archbishop, Cranmer was involved from the very first in some of the less pleasant aspects of Henry's career. He began by annulling the king's marriage to Catherine according to a slender majority of university judgments. This was followed rapidly by validation of Henry's secret marriage to Anne Boleyn, by her coronation, and by sponsorship of the infant Elizabeth at her baptism. Only two years afterwards Cranmer nullified Anne's marriage and issued the license for her successor. A third case of invalidation, that of Anne of Cleves, was to be presented later, and Cranmer finally

---

[19] *PS*, II, 216.

ended the marriage to Catherine Howard by breaking to the king the news of her infidelities. For all the mitigating factors, this side of Cranmer's work is squalid and distasteful. It helps us to understand the intrinsically absurd charge that Cranmer made a compact with Henry: "Give me the archbishoprick of Canterbury, and I will give you license to live in adultery."[20]

Cranmer's main duties as archbishop, however, were to see to his own diocese, to supervise the southern province, and to give ecclesiastical leadership. As a diocesan bishop, he proved able and conscientious, though he encountered great opposition. He also took his metropolitan duties seriously and carried out an early visitation. This was strenuously resisted by Gardiner, who alleged too much expense and infringement of the royal headship. Cranmer pertinently remarked: "I cannot persuade with myself that he so much tendereth the king's cause as his own."[21] In the third sphere, apart from his efforts at reform, he tended to be more an adviser and executive than a true administrator. He has been blamed for this, but he stepped into a crumbling position. Warham had already "given the supremacy to king Henry the eighth, and said that he had right to have it before the pope, and that God's Word would bear him."[22] Since an authority exceeding all episcopal jurisdiction was granted to Thomas Cromwell, the vice-gerent, Cranmer was hampered from the very outset.

A few unpleasant duties fell to him. As the ordinary, he had the task of examining and exposing Elizabeth Barton, the "maid of Kent" whose visions seduced not only "holy monks of Charter-house, obstinate (they should be called observant) friars of Greenwich, nice nuns of Sion, black monks (both of cowls and of conditions) of Christ's and St. Alban's, knights, squires, learned men, priests and many others,"[23] but also such notable figures as Fisher. Again, Cranmer headed the commission charged with

---

[20] *Ibid.*, p. 217.
[21] *Ibid.*, p. 304.
[22] *Ibid.*, pp. 214–15.
[23] *Ibid.*, p. 274.

administering the oath to Fisher and More. After an interview, he recommended that they be allowed to take the oath in an agreeable modified form, but the recommendation was rejected and the noble pair were vindictively brought to the block.

In other matters the archbishop's main task was to back up in convocation and parliament the radical legislation rapidly prepared by Henry and Cromwell. Cranmer had no difficulty here, for he was seeing the answer to a daily prayer of many years that he might "see the power of Rome destroyed" in England.[24] The successive measures from the Restraint of Annates and Appeals to the Dissolution of the Lesser and Greater Monasteries were, however, initiated and carried out by the crown rather than by the church. This is why Cranmer's detractors see in him the man who, by inaction, betrayed the freedom of the English church.

The overthrow of Cromwell enhanced the archbishop's power only formally, for it was accompanied by a diplomatic and ecclesiastical shift which gave the real initiative to others. Henry now abandoned the Lutheran alliance, made peace with Charles V, enforced the Act of Six Articles, and put the party of Gardiner in power. Though the office of vicegerent disappeared, Cranmer represented a disowned policy (apart from the antipapalism). Hence he was left hanging on a very slender bough. The general expectation was that his office, and possibly even his head, might be lopped off with it.

Much of his energy had in fact to be devoted to saving what could be saved. He made a brave struggle for clerical marriage, but Mrs. Cranmer had to retire for a while. He scored donnish points against the king's revision of the *Bishops' Book* ("I cannot perceive any manner of consideration why those words should be put in that place"[25]) but the *King's Book* could not be arrested. He defended the English Bible, and here experience told, for he managed to have revision put in the leisurely hands of a university

---

[24] *Ibid.*, p. 327.
[25] *Ibid.*, p. 88.

committee. Even so, restrictions were passed on private reading. In particular, Cranmer had to protect himself. Three main attacks came: the Prebendaries' Plot; the Privy Council Enquiry; and Gostwick's assault in parliament. Only Henry's personal intervention saved Cranmer. Henry ironically made Cranmer himself head of the commission to investigate the Canterbury charges. For the meeting with the council the king gave him the protection of a personal ring, and later berated Cranmer's opponents: "I would you well understand that I account my lord of Canterbury as faithful a man towards me as ever was prelate in this realm."[26] Finally he threatened Gostwick, a plutocrat of the dissolution, saying "if he do not acknowledge his fault . . . I will sure make him a poor Gostwick" (or, in another version, "I will pull the gostling's feathers").[27]

By 1546 the difficult period was ending. Alarmed by the war against the Protestants, Henry was reported to be planning a great French alliance which would include common reformation of the church. The king died early in 1547, and Cranmer, who was with him to the end, felt a keen sense of personal loss. Before his death, however, Henry had provided for the execution of his policy by giving control of the Council of Regency to the reforming party.

In consequence, Cranmer now enjoyed greater freedom than ever before. This was especially so under the Duke of Somerset, with whom he had much in common. The situation deteriorated under the Earl of Warwick (later Duke of Northumberland), who added to Somerset's fault of rapacity the further vices of ambition and ruthlessness, and whose tardy profession of Catholicism did more to embarrass than to encourage its proponents. Expediency led Warwick to support further and even more drastic reformation while in office. A few more naive extremists could even hail him as "that most faithful and intrepid soldier of Christ."[28] Cranmer was more realistic. The only virtue he perceived was that of allowing

---

[26] Cf. *NR*, pp. 254 ff.
[27] Cf. Foxe, *op. cit.*, VIII, 27.
[28] *OL*, I, 82. Cf. also p. 89.

reformation to proceed. At two points, however, Warwick was an obstacle. He blocked all reform of canon law, so that Cranmer's work here went for nothing. He also plundered the church in every possible way, prolonging vacancies, proposing exchanges, and confiscating released endowments which could have been used well in pastoral, educational and medical work. Cranmer protested sternly, but even when aided by the powerful voices of Latimer, Ridley, and the "runagate Scot," John Knox, he could not prevent extensive spoliation. Mary Tudor ran into similar trouble when she tried to get her traditionalist parliament to disgorge the proceeds of dissolution.

Within limits, however, Cranmer had considerable influence. He naturally used it to further his own reforming projects. Hence the ecclesiastic merges into the Reformer. It is from this angle that he must be studied for a proper appreciation of his very real achievements during this period. The untimely death of Edward in 1553 terminated Cranmer's ecclesiastical career as abruptly as it had begun. His part in the Jane Grey episode offered Queen Mary an easy excuse for the imprisonment which ended in execution.

III. THE REFORMER

Cranmer began his reforming work long before Edward's reign. At Cambridge, it may be recalled, he had tried to promote biblical study. He supported Henry's matrimonial suit primarily because he thought the marriage rested on an invalid dispensation from Scripture. He early rejected papal supremacy, so that as archbishop he welcomed the legislation which denied the Bishop of Rome any jurisdiction in the realm of England. He went further, for as occasion offered he sought to advance a more spiritual, doctrinal, and pastoral reformation.

A first concern was for the English Bible. Here he made a remarkable breakthrough. The start was poor. The bishops were more interested in keeping out Tyndale's allegedly erroneous work than in replacing it. Since they did not oppose the principle of translation, Cranmer forced the pace by committing the work to the episcopal bench (1534). But men like Stokesley, who said it was "abusing the people to give them liberty to read the Scriptures,"[29] frustrated the plan by simple inertia. Cranmer countered this in 1537 by securing permission for Coverdale's rendering. When in the same year he saw the so-called Matthew's Bible, he did even better. Preferring it "to any other translation heretobefore made" — did he read it closely enough to detect the hand of Tyndale? — he persuaded Cromwell to seek a royal license "until we the bishops shall set forth a better translation, which I think will not be till a day after doomsday."[30] Cromwell seems to have come to an arrangement with Henry, for they helped to finance the publication and made sure of their returns by ordering copies to be bought for all the parishes. For Cranmer the outcome brought a purer satisfaction: "You have shown me more pleasure herein, than if you had given me a thousand pounds."[31]

The victory was greater than Cranmer could have dared hope. Quite apart from official purchases, a new revised edition was already needed in 1538. The same year produced the injunction that "a copy of the largest volume" was to be purchased for each church, the cost to be shared by parson and parish. After various delays, the Great Bible came out with a preface by Cranmer, so that it sometimes bore the name of Cranmer's Bible. As noted, Cranmer parried the threat of withdrawal or revision in 1542, and in spite of temporary restrictions the Great Bible lived on into the days of Edward and Elizabeth. It thus began the work of instruction and edification effectively continued by the Bishops' Bible, the Geneva Bible, and finally the King James Bible.

Cranmer also made progress at the pastoral level. He brought men like Shaxton and Latimer to the episcopal bench. Out of the spoils of dissolution he founded the new see of Westminster, some

---

29 John Strype, *Memorials of Thomas Cranmer* (1840), I, 48.
30 *PS*, II, 344.
31 *Ibid.*, p. 347.

suffragan bishoprics (Dover, for example), and many schools. Certain plans such as that for the reconstruction of Canterbury Abbey, where the prebendaries "spent their time in much idleness, and their substance in superfluous belly cheer,"[32] aroused invincible opposition. The 1537 injunctions, however, discouraged images and pilgrimages, and provided for the support of poor scholars by the clergy. Inspection of shrines disclosed that the supposed blood of Becket was a "feigned thing, made of some red ochre or such like matter,"[33] that the miracles at Boxley were worked by mechanical gadgets, and other such frauds. The closing of these centers of pilgrimage followed.

Pastoral reform demanded new catechetical material, which in turn required a doctrinal statement. The *Ten Articles* of 1536 and the *Bishops' Book* of 1537 met the need. The articles were necessarily a compromise. Auricular confession and invocation of saints went hand in hand with only three sacraments and justification by faith. The same teaching dominates the *Bishops' Book,* except that the seven sacraments are back. Negotiations for a Lutheran alliance included an attempt to come to terms with the Lutheran dogmaticians attached to the embassage. Cranmer prepared the *Thirteen Articles,* which were far closer to the Augsburg Confession, but the whole project collapsed and the reactionary *Six Articles* of 1539 were passed instead. In spite of Cranmer's opposition, these were followed by a revised catechetical manual, the *King's Book* (1543), though Cranmer did manage to preserve here a few reforming elements.

Unexpected gains in the liturgical field offered compensation for temporary losses in the theological. The 1541 canons included a purging of the calendar and restriction of the use of lights. Three years later poor weather and bad harvests led to the ordering of special litanies. But Henry was worried that "the people had used to come very slackly to the procession,"[84] and so, faced by the new

---

[32] *Ibid.,* pp. 396–97.
[33] *Ibid.,* p. 378.
[34] *Ibid.,* p. 494.

crisis of war with France, he accepted the idea of litanies in English. At first, a bald translation was made from the Latin. Cranmer, however, asked permission to make a new version "using rather more than the liberty of a translator."[35] By royal injunction the version which he prepared replaced all others. It did so by merit as well as by command. Setting a standard and pattern for the offices to follow, it established itself so securely that apart from minor changes (for example, elimination of the petition for deliverance from the Bishop of Rome and his detestable enormities), it has continued in use right up to our own time.

While Henry lived, Cranmer could hardly do more than take advantage of whatever opportunities came his way. He had definite enough objectives and constantly sought to promote them. But others called the tune, while he worked what he could into the dance. Under the circumstances the surprising thing is not that he did so little, but that he accomplished so much.

With the accession of Edward he gained in stature as a Reformer. He now pushed through a massive program. Promptings came, of course, from others. The younger men, especially the forceful Ridley, supplied pressure. Cranmer had convictions awaiting expression, plans needing only the opportunity, and, for his years, an astounding openness to new developments. He also carried the final responsibility in the church, so that in a real sense the achievements of 1547–53 were his.

The first steps gave an intimation of what was to come. Preachers at Paul's Cross attacked images and ceremonies. The *Homilies* came out as preaching material for poorly qualified priests, of whom there were far too many. Prominent in the volume — a pet project of Cranmer's — were the great sermons on justification usually ascribed to his pen. New injunctions also ordered a sermon at least once a quarter; instruction in the Creed, Lord's Prayer and Ten Commandments; and the reading of the gospel and epistle in English.

More drastic reforms followed rapidly: communion in both

_____
[35] *Ibid.*, p. 412.

kinds; marriage of clergy; repeal of the *Six Articles;* and repeal of the heresy acts which stifled the free discussion "of things in the Church that needed reformation."[36] Chantries were also dissolved, though Cranmer opposed the first draft of this bill, not because he wanted chantries, but because he wanted more of the endowments for charitable causes. He had to accept only small concessions.

If anything, the pace increased in 1548. Candles, ashes, and palms were swept out of the churches, followed by holy bread and water, and images. Latimer preached against non-preaching prelates; he also had some serious words for rapacious landlords. Ridley, now at London, abolished the private mass and began to replace altars by tables. The catechism of Justus Jonas was translated; in spite of judicious changes, the Lutheranism disappointed those who were pressing for a Reformed doctrine of the sacraments.[37] Drafts were also prepared for liturgical revision. European scholars, harassed by the Augsburg Interim, found asylum and new employment in England.

This intense activity reached a first climax in the *Book of Common Prayer* of 1549. For years Cranmer had seen the folly of services in a language which, however noble, was not "understanded of the people." A high priority of his had been to put all the services into the "vulgar tongue." He had made a start with the litany, but the real advance came when discussion of the 1548 drafts led to specific proposals. After further revision these were embodied in the *Book of Common Prayer* and prescribed by the Act of Uniformity. The book was, of course, a compromise. Cranmer had wanted to maintain a balance between tradition and reformation. In parliament concessions had had to be made to get the act through at all. Severe censure came from more zealous reformers like Traherne: "The foolish bishops have made a marvellous recantation,"[38] or Hooper: "Very defective and of doubtful construction and in some indeed manifestly impious."[39] Even

---

[36] G. Burnet, *The History of the Reformation of the Church of England,* ed. N. Pocock (7 vols.; 1865), II, 92.
[37] *OL,* II, 380–81.
[38] *Ibid.,* I, 323.   [39] *Ibid.,* pp. 232–33.

friends like Bucer and Fagius could excuse some things only as concessions "to a respect for antiquity and to the infirmity of the present age."[40] Yet the gains far outweighed the losses. English services had been provided. There had been a great process of simplification and purification. Important doctrinal changes had been made. Above all, Cranmer had shown once again his genius in liturgical phrasing. Not merely had he avoided "translation English"; he had also created in his native tongue an instrument of worship which for power, beauty, and dignity ranks with the best in medieval Latin or any other liturgical tradition.

In some districts, however, the book had a poor reception. In Devon and Cornwall (the Cornish did not all speak English anyway) it contributed to the serious revolts which broke out in 1549. Cranmer found it child's play to refute the religious objections.[41] The economic difficulties were more stubborn. In fact, they toppled Somerset, and thus ended perhaps the smoothest working partnership Cranmer ever enjoyed. At one time, it seemed as though the revolts might endanger the whole work of reform, for Warwick looked both ways to see how his own plans could best be prospered.

As it turned out, the new regent decided for continued and even more drastic reformation. After a short lull, the work went ahead with new vigor. The ordinal of 1550 abolished minor orders and substituted an evangelical ministry of word and sacrament for medieval sacerdotalism. Hooper so disliked even the small relics of popery still remaining that he refused consecration when elected to Gloucester. He yielded only under combined pressure from Cranmer and Ridley, Bucer and Martyr, and a term in the Fleet prison. Ridley, though not accepting Hooper's principle, showed similar zeal in practice. When he pressed on with the elimination of altars in London, the council authorized a general replacement by tables, which Cranmer helped to implement.

The change had deep significance at this juncture. Eucharistic

---

[40] *Ibid.*, p. 535.
[41] *PS*, II, 163 ff.

doctrine had begun to emerge as the central issue of the English Reformation. Gardiner was championing transubstantiation and eucharistic sacrifice. Cranmer, with Ridley, had come to a clear-cut Reformed commitment. Cranmer published his teaching in *The True and Catholic Doctrine,* which he later substantiated in the more detailed *Answer.* In the light of these events, of the criticisms of Bucer and Martyr, and especially perhaps of the taunt of Gardiner that he could find his doctrine in the 1549 Communion Office, the sacramental inadequacy of the first *Book of Common Prayer* became increasingly evident. The replacement of altars by tables was thus a preparatory and symbolical step toward new liturgical revision.

The second *Book of Common Prayer,* authorized in 1552, made drastic changes. Medieval ceremonies were removed wholesale from the baptismal service. Reconstruction of confirmation laid new emphasis on confession of faith and prayer for the Holy Spirit. Objectionable relics were purged from the ordinal. Public confession and a declaration of remission replaced the penitential system. Above all, the communion service underwent reformation. Mass vestments were forbidden, the minister was put at the north side, ordinary bread came into use, reservation ceased, the canon or great central prayer was broken up, the *kyrie* found a new use, the *agnus dei* dropped out, the *gloria* was placed at the end, and "Take and eat [or drink] this in remembrance . . ." became the sentence of administration rather than "The body [or blood] of our Lord . . . preserve thy body and soul. . . ." A surprising amount of traditional material remained, and Cranmer's liturgical genius gave life and power to what might otherwise have been limp and faulty rearrangements. The most significant feature of the new book, however, was the translation, not now into another language, but into a new theology.

Ambitious for complete reconstruction, Cranmer would have liked to push through his canonical reform as well in 1552. Resistance in the council, which had no more taste for church discipline than had Geneva's Libertines, prevented the *Reformatio Legum* from ever passing into effect. Almost by accident, however, Cranmer did manage to crown his work with a confessional statement, the *Forty-two Articles*. He seems to have drafted these first (1549) as a disciplinary instrument in his own diocese. In altered form they were then submitted to the episcopal bench as a possible statement for the whole church. By order of the council, this statement was then exhibited and revised again in 1552. Finally, in 1553 the *Forty-two Articles* were authorized with a view to establishing "such a concord and quietness in religion . . . as else is not to be looked for many years."[42] Based upon the Augsburg Confession but with a more traditonal structure on the one side and yet also a definite Reformed element on the other, the articles aimed at comprehension within a distinctly evangelical understanding. Though conciliatory in general tone and in statement, they plainly rule out both Roman and Anabaptist beliefs. They also state plainly enough the fundamental convictions of the Reformation. In this connection, it may be recalled that at this very period Cranmer was in touch with Calvin and Melanchthon in the hope of holding a London conference which might draw up a common confession on behalf of the Protestant churches.[43] Unfortunately Melanchthon's lukewarmness frustrated this laudable project.

The astonishing thing about Cranmer is that, over the long haul and with substantial help from others, he accomplished reforms not quite so radical but just as comprehensive and far-reaching as those of the great Continental Reformers. He certainly did not have the same direct influence, or force, or many-sided genius, as Luther or Calvin. He started off without the clear-cut plans and convictions which may be seen in Calvin or Zwingli. On the ecclesiastical side he was often little more than a spectator or executive. He had to grasp opportunities as they came and postpone for long periods things he would have liked to do at once. His own understanding and projects grew as he went along, so that reformation was more of a developing process than the fulfillment

---

[42] *Ibid.,* pp. 440–41.
[43] *Ibid.,* p. 432.

of a set plan. Nevertheless, quite apart from what others did, he himself changed the face of the church beyond recognition during his tenure of office. He did this especially by his sponsorship of the English Bible, his liturgical work, to which he brought the surest element of genius, and his establishment of the articles. Even the sound and fury of Mary's reign could not finally overthrow his work. The essential features of the church of the Elizabethan Settlement were still the features impressed upon it by this most unassuming and apparently least effectual of all the Reformers.

IV. THE THEOLOGIAN

Although agreement does not come easily to scholars, there is almost an unbroken consensus that, as a theologian, Cranmer cannot be classed with Luther, Calvin, or even Zwingli. Though an eminent scholar, he made no outstanding or original theological contribution, and while points of interest and value may be discerned in his writings, it must be understood that as a theologian he played only a limited and secondary role.

Even the volume of his work is suggestive. Quantity, of course, is no indication of quality. Many unimportant figures have written at tedious length, while even a single work by a great dogmatician can make a decisive impact. Nevertheless, the true theologian usually has a doctrinal concern which leads him to write in breadth as well as in depth. Luther, no less busy than Cranmer, could leave the massive volumes of his German and Latin works. Calvin, almost unbearably harassed, could fill shelves with his commentaries, tractates, and editions of the *Institutes.* Even Zwingli in a short and hectic decade could bequeath substantial tomes. In contrast, Cranmer's output is very slight. Apart from the *True and Catholic Doctrine* and the weighty *Answer,* one can point only to occasional pieces like the *Homilies,* the disputation, and the contribution to official formularies.

Even more suggestive is the restriction of subject matter. Strictly, Cranmer dealt only with one dogmatic theme, the Lord's Supper. He touched incidentally on baptism. He has also left work on justification and Scripture. Drafting of the articles forced him to state his mind on traditional doctrines and the disputed points of his time. But there is no exhaustive examination or presentation of any subject apart from the eucharist. His other contributions are incidental and occasional.

A further point is that Cranmer has not much to offer which is genuinely distinctive. His doctrine of Scripture follows the familiar lines of Reformation understanding. In justification he is an apt pupil of Luther. Parallels to his view of baptism occur in Reformed writers. In basic essentials the *True and Catholic Doctrine* expounds the doctrine found also in Peter Martyr and in Calvin. This is not to say, of course, that Cranmer simply copied others. In sacramental teaching especially he wrote at a formative period of mutual interaction. Nevertheless, Cranmer certainly cannot be claimed as the author or even the leading representative of any particular doctrine.

To admit this is not to say that he was a theological nonentity. His work has many points of interest; he could even be regarded as one of the fathers of a broad theological trend or movement. He thus merits a niche in dogmatic history which neither the church in general nor his own church in particular has always been ready to grant.

The first point to note is his christological development of baptism and holy communion. He learned this primarily from the Fathers, and shared it especially with Peter Martyr. It has a twofold reference. On one side, the sacramental operation is set under the christological analogy. The sign corresponds to the human nature and the thing signified to the divine, though not with exact correspondence: "For the two natures of Christ be joined together in unity of person, which unity is not between the sacrament and the body of Christ."[44] On the other side, the presence in the sacra-

---

[44] *Ibid.*, I, 284.

ment is understood in terms of Christ's presence, not during the incarnation, the forty days, or the parousia, but during the time between the comings. It is a presence by the Holy Spirit: "Christ and his Holy Spirit be truly and indeed present."[45] This means that the presence is not just that of Christ's deity. It is the presence of the "whole Christ, his nativity, passion, resurrection and ascension."[46] But there is no transubstantiation or consubstantiation. This is a presence by the Spirit apprehended only in faith. Though Cranmer did not explore these themes very deeply, with the christological analogy and the interrelation of Christ and Spirit he undoubtedly opened up lines of fruitful theological reflection.

His discussion of justification also has its points of interest. Apart from the brief statements in the *Articles,* he dealt with this in the *Homilies.* This gave him a special, nontechnical context. He was offering popular instruction which would also serve the purpose of edification. He had not merely to give a presentation of the doctrine but also to show its ethical relevance. Hence good works play an important part in the discussion, negatively, because of their inability to justify, and positively, because they are an expression of justifying faith: "Faith is lively and fruitful in bringing forth good works;"[47] "the trial of all these things is a very godly and Christian life."[48] One is reminded here of Calvin's setting of the doctrine of justification in the broader context of sanctification. No less important is the example hereby given of true pastoral theology. Ethical exhortation is given a genuine foundation not just in faith, but in the grace in which faith itself reposes. The theological basis of pastoral work, and the pastoral relevance of theology, are plainly exhibited. To compare Cranmer's homilies on faith and good works with Hooker's later sermons on justification is instructive here.

In a very real way the prayer books bring out the same point.

---

45 *Ibid.,* p. 3.
46 *Ibid.,* II, 213.
47 *Ibid.,* p. 136.
48 *Ibid.,* p. 139.

These are not to be regarded as in themselves primary dogmatic sources. Nevertheless, they are undoubtedly applied theology. Cranmer always perceived that doctrinal issues were involved in liturgy. The very demand for a translation, the place granted to Scripture, the problem of ceremonies, all involved more than pragmatic or aesthetic considerations. At first Cranmer seems to have inclined to the Lutheran principle of reducing change to a minimum as long as right doctrine was taught. This suited his cautious nature and liturgical sense. Increasingly, however, he perceived that liturgy, too, is an expression of theology. Ordination must reflect a proper view of ministry; penitential exercises, a true understanding of justification; the communion office, a pure doctrine of presence and sacrifice. Cranmer was not in this respect a pioneer, for Zwingli had taken the same course more rapidly and more ruthlessly in Zurich. But in Cranmer the very delicacy of the solution gives added point to the underlying principle that Christian practice cannot be controlled by nontheological factors, and that theology must shape practice, not vice versa.

If Cranmer moved here more cautiously than many others, it was partly because he came more slowly to his final position. But this in turn was due to an inner conflict between conservation and reform which involved the whole question of authority. In this area Cranmer undoubtedly again shared the same conviction as other Reformers, but out of conflict he developed one of the common insights with particular force.

He seems never to have had any doubt as to the supreme authority of Scripture. Expression is given to this in the articles. Cranmer also practices it in his own works (for instance, in the *True and Catholic Doctrine*). Furthermore, he has left an interesting discussion of Scripture and tradition in the materials underlying the *Confutation of Unwritten Verities,* which was compiled by a later editor.

After devoting a first section to the self-witness of Scripture, Cranmer adduces many quotations from the Fathers to show that the early church unquestionably accepted the supreme normative-ness of Scripture. In further sections he then deploys biblical and patristic passages to refute the arguments for unwritten beliefs and practices. Finally he contrasts the role of the church on the one side and that of the Spirit on the other. The Spirit gave Christ's essential teaching a permanent form in the biblical records; the church has the duty of custodian or keeper of these records, with no more power than "the registers, recorders, stewards of courts, or town-clerks . . . to put to, or take away anything from, the first original writings."[49]

Asserting the primary and definitive authority of Scripture, Cranmer champions the common scriptural principle of the Reformation. But he does so with important nuances. He has no desire to be in the position of "reformers against the world." He is more ready to appeal to the Fathers than most of his contemporaries. This point must not be overstated, for all the Reformers, in varying measure, were ready to make the patristic appeal. Again, Cranmer himself never suggested that the Fathers could do more than support and confirm the scriptural testimony. Nevertheless, this patristic emphasis occupies both quantitatively and qualitatively a rather greater place in Cranmer's thinking than in that of most of the Reformers. His problems are solved as he comes to see that espousal of Reformation teachings, including the doctrine of Scripture, is not necessarily incompatible with true conservatism.

This leads Cranmer to make very strongly a common point, namely, that from the standpoint of the patristic as well as the biblical age, the reforming church is the church of restoration rather than of innovation. The Reformers, not the Romans, are the true heirs of the past. The protest of Cranmer is against medieval novelties. What his opponents "call the old (learning) is the new, and that which they call the new is indeed the old."[50] His heresy is simply that he would not consent "to words not accustomed in Scripture, and unknown to the ancient fathers."[51] His own con-

---

[49] *Ibid.*, p. 59.
[50] *Ibid.*, p. 450.
[51] *Ibid.*, p. 227.

fession is one of belief "in every article of the catholic faith, every clause, word, and sentence taught by our Saviour Christ, his apostles and prophets, . . . and also in all articles explicate and set forth in the general councils."[52] He is even confident that where there is patristic consensus in essentials, it must be accepted as in full agreement with the Scripture.[53] A patristic principle thus accompanies the predominant scriptural principle. The fact that Reformation theology is essentially that of the early church, as well as that of Scripture, is important.

In this respect Cranmer made a point which was particularly welcome in his own land. Ridley was already claiming Ratramnus as the writer who really opened his eyes to true sacramental teaching. Turner was composing a whole treatise on *The Old Learning and the New*. Jewel was amassing the stores of knowledge which would enable him to substantiate this position. Peter Martyr was contributing his interest and resources. Nor was this a passing phase. After the Marian period, Jewel returned to take up the work of his Edwardian heroes. In his famous sermons at Paul's Cross he issued again, in enlarged and more detailed form, the challenge of Cranmer. If on definite issues his opponents could show him to be wrong from Fathers and councils of the first six centuries, he would recant. That this was no idle boast Jewel showed in the *Apology* and its *Defense*. The principle that the Reformed church is the true patristic church, and that the patristic church recognizes and confirms the teaching and practice of Scripture, became an integral part of the Anglican position. Indeed, it was to have an even longer and broader history. Patristic interest and a sense of continuity with the early church have continued to characterize Anglicanism in almost all its different phases. Very generally, then, Cranmer might very well be regarded at this point as the initiator, or at least the first important representative, of a significant theological trend.

---

[52] *Ibid.*, p. 566.
[53] *Ibid.*, p. 59.

V. THE MARTYR

Rather oddly, Cranmer, the cautious and timid Reformer, was finally called upon to die for his cause. The robust Luther survived every crisis; the consistent and dedicated Calvin, though suffering a thousand deaths in Geneva, died finally of infirmity; Zwingli was killed, but on the field of battle. In so violent a century it is surprising that so few leading reformers, apart from Anabaptists, had to give the final witness. The peculiar course of reformation in England produced a disproportionate number of prominent martyrdoms. The death of Cranmer was in many ways the most crucial and most dramatic.

Cranmer did not make an ideal martyr. He hardly had the right qualifications. His virtues were those of meekness rather than of heroism. He had a respect for authority which urged him to comply, and a nimble mind which sought good reasons for doing so. The story of his martyrdom is not one of unbroken triumph, but of victory out of the very jaws of defeat. Perhaps this is its final secret, for Cranmer emerges as the ordinary man with no taste for violent death. In him men see themselves. They do not greatly like what they see, but they understand it, and take courage.

Cranmer began well enough. When Mary came to the throne, he did not flee, though Ridley warned him: "Therefore if thou, O man of God, do purpose to abide in this realm, prepare and arm thyself to die."[54] An attempt to discredit him by reporting that he had restored the mass provoked a forceful denial. When arrested and imprisoned on a charge of treason — the heresy laws were not yet back — he firmly defended his eucharistic teaching both in the Oxford disputation of 1554 and in a further refutation of Gardiner. He was probably strengthened by the fellowship of Latimer and Ridley, who shared a room with him in prison.

The re-enactment of the savage heresy laws was the first shock. An even greater shock was the burning of Latimer and Ridley,

---

[54] N. Ridley, *Works,* ed. Parker Society (1841), p. 62.

which he was forced to watch. Nevertheless, at the Oxford trial in 1555 he still made a good showing. When condemned, he argued powerfully for the royal supremacy and his view of the Lord's Supper in a letter to the queen. Like Luther, he expressed a willingness to recant — "I never was nor will be so perverse to stand wilfully in mine own opinion."[55] — but only if overpowered by plain arguments from Scriptures and the Fathers. Even after sentence he drafted an appeal to a general council, though now, in face of the question what he should go to the stake for, he was ready to abandon his own statements and simply to "use the same words that they (the Catholic church and most Holy Fathers of old) used . . . and to set my hand to all and singular their speeches, phrases, ways, and forms of speech, which they do use in their treatises upon the sacrament, and to keep still their interpretation."[56] It is revealing that this was thought to be inadequate.

Cranmer suddenly weakened early in 1556. The effects of imprisonment, the arguments of the friars, and natural fear of death probably induced him to sign his first and general recantation. Once the break came, skillful pressure was applied to exploit it. The degradation, hints as to the day of execution, and then a period of comparative ease with the suggestion of quiet retirement conspired to lead Cranmer further on the way of self-betrayal. Over the weeks he signed a series of increasingly specific and humiliating recantations. He finally described himself as "not only worse than Saul and the thief, but most accursed of all whom the earth has ever borne."[57]

But his enemies went too far. Not content with the final recantation, they planned that Cranmer should read it publicly and then be burned anyway (March 21, 1556). Perhaps this excess of cruelty was what brought Cranmer to his senses. We do not know the ultimate reason why he recanted of the recantations. Perhaps he considered that a church which could act thus stood self-

---

[55] *PS*, II, 453–54.
[56] *Ibid.*, p. 227.
[57] *Ibid.*, pp. 564–65.

condemned. Perhaps he decided he might just as well die for convictions if he had to die. Possibly he left the decision to the very last in case a pardon arrived. Perhaps he had more solemn thoughts of the account he must render to God. Be that as it may, he prepared in written or oral form a clever revision of his public statement. This enabled him, when the time came, to make a good profession before the assembled congregation, renouncing, not his doctrinal works, but "things written with my hand contrary to the truth which I thought in my heart, and written for fear of death . . . wherein I have written many things untrue . . . . And as for the pope, I refuse him as Christ's enemy and Antichrist with all his false doctrine. And as for the sacrament. . . ."[58] He could get no further, but he had said enough. At the stake he confirmed the verbal testimony with the sign he had promised: "And forasmuch as my hand offended in writing contrary to my heart, it shall be first burned."[59] Whatever the motivation, there could be no missing the message of the outstretched hand and the words: "This hand hath offended." It need cause no surprise that when Mary's unhappy reign ended in fanaticism and disaster, the sign Cranmer had given was not forgotten. He himself went down in a cruel death, but his work found new and enduring form in the English Bible, the majestic liturgy, and the evangelical confession which were the constitutive elements in the Elizabethan Settlement.

BIBLIOGRAPHY

PRIMARY

Acts of the Privy Council. Ed. J. B. Dasent and H. Nicolas.
Burnet, G. *The History of the Reformation of the Church of England.* Ed. N. Pocock. 7 vols. 1865.
Cranmer, T. *Remains.* Ed. Jenkyns. 4 vols. 1833.
————. *The Work of Thomas Cranmer.* Ed. G. E. Duffield. Philadelphia, 1965.
————. *Works.* Ed. Parker Society. 2 vols. 1844, 1846.
Formularies of the Faith under Henry VIII. Ed. Lloyd. 1856.
Foxe, John. *Acts and Monuments.* Ed. G. Townsend. 8 vols. 1843–49.

---

[58] *Ibid.,* p. 566.
[59] *Ibid.*

Letters and Papers. Ed. J. Brewer and J. Gairdner. 1862–1910.

Narratives of the Reformation. Ed. Camden Society. 1859.

Original Letters. Ed. Parker Society. 2 vols. 1846, 1847.

Ridley, N. *Works.* Ed. Parker Society. 1841.

Strype, John. *Annals of the Reformation.* 1824 ed.

_____. *Ecclesiastical Memorials,* 1822 ed.

_____. *Memorials of Thomas Cranmer.* 1840 ed.

SECONDARY

Brooks, P. *Thomas Cranmer's Doctrine of the Eucharist.* London, 1965.

Bromiley, G. W. *Thomas Cranmer.* London, 1956.

_____. *Thomas Cranmer: Theologian.* London, 1956.

Deane, A. C. *The Life of Thomas Cranmer.* London, 1927.

Hutchinson, F. E. *Cranmer and the English Reformation.* London, 1951.

Innes, A. D. *Cranmer and the Reformation in England.* Edinburgh, 1900.

Mason, A. J. *Thomas Cranmer.* London, 1898.

Pollard, A. F. *Thomas Cranmer and the English Reformation.* London, 1926 ed.

Ratcliff, E. C. "The Liturgical Work of Cranmer," *Three Commemorative Lectures.* Westminster, 1956.

Richardson, C. C. *Zwingli and Cranmer on the Eucharist.* Evanston, 1949.

Ridley, Jasper. *Thomas Cranmer.* Oxford, 1962. (Has full bibliography.)

Rupp, E. Gordon. *Studies in the Making of the English Protestant Tradition.* Cambridge, 1947.

Smyth, C. H. *Cranmer and the Reformation under Edward VI.* Cambridge, 1926.

Timms, G. B. *Dixit Cranmer.* London, 1946.

Part Four

RADICAL REFORM

CHAPTER EIGHT

MENNO SIMONS

J. C. WENGER

I

Many strands were united in bringing the Reformation to the Netherlands. Among the pre-Reformation factors which ultimately contributed to the rise of the Protestant movement in the Lowlands may be mentioned the Brethren of the Common Life and their attractive devotional monographs such as the *Imitation of Christ*. Humanists, led by the brilliant scholar Erasmus, also made their contribution toward more evangelical thought. Of great influence were the writings of Luther. Not long after the publication of his theses on indulgences (1517), Luther's writings were being read in the Netherlands and his hymns were being used. Many editions of Luther's Testament and Bible were also printed in the Low Countries. And as early as 1523 two Lutheran martyrs were burned at the stake in Belgium. There also arose in the Netherlands a group of reformers who came to be known as Sacramentarians because of the attention which they gave to the sacrament of the mass. Worthy of special mention is Cornelis Hoen, also known as Honius, who before 1520 produced a definitive treatise on the Lord's Supper which Luther rejected but which Zwingli found attractive and convincing. Zwingli published this treatise in 1525 without indicating its source. In this treatise Hoen maintained that the word "is" in "This is my body" means "signifies." He felt that the main point of the dominical words was the memorial significance of the bread and the cup.

Finally, another type of reform movement came to the Netherlands. The chief promoter of this radical reformation was a former Lutheran preacher of Swabia named Melchior Hofmann (also spelled Hoffman). An indefatigable man, Hofmann labored in Sweden in 1526, in Northern Germany in 1527, and in Alsace in 1529. In 1530 he established a congregation in Emden in East Friesland. He left in charge there a man named Jan Volkerts or Volkertszoon (also known as Trijpmaker from his occupation of making slippers), while he himself went on to other fields. After being in Strassburg for a time, Hofmann appeared in the Netherlands in 1531. He taught the same view of the sacrament as Cornelis Hoen, as well as such Anabaptist ideas as believer's baptism, the rejection of oaths, and biblical nonresistance. Yet Hofmann could not bring himself to unite with the Swiss Brethren, the Anabaptist left wing of the Zwinglian movement, for the Swiss Brethren rejected Hofmann's apocalypticism as well as his preoccupation with the mysteries of Daniel and the Revelation. Volkerts went to Amsterdam in 1530 and the next year died as a martyr in the Hague. Hofmann in turn went back to Strassburg where he was imprisoned and languished in jail for the last decade of his life, 1533–43. The followers of Hofmann were commonly known as Melchiorites.

Hofmann held confidently that Christ was about to return to earth to set up a kingdom of glory with his capital at Strassburg. And when Christ came, all God's enemies would be destroyed. In the meantime, the saints of the Lord would wait patiently, and bear their sufferings quietly. They would also be obedient to earthly governments. The disciples of Christ could inflict no harm on anyone.

All this sounds innocent enough, but some of the Melchiorites carried Hofmann's apocalypticism to a quite unanticipated position. One of the disciples of Volkerts was a certain Jan Matthijs of Haarlem, through whom two quite dissimilar religious movements emerged. Matthijs himself went to Muenster in Westphalia in 1534 and there helped promote a radical revolutionary type of Anabaptism, the adherents to which took over the government of the city and resisted the forces of the Catholic prince-bishop. Killed in a skirmish with the bishop's forces at Easter, 1534, Matthijs was succeeded by a carnal opportunist named Jan of Leiden, who added polygamy to the revolutionary Anabaptist principles of his subjects, and even accepted coronation. Perhaps he reasoned that he was but preparing the way for another king who was destined to appear, the Lord Jesus, but it is more likely that he was a shrewd leader who rode to power, luxury, and personal indulgence on a wave of fanaticism and gross delusion. Meanwhile, the bishop's army continued to besiege Muenster, effectively cutting off the importation of foodstuffs. While his miserable subjects were starving, King Jan lived in a riotous manner with his harem; he had seized control of the food supplies of the city and he doled them out sparingly. By the spring of 1535 conditions in the city were beyond description; the people were eating cats, dogs, mice, shoes, and even human flesh. Finally, the city was betrayed into the hands of the bishop on the night of June 24–25, 1535, and the so-called Anabaptist kingdom came to an abrupt end.

The Muenster type of "Anabaptism" stood in stark contrast with the sober biblical program of the Swiss Brethren, the free church-men of Zurich who originated under the leadership of Zwingli's young colleague, Conrad Grebel, in 1525. But from the beginning, the Swiss Brethren had stressed sharing with those in need in such a way that they were accused of some sort of radical "commu-nism." And the Muenster debacle furnished the anti-Anabaptist polemicists of the sixteenth century with excellent materials to "prove" that the very genius of Anabaptist thought was revolu-tionary in character and sought to overthrow all civil order and concord. Such polemics were of course not just, for even Melchior Hofmann would have stood in horror before such a program as the two Jans launched in Muenster. Yet it must be observed that a more sober attention to the heart of the gospel would have kept Hofmann from the vagaries of his apocalypticism — and might have avoided the thrust which sent Jan Matthijs into the whirlpool of revolutionary fanaticism.

Meanwhile a second, and quite different, type of Anabaptist movement arose in Friesland. This movement owed its origin to several "apostles" of Jan Matthijs who arrived in Leeuwarden, the capital of Friesland, in December of 1533. Included in the small circle of their converts were two brothers, Obbe and Dirk Philips. The Matthijs "apostles" baptized the Philips brothers and also ordained them. Among other things, the "apostles" promised that no Melchiorites would ever have to endure persecution. God would watch over his own and preserve them from suffering and execution. If anyone questioned this theology of non-suffering he was denounced as resisting the Spirit. The Matthijs "apostles" assured the little band of Leeuwarden believers that God was about to destroy all the godless of the earth. Obbe and Dirk had their mental reservations about this promise, but said little.

In a few months the theology of non-suffering was rudely shattered. On March 26, 1534, the civil authorities tortured some sixteen or seventeen Melchiorites on the wheel, and put them all to death. Obbe went to the place of execution, but the torture and the fire had so disfigured the dead that they were not recognizable. These executions were a traumatic experience for the Melchiorites. Could Matthijs be a false prophet? They hardly knew what to think. They turned to the Scriptures for guidance and the illumination they craved, and found direction there. Obbe and Dirk Philips came to a position remarkably similar to that of the Swiss Brethren of Zurich, although without knowledge of Grebel and his program.

On only one major point did Obbe and Dirk differ from the similar Anabaptists in Switzerland. Melchior Hofmann had pondered long and hard over the question of how Jesus Christ could be a true man and yet sinless. He found nothing in the Scripture about the Roman Catholic doctrine of the immaculate conception of Mary. How then could Christ be human yet sinless? Hofmann finally decided that the real explanation must lie in the virgin birth of the Lord. Since Christ had no human father, and since Christ was conceived in Mary by the Holy Spirit, Mary must have sustained a unique relation to her holy son. Christ was conceived, taught Melchior, *in* Mary's body, yet was not *of* Mary. Obbe and Dirk Philips accepted this explanation, for it seemed to them to be a satisfactory explanation for an otherwise inexplicable situation.

In the course of time a difference in program began to be apparent between Obbe Philips and his sturdy brother Dirk. Obbe began to stress increasingly the importance of one's own inner relationship to God. The important thing is the state of one's soul. Like the later Lutheran Pietists, Obbe was much concerned to cultivate true love for Christ and holiness of heart. Dirk on the other hand tended to emphasize the establishment of disciplined Christian congregations, true disciples of the Lord Jesus who placed themselves under the authority of the word of God and under the discipline of the church.

II

This, then, was the background of the religious milieu which ultimately enveloped Menno Simons of Friesland. We cannot be sure of Menno's birthdate. Karel Vos, one of his finest biographers, thought that Menno had been born in January of 1496 or perhaps late in 1495. At this point there seems to be no way to resolve this difficulty. The place of Menno's birth was a village called Witmarsum, about thirty miles southwest of Leeuwarden and about eight miles northwest of Bolsward. The name of the man was simply Menno; Simons is a patronymic, a common way of designating people in the Netherlands in those days. Of Menno's youth nothing is known. Nor do we know why he entered the priesthood. Because Menno was born in the western section of Friesland, his native tongue was not Dutch, but Frisian, a language somewhat akin to ancient Anglo-Saxon. If the usual practice of the period was followed, Menno was ordained as a Roman priest by the suffragan bishop, Joannes Heetveld, representing the Bishop of Utrecht, during Passion Week, on or about March 26, 1524. Menno himself reports that his first charge was in his father's native village, Pingjum, about three miles from Witmarsum. Here he served as a priest from 1524 until 1531; from 1531 to 1536 he served in his native Witmarsum.

Three quite unrelated events conspired to cause Menno ultimately to leave the Roman Catholic church. The first happened in
1525, within a year of his ordination as a priest. From time to
time, as Menno officiated at mass, he was haunted by a doubt
about the truth of transubstantiation. Does the holy wafer really
become the body of the Lord? Menno speaks of this doubt as if
at the time he considered it a special onslaught of the Evil One;
there is no hint whatsoever that he was familiar with the views of
Cornelis Hoen, for example. In any case Menno found himself
unable to shake off this doubt. At this point Menno knew Latin
and evidently some Greek, and had some knowledge of patristic
writings. But by his own admission he had never taken up the
Scriptures and read them for himself. (He would have read many
citations, of course, in secondary sources.) Of this fact he was
later heartily ashamed: "Lo, such a stupid preacher was I!"
Menno confessed his nagging doubt to his father confessor, but
received no release from his distressing temptation. "I could not
shake off the idea," he writes.[1] With a charming simplicity Menno
reports that he decided to read the New Testament: he had not
gone very far, he confesses, until he saw that "we were deceived."[2]
He came to reject completely the doctrine of transubstantiation.

Menno's distress was great. What should he do? To leave the
Roman Catholic church, he believed, would be to bring eternal
damnation upon himself. It was not until the year 1528 that he
was relieved of anxiety on this score. Through the reading of
Luther's writings, Menno came to the happy awareness that no
one would be lost spiritually through rejecting merely human doctrines. Yet he decided at that point to remain in the Roman church
and go on with his pastoral work.

A second disturbing incident occurred in 1531. Menno happened to learn of the execution of a godly man named Sicke
Freerks (or from his occupation, Sicke Snijder, tailor) for having

---

[1] *The Complete Writings of Menno Simons,* trans. by Leonard Verduin
and ed. J. C. Wenger (corrected edition; Scottdale, Pa., 1966), p. 668.
Hereafter cited as *Complete Writings.*
[2] *Ibid.*

accepted rebaptism — in short, for Anabaptism. This was deeply disturbing to the young priest. Could the holy church be wrong on its doctrine of baptism, just as Menno now believed it to be wrong in its doctrine of the sacrament of communion? Thus began another round of suffering and searching. Menno timidly approached his fellow priest and pastor who finally admitted to him that infant baptism actually had no basis in Scripture. Menno searched the writings of the ancient Fathers as well as those of such contemporaries as Luther, Bucer, and Bullinger. But he was not satisfied with their answers. Again, as a final resort, he turned to the New Testament, only to come to the same conclusion about infant baptism as he had about transubstantiation. Menno felt that his pastor was correct. The only baptism which the New Testament knows is that of those who respond to the proclamation of the gospel, repent of their sins, and turn to the Lord Jesus Christ as Saviour and Lord. Yet Menno was still hesitant to leave his church and follow the light of the truth which he had discovered.

The year of decision was 1535. To Menno's intense shame and inner suffering, his own brother was taken up in a revolutionary religious movement in that year, and died in the spring in a futile attempt to defy the government. This broke Menno's heart. For years Menno had known basic truth which he had not been courageous enough to follow. His poor deluded brother had not found the light, yet he had been man enough to die for what he thought was truth. With bitter tears Menno turned to the Lord in profound penitence and faith. He was then a converted and evangelical pastor. For nine months he followed the example of various other religious leaders and tried to bring his congregation with him into an evangelical faith and obedience. But in the end he considered this impossible. On or about Sunday, January 30, 1536, Menno renounced the Roman Catholic church and fled for his life. Probably in that same year he was united in marriage with a good and faithful woman named Geertruydt, of whom nothing more is known with certainty. She may have come from Friesland or from Groningen, the province to which he likely fled when he renounced

Catholicism. He speaks of his daughters in 1558; he is reputed to have lost a son named Jan.

Menno's own account of his conversion reads as follows:

> After this had transpired the blood of these people, although misled, fell so hot on my heart that I could not stand it, nor find rest in my soul. I reflected upon my unclean carnal life, also the hypocritical doctrine and idolatry which I still practiced daily in appearance of godliness, but without relish. I saw that these zealous children, although in error, willingly gave their lives and their estates for their doctrine and faith. And I was one of those who had disclosed to some of them the abominations of the papal system. But I myself continued in my comfortable life and acknowledged abominations simply in order that I might enjoy physical comfort and escape the cross of Christ. . . .
>
> My heart trembled within me. I prayed to God with sighs and tears that He would give to me, a sorrowing sinner, the gift of His grace, create within me a clean heart, and graciously through the merits of the crimson blood of Christ forgive my unclean walk and frivolous easy life and bestow upon me wisdom, Spirit, courage, and a manly spirit so that I might preach His exalted and adorable name and holy Word in purity, and make known His truth to His glory.[3]

About a year after his renunciation of the church of Rome, Menno reports that he was one day exercising himself in the word of God, reading and writing, when

> some six, seven, or eight persons came to me who were of one heart and one soul with me, beyond reproach as far as man can judge in doctrine and life, separated from the world after the witness of Scripture and under the cross, men who sincerely abhorred not only the sect of Muenster, but the cursed abominations of all other worldly sects. [The delegation represented the so-called Obbenites, the followers of Obbe Philips.] In the name of those pious souls who were of the same mind and spirit both with themselves and with me, they prayerfully requested me to make the great sufferings and need of the poor oppressed souls my concern, seeing that the hunger was very great and the faithful stewards al-

---

[3] *Ibid.*, p. 671.

together few. They urged me to put to good use the talents which I, though unworthy, had received from the Lord.[4]

That is, the delegation wished Menno to accept ordination to the office of bishop in the Obbenite Brotherhood. Menno at first refused, feeling that his talents were too limited, and also dreading the persecution which he knew would be his lot as an Anabaptist bishop. On the other hand the obvious need of the nonresistant and nonrevolutionary Anabaptists rested heavily on his conscience. Finally, after much prayer, Menno yielded and accepted ordination. Obbe Philips, who likely baptized him in 1536, now early in 1537 committed to him the office of bishop or overseer. The ceremony was, says Obbe, performed in the province of Groningen.

Almost twenty years later, in 1554, reflecting back over his service, Menno marveled at the way in which God had blessed his ministry and made it fruitful:

> The great and mighty God has made known the word of true repentance, the word of His grace and power, and the salutary use of His holy sacraments [baptism and the Lord's Supper], through our humble service, doctrine, and unlearned writings, together with the diligent service, labor, and help of our faithful brethren in many towns and countries. It has been made known to such an extent, and He has made the fashion of His churches so glorious, and has bestowed upon them such unconquerable power that many proud and lofty hearts not only have become humble; the impure, chaste; the drunken, sober; the avaricious, benevolent; the cruel, kind; and the ungodly, pious; but they also faithfully left their possessions and blood, life and limb, with the blessed testimony they had, as it may be seen daily still.[5]

From the time of his withdrawal from Roman Catholicism early in 1536 until 1543 Menno lived in Holland: Groningen, West Friesland, and near Amsterdam. About the year 1539 a man named Tjaert Reynerdson of West Friesland was put on the torture wheel because he had dared, out of compassion, to take Menno into his

---

[4] *Ibid.*
[5] *Ibid.*, pp. 672, 673.

house. In 1542 Emperor Charles V issued a severe edict against the heretic "Minne," as he was known in the Frisian tongue, his crime being Anabaptism. Menno, declared the placard, was guilty of "endeavoring at night and other unseasonable times . . . to seduce by his false teachings and sermons the simple people, our subjects."[6]

For a time, 1543–44, Menno lived and labored in East Friesland. Then he transferred to the diocese of Cologne on the Lower Rhine, where Archbishop Herman took a remarkably tolerant attitude toward the Reformation. After his death, Menno spoke of him as "Archbishop Herman, the Elector of Cologne, of lovely memory." About 1545 Menno ventured to ask the clergy of Bonn for the privilege of a debate with them on the religious issues of the day, under Archbishop Herman, but the request was denied. (On later occasions Menno made the same attempt at Emden and at Wesel, but was turned down at both places. Those at Wesel remarked that they wished that the hangman might treat with him.) Finally, in 1546 Menno removed to the territory of Holstein, then under the King of Denmark but now in northern Germany; there he lived most of the remainder of his life, 1546–61, although he sometimes moved about in what is now northern Germany. In 1553–54, for example, he dwelled in Wismar in Mecklenburg. His final residence was at a place called Wuestenfelde near Oldesloe, north of Hamburg and west of Luebeck.

Menno served as a bishop in his brotherhood from 1537 until his death in 1561. There were many bishops in the church in that generation, for the office as such did not involve the oversight of vast territories which we today associate with the office. But although there were many bishops, there were four in Menno's time who, by virtue of their gifts and personal effectiveness, did serve more or less as district superintendents. Gillis of Aachen, born about 1500 and beheaded in 1557, served effectively in the Rhineland. Leenaert Bouwens looked after the congregations in

---

6 Karel Vos, *Menno Simons, 1496–1561. Zijn Leven en Werken* (Leiden, 1914), p. 236; John Horsch, *Menno Simons: His Life, Labors, and Teachings,* (Scottdale, Pa., 1916), p. 56.

Holland, baptizing in a thirty-year period no fewer than 10,252 persons. Dirk Philips, perhaps Menno's staunchest colleague and co-worker, looked after the churches of Danzig and the Baltic area. Menno, the most outstanding of them all, cared for the congregations in East Friesland, Oldenburg, Holstein, Mecklenburg, and possibly Pomerania. It will be noted that Obbe Philips was not included among the outstanding bishops. The reason is that Obbe lost heart, partly perhaps because the emphases of Dirk and Menno became dominant in the Anabaptist Brotherhood (that is, a strict congregationalism, with vigorous church discipline, rather than Obbe's mild program of stressing inner piety) and partly because of anxiety and discouragement due to his ordination by representatives of Jan Matthijs, who later proved to be a false prophet. Obbe retired from the ministry about 1540 and withdrew to Rostock on the Baltic where he lived a quiet and secluded life. For this step Menno charged him with being a Demas!

From time to time the leading bishops held consultations to seek to maintain more or less uniform disciplinary standards. Such a meeting was held at Wismar in 1554. Among the seven present were four great leaders, Menno Simons, Dirk Philips, Leenaert Bouwens, and Gillis of Aachen. The bishops decided that members should be expected to marry only within the Brotherhood; those who were disobedient were to be expelled until they demonstrated their true Christian faith by the honesty of their life. It was also considered improper to do unnecessary business with an excommunicated person. (This practice of breaking social relations with expelled persons until they repented and were again received into the church was called shunning or avoidance. It was instituted by Obbe Philips as a safeguard against the fanatical Anabaptist sects such as the Muensterites, and was later extended to include all excommunicated members.) The bishops held in 1554 that marital avoidance applied even to the marriage bed, provided the faithful member accepts this as his Christian obligation. The bishops also decided that adultery broke the marriage bond, and if there was no penitence on the part of the guilty party, the spouse was free to remarry. If an unbelieving spouse abandoned his believing mate, the latter should remain unmarried unless the unbelieving spouse commited adultery or married someone else, in which case the abandoned believer might also remarry, subject to the approval of the elders of the congregation. The bishops advised that young people should seek the approval of their parents before getting married, but also advised the parents not to attempt to prevent valid marriages on the part of their believing children. Just debts could be collected by law "where no wickedness results therefrom" (this qualification is not further clarified). Finally, the bishops took a stand against the bearing of arms, although it was considered permissible to carry "an honest staff or rapier" when on a journey, "according to conditions of the land." These ethical applications indicate the deep pastoral concern of the bishops, and perhaps also the rising prestige of the office.

III

What were the major doctrinal emphases of Menno? Here are a number of statements which reflect his doctrinal position:

Scripture Alone. "I have written this out of pure love, and in the interest of peace, according to the direction of the holy Word, before my God who shall judge me at the last day. . . . To some what I have written will be too stringent and to others too lenient. . . . Whatsoever any person can advance and prove I will gladly hear and obey; but I dare not go higher nor lower, be more stringent or lenient, than the Scriptures and the Holy Spirit teach me; and that out of great fear and anxiety of my conscience lest I once more burden the God-fearing hearts who have renounced the commandments of men with more such commandments. Willfullness and human opinions I roundly hate, and do not want them. I know what tribulation and affliction they have caused me for many years."[7]

---

[7] *Complete Writings,* p. 484.

Saving Faith. "Behold, my reader, such a faith as mentioned is the true Christian faith which praises, honors, magnifies, and extols God the Father and His Son Jesus Christ through loving fear and fearing love, for it recognizes the good will of the Father toward us through Christ. It recognizes, I say, that all the promises to the fathers, the expectation of the patriarchs, the whole figurative law, and all the prophecies of the prophets are fulfilled in Christ, with Christ, and through Christ. It acknowledges that Christ is our King, Prince, Lord, Messiah, the promised David, the Lion of the tribe of Judah, the strong One, the Prince of Peace. . . . In short, our only and eternal Mediator, Advocate, High Priest, Propitiator, and Intercessor; our Head and Brother.

"And since faith confesses all this, therefore, I say, it also observes His Word aright, hears His voice, and faithfully follows His example and counsel, and departs from ungodliness. For the heart is changed, the mind is renewed, and with Moses it clings to the promises as if they were in sight."[8]

Voluntarism. "If you want to be a true member of the church of Christ, you must be born of the Word of God; be Christian-minded; bring forth Christian fruits; walk according to His Word, ordinance, and command; die unto the flesh and the world; lead an irreproachable life in the fear of God; serve and love your neighbors with all your heart; confess the name and glory of Christ, and be prepared for all manner of tribulation, misery, and persecution. . . .

"But if you refuse this, and remain unchanged in your first birth, if you lead an impenitent easy life, neglect the Word and ordinance of the Lord, act the hypocrite with the world, and spurn the cross, then you cannot be a member of the church of Christ. . . ."[9]

The Obedience of Faith. "For all the regenerated and spiritually minded conform in all things to the Word and ordinances of the Lord. Not because they think to merit the atonement of their sins and eternal life. By no means. . . . For a truly believing Christian

---

[8] *Ibid.,* p. 339.
[9] *Ibid.,* p. 744.

is thus minded that he will not do otherwise than that which the Word of the Lord teaches and enjoins. . . ."[10]

Grace Alone. "Think not, beloved reader, that we boast of being perfect and without sins. Not at all. As for me, I confess that often my prayer is mixed with sin, and my righteousness with unrighteousness; for by the grace of God I feel, if I but observe the anointing which is in me, when I compare my weak nature to Christ and His commandment, what kind of flesh I have inherited from Adam. If God should judge us according to our deserts, and not according to His great goodness and mercy, then I confess with the holy David that no man could stand before His judgment. . . . Therefore it should be far from us that we should comfort ourselves with anything but the grace of God through Christ Jesus. For He it is, and He alone, and none other, who has perfectly fulfilled the righteousness required by God. . . .

"For Christ's sake we are in grace; for His sake we are heard; and for His sake our faults and failings which are committed against our will are remitted. For it is He who stands between His Father and His imperfect children with His perfect righteousness, and with His innocent blood and death. . . ."[11]

The True Saints. "Therefore my very precious brethren and sisters in the Lord, do take the crucified Jesus as your example, and the righteous apostles and prophets of God. Learn through them. . . . They had their hearts trained there, and they were so endowed and drawn by God that they knew nothing, sought nothing, loved and desired nothing save the eternal, heavenly, and imperishable treasure and existence, that is, God and eternal life. They were so grounded in love and driven by love, and were so firm and immovable, that neither life nor death, angels nor empires nor rulers, neither hunger nor sword nor any other torture, pain, or means, could frighten them away from the love which is in Christ Jesus. Their thoughts, their words, their acts, their life, and their deaths were Christ's. Their kingdom and rest they sought not upon this

---

[10] *Ibid.,* pp. 396, 397.
[11] *Ibid.,* p. 506.

earth, for they were spiritually, heavenly minded, and all their fruit was righteousness, light, and truth. Their whole lives were pure love, chastity, humility, obedience, and peace. The transient wicked world with all its works was to them an offense and an abomination. They loved their God with all their soul, and therefore they rebuked all that was against His holy will, His honor, and His Word. They loved their neighbors as themselves, and therefore they admonished and rebuked them in love, served them, and pointed out and taught God's pure will, Word, and truth with all diligence, and sought their salvation with all their power, and at a great cost to their own name and life."[12]

Restitution of the Primitive Church. "Here you have, most pious reader, how baptism ought to be practiced in the church of God, the baptism that by lengthy deterioration was corrupted, but now by the generous gift of God restored. Let the rulers oppose as they will. Let the learned doctors by their wisdom do as they may. Let the whole world, by every means available to it, resist. This [believer's baptism] is the one and only manner of baptism which Christ Jesus has instituted, and the apostles taught and practiced. Truth will remain forever unconquered, no matter how violently many fight against her. Whoever reads with Christian discernment, and judges properly, will welcome this heavenly truth of Christ, for so many ages lost, and now regained. . . ."[13]

Ceremonies Secondary. "If you are a genuine Christian, born of God, then why do you draw back from baptism, which is the least that God has commanded you? It is a weighty and important command to love your enemy, is it not? to do good to those that hate you . . . , to crucify your wicked and ungodly flesh. . . .

"It seems to me that these and the like commands are more painful and difficult for perverse flesh . . . than to be the recipient of a handful of water."[14]

---

12 *Ibid.,* p. 598.
13 *Ibid.,* p. 287.
14 *Ibid.,* pp. 138, 139.

The Two Kingdoms. "The Scriptures teach that there are two opposing princes and two opposing kingdoms: the one is the Prince of peace; the other the prince of strife. . . . The Prince of peace is Christ Jesus; His kingdom is the kingdom of peace; His Word is the word of peace; His body is the body of peace; His children are the seed of peace. . . . In short, with this King, and in his kingdom and reign, it is nothing but peace. Everything that is seen and heard, and done is peace. . . .

"Peter was commanded to sheathe his sword. All Christians are commanded to love their enemies; to do good unto those who abuse and persecute them; to give the mantle when the cloak is taken, the other cheek when one is struck. Tell me, how can a Christian defend Scripturally retaliation, rebellion, war . . . ?"[15]

Why We Are Persecuted. "These miserable men cruelly cry against us, saying, Heretics! heretics! Drown them, slay them, and burn them! And this for no other reason than that we teach the new life, baptism on confession of faith, and the Supper in both elements in an unblamable church. . . . We rebuke all false doctrine, idolatry, and the damnable carnal life, and point to the blessed Christ Jesus alone, and to no other means of salvation. . . ."[16]

IV

In January of 1561 Menno lay on his deathbed. He ventured, however, to deliver a brief sermonette to those around his bedside. On the twenty-fifth anniversary of his renunciation of the Roman church he took a turn for the worse; he died the next day, Friday, January 31, 1561. (The old books which give his dates as 1492–1559 are in error, as are those sources which indicate that he died on January 13, 1561.) Menno's body was interred in his own lawn, or "garden," as the Europeans say. The exact spot was lost in the destruction of the Thirty Years' War.

---

15 *Ibid.,* pp. 554, 555.
16 *Ibid.,* p. 232.

In all essential points Menno was an evangelical believer in Christ, a man who emphasized human sin and need, the importance of repentance and faith, the reality of the new birth and of sanctification, the great significance of the church as a converted body of earnest disciples of Christ, living under the dicipline of the word of God and the spirit of God. He took a strong stand for believer's baptism and for a life of nonresistance to violence and unjust suffering. The only oddity in his theology was his quiet espousal of the Melchiorite doctrine of the incarnation which taught the reality of Christ's humanity along with the fact that he was the eternal Son of God who became incarnate, but emphasized that Christ was conceived *in* Mary, yet was not *of* Mary. (Menno was not aware that the female has an ovum which is fertilized by the male; he thought that the woman passively received seed of the male, which seed then developed into the child to be born.)

During the past several centuries various portraits of Menno have been made by a number of different artists, but none of them was made from actual knowledge of how Menno looked. Among the artists who made portraits of Menno were Christoffel van Sichem, 1608; Jacob Burghart, 1683; Jan Luyken, 1681 (in *Opera* of Menno); Alex Harder, 1935; Arend Hendriks, 1948; and Warren Rohrer, 1961. A memorial shaft, a stone obelisk about ten feet in height, was erected to Menno's memory at the site of the old Witmarsum Mennonite Meetinghouse and dedicated on September 11, 1879. Another granite monument, with a bronze plaque to Menno's memory, was erected near Fresenburg in northern Germany in 1902 and dedicated on August 26, 1906. In 1953 eight young men in *PAX* service (humanitarian work abroad under the administration of the Mennonite Central Committee) moved the 1906 monument to the main highway between Bad Oldesloe and Bad Segeberg, about two kilometers from the former location. Sometime after World War II the plaque was removed from the monument; in 1958 a new plaque was placed on it by German university students in appreciation for the relief program of the Mennonite Central Committee after World War II. But the real "monument" to the memory of Menno is the conviction with which his vision of Christianity as earnest discipleship to Jesus Christ is today held by a half-million Mennonites around the globe.

BIBLIOGRAPHY

PRIMARY SOURCES

Menno was the author of twenty-five books and booklets which together make a volume of something over a thousand pages. As early as 1535, the year of his conversion, he wrote a vigorous polemic against Jan of Leiden, the "king" of Muenster. For most of the next twenty years Menno's writings were positive, edifying treatises to clarify for the public the doctrinal position of his Anabaptist church and to build up that church in faith and holiness. In this category are:

The Spiritual Resurrection
Meditation on the Twenty-fifth Psalm
The New Birth
Foundation of Christian Doctrine (his masterpiece)
Christian Baptism
Why I Do Not Cease Teaching and Writing
The True Christian Faith
A Kind Admonition on Church Discipline
A Clear Account of Excommunication
Confession of the Triune God
Confession of the Distressed Christians
A Pathetic Supplication to All Magistrates
Brief Defense to All Theologians
The Cross of the Saints

After 1554, however, Menno became involved in controversy with Martin Micron, John à Lasco, Gellius Faber, and with Sylis and Lemke, Anabaptist leaders from the Rhineland. In his polemics with these men Menno developed a sharp and bitter style which, while common in the sixteenth century, mars his otherwise Christlike spirit and gentle style.

In 1558 Menno published eight of his writings under the title *Foundation of Christian Doctrine*. In 1600 and 1601 two additional collections of his writings were published. These collections, together with that of 1558 and six additional works (a total of twenty-one writings), were published in 1646. Finally, in 1681, his *Opera omnia theologica*, containing twenty-two writings and ten letters, was published. An English edition was published at Elkhart, Indiana in 1871. The most recent English edition is *The Complete Writings of Menno Simons,* trans. Leonard Verduin, ed. J. C. Wenger (Scottdale, 1956; corrected ed., 1966).

SECONDARY SOURCES

Behrends, Karl. *Der Ketzer Bischof.* Basel, 1966. Delightful reading but adds no real factual information to Menno's life. Some of the interpretation is debatable.

Bender, Harold S. and John Horsch. *Menno Simons' Life and Writings.* Scottdale, Pa., 1936.

Brandsma, J. A. *Menno Simons van Witmarsum.* Drachten, 1960.

Dyck, C. J. (ed.). *A Legacy of Faith: The Heritage of Menno Simons.* Newton, Kansas, 1962. One of the finest collections of essays on Menno.

Horsch, John. *Menno Simons: His Life, Labors and Teachings.* Scottdale, Pa., 1916. The most complete English work on Menno, and the best general interpretation.

Horst, Irvin B. *A Bibliography of Menno Simons, ca. 1496–1561: Dutch Reformer.* Nieukoop, The Netherlands, 1962. A scholarly tabulation of various editions of Menno's writings, with a listing of known copies.

Klaasen, Walter, et al. *No Other Foundation: Commemorative Essays on Menno Simons.* North Newton, Kansas, 1962. Articles of excellent quality.

Krahn, Cornelius. *Menno Simons (1496–1561). Ein Beitrag zur Geschichte und Theologie der Taufgesinnten.* Karlsruhe, 1936. The most thorough German monograph on Menno, a doctoral dissertation at the University of Heidelberg.

Littell, Franklin H. *A Tribute to Menno Simons.* Scottdale, Pa., 1961. Creative and stimulating.

Meihuizen, H. W. *Menno Simons: Ijveraar voor het Herstel van de Nieuwtestamentische Gemeente.* Haarlem, 1961. A good piece of research.

Smith, C. Henry. *Menno Simons. Apostle of the Nonresistant Life.* Berne, Ind., 1936. A readable, brief biography of Menno by a good historian.

Van der Zijpp, N. *Menno Simonsz.* Amsterdam, 1947. A brief interpretation, less significant than the monographs of Vos, Horsch, Krahn, and Bender.

Visser, M. S. E. *Minne Simens en de Minnisten.* Bolswert, 1960. A treatise in Frisian.

Vos, Karel. *Menno Simons, 1496–1561. Zijn Leven en Werken.* Leiden, 1914. The most thorough Dutch monograph on Menno's life.

CHAPTER NINE

THOMAS MUENTZER

HANS J. HILLERBRAND

Thomas Muentzer was both a competent theologian and an ardent reformer; as such, he had few equals in the early sixteenth century. And even though the aim of this volume is to portray the rich variety of ecclesiastical reformers, each with his individuality and significance, one must say that both as theologian and as reformer Muentzer is unthinkable without Martin Luther. "The Pope of Wittenberg," as he called Luther, was his mortal enemy. For him Muentzer reserved his most abusive epithets; against him he levied the most devastating charges. He did this to stem the tide of Luther's reformatory renewal, which he considered as despicable an abomination as Roman Catholicism. He fought for his cause with an intense personal involvement to the point of participating in a radical revolutionary upheaval of society. But his frenzied pronouncements and feverish activity did not save his cause from defeat nor his head from the executioner's block.

His voice was silenced less than two years after its protest had first been sounded. It had little if any direct impact upon the subsequent course of ecclesiastical events. For four centuries following his death, Thomas Muentzer was cited mostly as a case history for precisely the kind of unbiblical and satanic abomination which he believed he saw in his contemporaries. Only in our own day has there been a reappraisal of Muentzer's place in the sun. A few theologians have discovered a bit more theological substance than has heretofore been assumed and Marxist historians have bestowed lavish praise upon a man to whom they attribute a major place in the turbulent effort at social reconstruction undertaken by the peasants in 1524–25. While most theological assessments of Muentzer err by measuring him too strictly by standards

213

set by Luther, Marxist interpreters surely err by overestimating his significance. But that Thomas Muentzer played a more important role in the early Reformation than has traditionally been accorded him seems clear enough; he was better than his reputation.

I

Muentzer's childhood and early life do not seem to have been particularly unusual. If born in 1498, which seems the most probable date of several suggested, he was, as were most of the Protestant Reformers, in his youth when the forceful issues of ecclesiastical renewal came to the fore. He took some university work and in all likelihood received a theological degree, but his studies appear to have been a bit erratic and disorganized, characteristic of the brilliant and sensitive student who can't quite adjust to the pedestrian routine of academic procedure. We know far too little about him, although one fact is, interestingly enough, attested: he was an avid reader of everything he could lay his hands on — Plato, Augustine, Jerome, to name but a few.

Muentzer decided on an ecclesiastical career and, not surprisingly, became a follower of Martin Luther once the indulgences controversy had begun to be the number one topic among theologians. In 1520 he went as minister to Zwickau, a small town in the eastern part of Saxony, where for the next twelve months he showed himself a rabid and aggressive disciple of the Wittenberg Reformers. Zwickau had its share of social and economic problems at the time; even without Muentzer's determined effort to preach a new kind of gospel, there were tensions enough in the city. It is a pity that we do not know more about Muentzer's preaching in Zwickau, for if we could assess his theological orientation of that time his subsequent theological development would come into sharper focus. Fragments of sermons show an astoundingly conservative orientation, however; this counsels restraint in the face of the temptation to make Muentzer a radical theologian from cradle to grave.

True, he ran headlong into troubles in Zwickau, but there is no reason to attribute this solely to a rabble-rousing temperament or to a radical theology. Probably it was a clash between the Roman Catholics and the proponents of the "new faith," such as occurred any number of times wherever the "new faith" was propagated, the intensity of the clash being determined more by the local reformer's temperament than by his theology. Muentzer wanted a forthright acceptance of the "new faith"; although the leading minister of the town was an irenic and erudite Erasmian Humanist, the two men clashed. This precipitated Muentzer's somewhat abrupt departure in the summer of 1521. The failure of his work at Zwickau set a pattern. From the beginning Muentzer's quest for reformatory renewal was marked by defeat and disappointment.

At Zwickau, Muentzer may have come into contact with Hussite thought — the possibility is enticing — for when he left the city he headed southward to Bohemia, that old Hussite hunting ground, to preach the "new faith." He called himself an *emulus*, a messenger, of Luther and propagated theological theses which he had taken straight from Melanchthon.[1] This was the time of stark uncertainty after Luther's disappearance and secret stay at the Wartburg. Muentzer's southward journey may have reflected ongoing enthusiasm for the "new faith" or even his intent to propagate this faith in the relative safety of a heretical region.

From Muentzer's Bohemian sojourn comes one important document. On All Saints' Day, 1521, Muentzer published what is known as his *Prague Manifesto*, a fiery ultimatum to the people of Prague to accept the "new faith": "If you will not do this, God will let you be smitten by the Turks within a year. Indeed, I know that my words are true. I will suffer for them even as Jeremiah suffered."[2] The *Manifesto* was but another reformatory treatise and to go over it with the fine-toothed comb of theological sophistication in order to detect radical notions is a misguided effort. If

---

[1] Heinrich Böhmer and Paul Kirn (eds.), *Thomas Münzers Briefwechsel* (Leipzig, 1931), p. 138.
[2] *Ibid.*, p. 142.

Muentzer parted company here with Luther, then it was more in degree than in kind. And more noteworthy than any kind of radical theology was the mood of his pronouncement — its dramatic character, its explosively exuberant tenor. Luther never issued this kind of ultimatum. There was a theocentric motif present here, an unerring conviction of divine presence, a profound knowledge of God's imminent intervention in man's affairs.

Afterward the curtain fell on Muentzer, and his whereabouts for almost two years remain unknown. What was he about during this time? Did he read and study, or perform the routine chores of a minister? Our questions must go begging. Early in 1523 Muentzer appeared again in the small Saxon town of Allstedt; by that time his theological position was complete. How he got to Allstedt no one knew even at the time, though the city fathers of Allstedt afterward must have come to regret his appointment.

Somewhere along the line Muentzer must have grown weary of the Wittenberg program of ecclesiastical reform — perhaps that other unhappy reformer, Andreas Bodenstein of Carlstadt, did his share to disenchant him — for by the end of 1523 his theological declaration of war against Luther was ready and promptly appeared in print in the form of two pamphlets, one entitled *On Phony Faith* and the other *Protestation and Declaration*. These two pieces were also a relatively detailed statement of his thought. They were sensational inasmuch as they constituted the first public and spectacular dissent from the Wittenberg Reformer from within the ranks of his followers. Open disunity was thus introduced into the camp of those who strove for reformatory renewal. Muentzer's dissent from Luther must have taken place sometime in the fall of 1523; in the summer of that year he had still assured Luther in a letter, "I have known for a certainty that you did not pursue your own cause but that of all men."[3]

On the face of things little happened for the time being. Muentzer sought to translate his theory of ecclesiastical renewal into practice and, as became his temperament, he did so forcefully and

---

[3] *Ibid.*, p. 42.

exuberantly. Some of his reformatory efforts were on the innocuous side; they establish his stature as a practical churchman, but say little about his place in the ongoing course of ecclesiastical renewal. His most eminent contribution was the writing of several orders of worship — the first ones, incidentally, to come from the pen of a Protestant reformer. His liturgical effort was perceptive. While it largely retained the traditional form, it creatively remolded the worship of the church in line with the new Protestant teaching. Another facet of Muentzer's reformatory activity at Allstedt, one embarrassingly enigmatic, was the founding of a *Bund,* or league, members of which were those who pledged themselves "to stay true to God and his gospel."[4] To use a bit of Churchillian prose, this *Bund* is "an enigma wrapped in a mystery"; probably it was nothing but Muentzer's own way of expressing the age-old sectarian impulse to separate the truly faithful from the mass of nominal believers.

Muentzer's proclamation involved him in a running feud with Count Ernst of Mansfeld, in whose territory Allstedt was situated. The two men exchanged a goodly number of uncomplimentary epithets and while they never got around to stating specifically why they were so furious with one another, one suspects that Muentzer's somewhat impulsive and aggressive demeanor must have been a thorn in the count's flesh. The quarrel between the two men soon also involved the Saxon authorities, whose critical eye remained on Allstedt throughout the subsequent months. Then, in March of 1524, a pilgrimage shrine near Allstedt was burned down by a group of incensed Allstedt burghers. Muentzer himself had not participated in this exhibition of reformatory zeal, but his preaching undoubtedly had laid the groundwork. The Saxon authorities promptly intervened and initiated an investigation which dragged on inconclusively for some time, since suddenly no one at Allstedt seemed able to remember what had happened. Muentzer staunchly defended the burning, since, as he put it, the devil had been wor-

---

4 Carl Hinrichs, *Luther und Müntzer. Ihre Auseinandersetzung über Obrigkeit und Widerstandsrecht* (Berlin, 1962), p. 19.

shiped in the shrine. Eventually the Saxon authorities issued a stern reprimand not to use force for the proclamation of the gospel.

This turbulent state of affairs prompted Duke John and his son John Frederick to pay a visit to Allstedt. Muentzer was asked to preach a sermon for the occasion and he took his text from the second chapter of the book of Daniel, that awesome passage in which Daniel enlightens King Nebuchadnezzar about the handwriting on the wall. Muentzer similarly sought to enlighten the two rulers on God's place in history — perhaps even on his own place, for he candidly told his distinguished audience that "a new Daniel must arise and interpret for you your vision."[5] He meant to unfold God's plan before their eyes and he challenged them to take their place in this plan. The Saxon rulers were not impressed, however, and Muentzer had to realize that his challenge had been a failure. Indeed, as subsequent events were to show, the rulers increasingly hindered the proclamation of his gospel; for him, this was unmistakable evidence that they were siding with the godless. Martin Luther did his share to pour oil on the fire by publishing his *Letter to the Rulers of Saxony Concerning the Rebellious Spirit,* which vehemently denounced Muentzer (without mentioning him by name) for advocating civil insurrection under the guise of preaching the gospel.

For a short while Muentzer's known activities consisted in an explosive exchange of letters with various rulers. Examined at Weimar early in August, he bluntly denied that he had ever advocated insurrection or that he had preached against the rulers. He must have realized, all the same, which way the wind was blowing, for within days of his return from the interrogation he left Allstedt. After a brief stay at Muehlhausen, he went on to southern Germany. There he published two tracts, the *Explicit Revelation* and the *Highly Occasioned Defense;* as it turned out, these were the last ones from his pen.

---

[5] Otto H. Brandt, *Thomas Münzer. Sein Leben und seine Schriften* (Jena, 1933), p. 59.

By the spring of 1525 he was back in central Germany. There he met his downfall, both personally and theologically. When he returned North, the peasants' uprising, which had broken out the previous summer and fall in southwestern Germany, had spread there and he found himself embroiled in it. Exactly how much he was involved is a mystery. Scant sources require this cautious statement, even though he is customarily seen as the chief ring-leader of the peasants in central Germany. What can be definitely established is that Muentzer was in the peasants' camp, that he preached to the peasants, and that he wrote bold letters to several rulers which he signed "Thomas Muentzer with the Sword of Gideon."[6] All sorts of stories about Muentzer's doings made the rounds afterward — for example, that he had assured the peasants that he would catch the enemy's bullets in his coat sleeves — but they seem to be apocryphal and to belong to the realm of fiction.

The decisive battle of Frankenhausen in the middle of May, 1525, which ended the uprising in Thuringia, found Muentzer hiding in a bed in the attic of a house. Whatever else may be said about him, he was not exactly a hero. Discovered by marauding soldiers, he was taken prisoner, tortured, forced to confess anything and everything, and executed within a week. His confession dutifully acknowledged that he had "incited this rebellion so that all Christendom should be equal and that the lords and nobles who do not stand by the gospel should be killed."[7] He also confessed that he had advocated that "all things should be held in common."[8] At the same time he pleaded with the peasants still in the fields to lay down their arms and cease the shedding of blood. On May 27, 1525 he was beheaded.

Such was the end of Thomas Muentzer — catastrophic, abrupt, ignominious. On the face of things, his life had hardly been spectacular: a reformatory work in a small and insignificant Saxon town; a few pamphlets; a cursory and enigmatic involvement in

6 *Ibid.*, pp. 77, 78.
7 *Ibid.*, p. 82.
8 *Ibid.*

the peasants' uprising in Thuringia. His public activity had been brief indeed, and by no means did he ever rise to be the spokesman for the social and economic yearnings of the German people.

II

If the famous Sichem engraving depicts an authentic "Muentzer," it shows an unintellectual face and portrays features that seem to combine sadness and determination. And such was Muentzer's temper. Like a meteor he had appeared on the firmament of the Reformation and he had compressed into two brief years a noteworthy sequence of activity. One dramatic appeal, one daring involvement, one striking theological insight followed the other: this is the story of Thomas Muentzer between 1523 and 1525. It was as if Muentzer breathlessly raced from one engagement to the next, knowing his time to be short. His abiding concern was to understand the Christian faith more fully and to effect ecclesiastical renewal more comprehensively. His whole being was involved and his quest was more than an intellectual exercise. He remains one of the eminent names of the early sixteenth century, without whom the history of the Protestant Reformation cannot be written.

And Muentzer's story cannot be written without Martin Luther. Muentzer called him "Brother Fattened Swine," "Brother Soft Life," "Dr. Liar," the "Pope of the Lutheran Scripture Perverters," the "Soft-living Flesh of Wittenberg" — and in each instance more was at stake than personal insult or abusive epithet.[9] A theological *raison d'être* stood behind Muentzer's labels and it may well have been for this reason that they were so poignant and devastating.

The relationship between the two men had not always been of this sort. In 1521 Muentzer had called Luther "sweetest father," "paradigm and light of the friends of God," and perhaps he had even acknowledged himself one "whom you have created through

---

[9] *Ibid.*, pp. 187, 190, 201.

the gospel."[10] What echoed here was a comment widely heard in the early years of the Reformation: the acknowledgment of having received from Luther the stimulus for an incisive theological reorientation. Thus Luther was to Muentzer both a mortal enemy and an important theological influence. In helping him to reject the idea of man's merit, Luther had shown Muentzer the path away from Roman Catholicism. If Muentzer afterward became furious with Luther, then surely it was because he knew that he owed so much to him, but on second thought found him so abominably wanting.

Alongside Luther were other sources of Muentzer's thought. One of them, Joachim of Fiore, that fiery Franciscan philosopher of history, was singled out even in his lifetime. But Muentzer discounted that influence and noted that he had read Joachim "only on Jeremiah," adding "my teaching is from high above."[11] Needless to say, the historian can make little of spatial-metaphysical statements of this latter sort, though Muentzer's point may only have been to express his conviction that his teaching was from God rather than from men.

Surely Muentzer had imbibed the mystic tradition and he employed its vocabulary no less than its ideals to describe man's relationship with God. Whether his exact sources can be established must remain doubtful, but that he had been influenced by the late medieval German mystics is clear enough. From the mystics, Muentzer derived the stress upon the spiritual significance of man's suffering. He put it this way: "No man can come to the proper Christian understanding without suffering, for the heart has been torn away from the clinging to this world through wailing and pain, until one comes to hate this life completely."[12] In a letter of 1523 Muentzer expressed it even more picturesquely:

> But before a man becomes certain of his salvation come many streams of water and their cruel roar. Man loses his will to

---

[10] Böhmer and Kirn, op. cit., p. 14. See also H. Gerdes, "Der Weg des Glaubens bei Müntzer und Luther," Luther 26 (1955), 153.

[11] Brandt, op. cit., p. 132.

[12] Ibid., p. 68.

live, for the billows of the wild sea devour many who think that they have already won. Therefore, one should not run away from these billows, but break them in a masterful way as the experienced sailors do, for the Lord will not grant his sacred witness unless man has first of all worked through to wonderment.[13]

Here was the imagery and the vocabulary of the mystics together with a theology that stressed the abandonment of all creaturely desire and love of self.

Muentzer possessed deep yearning for the renewal of the church. One of his favorite phrases was "poor, miserable, pitiful, and wretched Christendom."[14] He must have used this phrase a hundred times, for it came from his lips whenever he reflected on the state of the church and his place in it. His *Prague Manifesto* was an ardent lamentation for the church which had "through spiritual adultery become a harlot."[15] Muentzer informed his readers that he "had taken this miserable and pernicious damage of Christendom to heart" and in one of his early letters to Elector Frederick of Saxony he confessed that the "zeal for poor, miserable, wretched Christendom has consumed me."[16] He was an ardent reformer, and for ecclesiastical reform he worked, pleaded, exhausted himself and died.

Muentzer regarded himself as God's tool for the reformation of the church. This gave him boldness and determination. Audaciously, he demanded a hearing "before all the nations of men," calling himself a "prophet" and a "serious servant of God."[17] During the height of the peasants' uprising in May of 1525, he told Count Ernst of Mansfeld with unsurpassable candor that "the eternal and living God has commanded us to push you from the chair with the power that is given us. You are unprofitable to Christendom, a pernicious dust-broom to the friends of God."[18]

---

[13] *Ibid.*, p. 62.
[14] *Ibid.*, pp. 115, 128, 133.
[15] *Ibid.*, p. 61.
[16] *Ibid.*, p. 64.
[17] *Ibid.*, p. 71.
[18] *Ibid.*, p. 78.

Muentzer never wavered in this conviction of having been called by God to reform the church.

Such intensity of conviction and commitment was characteristic of him from the first time of which we have a record to the very last. His words always seem to have been written with anguish. The zeal for the Lord consumed him and if he was so fond of the Old Testament and so close to the Prophets, it was because he found there the same zeal and the same singlemindedness of purpose. Few men in the early years of the Reformation exhibited such qualities; for this reason, if for nothing else, Muentzer's name deserves to be recalled.

III

How did he envisage a true reform of the church? His answer was simple. It entailed a distinctive understanding of the Christian faith. This understanding was somber, serious, heavy. When Muentzer wished the recipients of his letters "the fear of the Lord," he expressed thereby, as Gordon Rupp has so aptly noted, a theological program. He found the phrase in Psalm 111:10 which calls such fear "the beginning of wisdom." For him fear was obedience and consequently he talked much about the divine law and God's demands upon man. Such obedience was profoundly prefigured in Christ, who at the same time "removed the sins of the world." Still, this historical recollection was of secondary importance, even as Angelus Silesius put it later on: "If Christ were born a thousand times, but not in me, it be in vain." Muentzer wrote, "The will of God and his work must be fulfilled through a consideration of the Law. Otherwise no one could separate faith from unbelief."[19] What Muentzer meant to say here was that the Law justifies, even as Christ proclaimed the Law. It had been fulfilled by Christ and each believer was called upon to fulfill it also.

---

[19] Carl Hinrichs, *Thomas Müntzer: Die Politischen Schriften mit Kommentar* (Halle, 1950), pp. 78, 134.

This meant that one must know the "whole Christ," which included the knowledge of the "bitter Christ" — the experience of suffering even as Christ suffered. Such suffering was not primarily physical, but spiritual and theological. At one place Muentzer spoke of "suffering" the word, and what he had in mind was the accusing function of the word which confronts man as the demanding Law.[20] The scriptural characterization of the word as a "two-edged sword" was important for Muentzer since, as he put it, "everything in it kills rather than quickens us."[21] The demands of God lie heavily upon man; they lead him to despair and to a complete renunciation of all creaturely confidence. Suffering was the profound awareness of one's distance from God. It was, he had learned from the mystics, the pain and anguish that comes with giving up all desire and love of self.

Tellingly, Muentzer remarked at one time that he had read Augustine and one suspects that the Church Father's notion of the fulfillment of the Law on the part of those filled with the spirit made a profound impact upon him. That the Law must be fulfilled by the elect of God was for Muentzer a corollary of his notion of suffering. It was not man himself, however, who performed the works, but man together with God. The message of Scripture is not Law *or* gospel, but Law *and* gospel. Man who has abandoned all love of self and who looks solely to God knows that the immutable divine will must be fulfilled. This is what Christ did — and to this Christ's followers are also called. Augustine's dualism of letter and spirit may have exerted considerable influence upon Muentzer, who may well have taken his own stress on the spirit from the Church Father, making statements which seemed to suggest that he meant to discount Scripture in favor of the direct inspiration of the spirit. But, while he always insisted that without the guidance of the spirit the Bible is a dead book, he did not depart radically from what might be called the Protestant consensus of the time. He denounced Luther only after he became

---

[20] Brandt, *op. cit.*, pp. 126, 129.
[21] *Ibid.*, p. 126.

persuaded that the Wittenberg Reformer seemed to make the "dead" Bible into an empirically objective source of faith. Thereby he misunderstood Luther, but he anticipated the future development in Protestant theology.

The quintessence of Muentzer's reformatory work was thus the call for an empirical dimension of the Christian faith. He demanded that this faith should not be "monkey play," but serious business. Muentzer's protestation against the "phony faith" of Wittenberg charged that Luther propounded a faith without empirical consequences. And he would have none of it.

If this much can be said about Muentzer's theological reform, a few words need to be added about his vision for society. We do well to begin with his firm conviction concerning God's plan for history. It was as if he had become party to this plan and he was shouting himself hoarse with threats, admonitions, and pleas. A first and telling expression had appeared back in 1521 in the *Prague Manifesto* where he had threatened the Prague burghers with these words: "If you will not do this, God will suffer you to be smitten by the Turks in the coming year. Truly, I know what I say is true and I will suffer for it what Jeremiah also suffered."[22]

"I know what I say is true and I will suffer for it." Here spoke a prophet — a false one, as it turned out, both in Prague in 1521 and in Thuringia four years later, though only after the events had passed were men wiser for this insight. In the midst of events, Muentzer claimed to be a seer, one who had folded back the mantle of the future, who had deciphered, as his sermon on Daniel so cogently argued, the handwriting on the wall. Muentzer's earnestness grew from his conviction that a catastrophe might be avoided if men would only listen. This was especially true as far as the rulers who failed to support the proclamation of God's word and who actually thwarted it were concerned. Carl Hinrich's fine study on the relationship between Muentzer and Luther has shown how Muentzer sought to challenge the rulers to take their place in the

---

[22] Böhmer and Kirn, *op. cit.*, p. 142.

realization of ecclesiastical reform and, thereby, of God's purpose. This is what he aimed for. For a long time he talked about the struggle of the elect against the godless, inviting the rulers to take their place among the former. Revolutionary upheaval was not his intention, at least not in the sense of pitting the people against the rulers. "I could have played a nice game with those of Nuremberg," he wrote in the fall of 1524, "if I had meant to incite an insurrection, as the deceitful world accuses me."[23]

But afterward Muentzer came into contact with the rebellious peasants, and this proved to be his theological undoing. For two years he had experienced with increasing dismay and frustration the unwillingness of the rulers to take their place in the realization of the divine purpose. His words to them became more and more demanding. "The people have great hope in you," he told Elector Frederick in the summer of 1524, but he was to be sorely disappointed in the rulers.[24] The peasants, on the other hand, apparently advocated what he himself stood for. Their slogan of the "divine law," the basis for their various economic and political demands, seemed to point in the direction of his own goals. Indeed, they opposed the same rulers whom he had come to see as godless.

The consequence was both natural and inevitable. Thomas Muentzer identified the cause of the peasants with his own. The peasants' uprising meant that his own grim prophetic anticipation of what God would do had become stark reality: the elect had risen against the godless and the final triumph of God was at hand. There were to be no more rulers or subjects, no more high or low estates. All these had passed; only the elect and the godless remained. Muentzer found ample scriptural references for his argument — Hosea 8 and 13; Luke 1; Daniel 7 — and he pointedly enumerated them in his appeal to "Brother" Albert of Mansfeld. Social overtones found expression in Muentzer's increasingly aggressive pronouncements. "To it, to it, while the fire is hot," he shouted to the people of Allstedt in April of 1525, and in his last

---

23 *Ibid.*, p. 104.
24 Brandt, *op. cit.*, p. 72.

major pronouncement, the *Highly Occasioned Defense,* he spoke about the oppression of the common people by the rulers.[25] But there was still nothing of a comprehensive social program here, nothing of a blueprint for the future.

The involvement in the peasants' uprising, no matter how cursory, meant that Thomas Muentzer was a revolutionary after all — his own demurrers notwithstanding. What is more, one can hardly ignore that Muentzer's proclamation had unmistakable social and political implications. He might not himself have realized them fully and might actually have done little to translate them into practice. But there they were, a distinct expression of his basic insight that those who had accepted the call of God stood in a new and different relationship to society.

A telling expression came in a letter to Count Ernst of Mansfeld dated May 15, 1525, the day before the catastrophe of Frankenhausen: "Tell me, you miserable bag of worms," Muentzer wrote, "who has made you a ruler of the people whom God has redeemed with his precious blood?"[26] Here was the conviction that God's acceptance of man, expressed in the coming of Jesus Christ, had definite social and political implications. A new way of governmental rule was to characterize the elect of the Lord. No longer was there to be inequality, since redemption had brought freedom and equality. Muentzer's dramatic pronouncements were far too cursory to allow a systematic delineation and one can hardly argue any influence of his thought upon the subsequent development of Western democracy. But the thought is there, perhaps for the first time in modern history — the notion of a new political dignity of man because of his religious stature. Muentzer himself may not have realized it. But here was a new idea which, once cleansed of its sectarian and even religious tinge, became a most powerful force in the West.

But, above everything else, Thomas Muentzer was a religious reformer, though with the exception of his brief sojourn at All-

---

25 *Ibid.,* p. 75.
26 *Ibid.,* p. 78.

stedt, he never had a chance to put his reformatory ideas into practice. We do not know whether the realization of Muentzer's
reformatory program would have made any significant impact
upon the spirituality of Christendom. Like many another figure in
the long and eventful course of church history, he has been
maligned, and his attempts to contribute to the spiritual enrich-
ment of Christendom have been overshadowed by the violence and
polemics which filled his last years.

BIBLIOGRAPHY

The literature on Thomas Muentzer is astoundingly extensive. Per-
ceptive historiographical essays are: George W. Forell, "Thomas
Münzer, Symbol and Reality," *Dialog*, 2˙ (1963); Abraham Friesen,
"Thomas Müntzer in Marxist Historiography," *Church History*, 34
(1965). The literature to 1962 is listed in Hans J. Hillerbrand, A
Bibliography of Anabaptism (Elkhart, 1962).

A definitive edition of Muentzer's writings is now being prepared
under the auspices of the Verein für Reformationsgeschichte in Germany, under the editorship of Günther Franz. In the meantime the
following are to be noted: Otto H. Brandt, *Thomas Münzer. Sein
Leben und seine Schriften* (Jena, 1933) offers, in modern German, a
good sampling of Muentzer's letters, tracts, and other contemporary
documents. *Thomas Münzers Briefwechsel*, ed. Heinrich Böhmer and
Paul Kirn (Leipzig, 1931) is a collection of Muentzer's letters. Carl
Hinrichs, *Thomas Müntzer. Politische Schriften* (Halle, 1950), has
edited *Auslegung des 2. Kapitel Danielis, Ausgedrückte Entblössung,*
and *Hochverursachte Schutzrede.*

English translations are available of only two tracts — the sermon
on Daniel, in George H. Williams (ed.), *Spiritual and Anabaptist
Writers* (Philadelphia, 1957); and the *Hochverursachte Schutzrede,*
in Hans J. Hillerbrand, "Thomas Müntzer's Last Tract Against
Luther," *Mennonite Quarterly Review*, 38 (1964).

Of the older, but still valuable, studies on Muentzer, we note Fried-
rich Engels, *Der deutsche Bauernkrieg* (Moscow, 1956) which was
first published in 1850 and which programmatically set the stage for
subsequent Marxist scholarship. The essays of Karl Holl, "Luther und
die Schwärmer," *Luther. Gesammelte Aufsätze*, I (Tübingen, 1923),
and Heinrich Böhmer, "Thomas Müntzer und das jüngste Deutsch-

land," *Gesammelte Aufsätze* (Gotha, 1927), were the initial attempts on the part of Protestant historians to arrive at a more penetrating understanding of Muentzer. Annemarie Lohmann, *Zur geistigen Entwicklung Thomas Müntzers* (Leipzig, 1931) is brief and hardly penetrating, but still helpful for its over-all assessment of Muentzer's theological genius.

The most extensive biographical effort comes from the pen of the Russian historian M. M. Smirin: *Die Volksreformation des Thomas Münzer und der grosse Bauernkrieg* (Berlin, 1952). It seeks especially to place Muentzer in the stream of late medieval thought. The first major biographical effort in non-Marxist scholarship is by Eric Gritsch, *Reformer Without a Church* (Philadelphia, 1967). A shorter biographical essay is by Hans J. Hillerbrand, *A Fellowship of Discontent* (New York, 1967).

The most incisive analysis of Muentzer's thought is Walter Elliger, *Thomas Müntzer* (Berlin, 1960), which stresses his eminently theological concerns. Shorter, but full of stimulating suggestions is E. Gordon Rupp, "Thomas Müntzer, Prophet of Radical Christianity," *Bulletin of the John Rylands Library*, 48 (1966).

PART FIVE

ROMAN CATHOLIC
REFORM

CHAPTER TEN

IGNATIUS LOYOLA

ROBERT E. MCNALLY, S.J.

One hundred years before Martin Luther published his celebrated theses the Council of Constance (1414–18) closed. Inspired and animated by the conviction that the church should be reformed in head and in members, this synod concentrated its efforts on repairing the scandalous disunity of the Great Western Schism. With the election of Martin V (1417–31), who was accepted by the universal church, unity was restored to the Holy See; the way seemed opened to reform by the decree *Frequens* (Oct. 9, 1417) with its provisions for subsequent councils to continue the renewal of the church. Purified of excesses, conciliarism had proved that an ecumenical synod could be a valuable instrument of church reform. No one who grasped the significance of the service to unity which the Council of Constance had rendered could deny that. Reform was in the air in the fifteenth century. From all sides the slogan, *Reformatio ecclesiae tum in capite tum in membris* ("reformation of the church in head and in members"), echoed and re-echoed. That this urgent cry faded finally and died unheeded proved tragic.[1]

Before the century ended, reform councils had assembled at Basel (1431–39) and at Florence (1438–45); under Pope Julius II (1503–13) and Leo X (1513–21) the fifth Lateran Council was held at Rome. These four synods asserted their ecumenicity, they claimed the inspiration and guidance of the Holy Spirit, and they resolutely declared their determination to undertake the reform of the church in head and in members. That they neither renewed nor reformed the church is a matter of history. It is, in fact, a

---

[1] On the problematic of the church on the eve of the Reformation, cf. Robert E. McNally, S.J., *The Unreformed Church* (New York, 1965).

bitter chapter in the chronicle of Western Christianity that the hierarchy at this time did not heed its vocation to provide for the church and its needs. The Lateran Council closed in the spring of 1517; seven months later (Oct. 31, 1517) Martin Luther brought his theses before the public forum of Christendom. Without anyone, even Luther himself, realizing the full significance of what was happening, the Reformation was inaugurated.

In the course of the subsequent hundred years the Western church was filled with reformers of every nationality, conviction, method, and ideal. Each, inspired by a distinct interpretation of the gospel, strove to shape Christianity into a living reality. This essay is concerned with one of them, Ignatius of Loyola (baptized Iñigo López de Loyola), who had his own characteristic concept of reform and of the part that the Christian should play in it. His influence on the renewal of the church of his own day was powerful; it has lasted, and is worthy of consideration.

I

Martin Luther was born in 1483 at Eisleben in Saxony; eight years later Iñigo López de Loyola was born in Azpeitia in the province of Guipúzcoa, a relatively obscure part of Spain. Aside from the fact that both men were ordained priests and both were church reformers, they had little in common. One was a Saxon peasant, the other a Basque nobleman. At the time of their conversions, one was a learned professor, the other an uneducated soldier. Luther laid down his priesthood and set aside his religious vows, while Ignatius had himself ordained and embraced the religious life. Each took this decisive step in terms of his concept of the gospel; both claimed the inspiration of an overpowering experience of God. Both were born and matured as members of the late medieval church; each responded to it differently. Luther found it impossible to work within its structure; Ignatius would have found it impossible to work apart from it. The two grew up totally unaware of one another and their paths never crossed; yet for centuries their basic ideas were in sharp conflict.

The character of the response which these men made to the word of God has determined their historical greatness within the broad context of Christian history. That the late medieval church could produce two personalities so heavily endowed with a sense of true religion and with deep concern for it is a sign of its peculiar richness. But at the same time the striking diversity in ways and means, ideals and inspirations, which distinguishes the lives of these two Christians, is a vivid reminder that the ultimate meaning of church reformation is a mystery. Its full significance is elusive because it is rooted in the charity of the Holy Spirit — the only true reformer of God's church — whose healing activity knows no rule or measure.[2]

Ignatius was not born into a great noble family, but his lineage was noble, and his parents took special care that their son be educated in the ancient traditions of this nobility.[3] As a mere boy, he was turned over to a relative, Juan Velázquez de Cuéllar, a high official of the Catholic court, to be formed according to a knightly and courtly pattern, one calculated to mature him into a gentleman and a knight of honor. This program provided nothing bookish or academic; it was oriented toward the practical and the useful, and aimed at the inculcation of manly virtue, aristocratic refinement, and military courage. It was a masculine education for life in a man's world.[4]

---

[2] Cf. M. Schmidt, "Who Reforms the Church?" in *Ecumenical Dialogue at Harvard* (Cambridge, Mass., 1964), who writes (p. 191): "The reform of the Church is the work of God himself, who works through 'spiritual men,' that is, through such members of the Body of Christ as are quickened by his spirit and are able to contribute to the quickening of the whole body." Basically this is the Ignatian ideal of reform.

[3] P. Leturia, S.J., *El Gentilhombre Iñigo López de Loyola* (Barcelona, 1941), trans. A. J. Owen under the title, *Iñigo de Loyola* (Syracuse, 1949), is the most careful study of the career of the young Ignatius.

[4] From the point of view of source material it is possible to study the life of Ignatius in great detail. In addition to the *Constitutions* of the Society of Jesus and the *Spiritual Exercises*, he composed almost seven thousand letters, part of a spiritual diary, and an account of his early life. This last work, ranked as one of the best autobiographies of the Renaissance period,

In 1517, in his twenty-sixth year, Ignatius turned aside from the dissolute existence of court life. Fatigued with the pompous character of its style and manner, he entered on a new career — the military. Under the command of Antonio Manrique de Lara, Duke of Nájera and Viceroy of Navarra, he took up sword and shield, was commissioned and became a soldier. His military service lasted only four years, for in the course of the furious siege of the castle of Pamplona by the army of Francis I of France, Ignatius was struck by a cannon ball. Acutely wounded in both legs and almost overcome by sheer pain, he was carried from the field of battle. In terms of the chivalry of sixteenth century Spain, the scene was highly moving and dramatic. Here was the courageous young soldier who had fought hard and who fell a hero in the service of his lord. May 20, 1521 was a memorable day for Ignatius, the last day of his military career, the closing chapter of the first phase of his life (1491–1521).

There was nothing about the intellectual and spiritual development of the crippled soldier then in his thirtieth year to suggest the character of his future career. His education was very limited; he had indeed learned to read and write, but not much more than that. He had not been schooled in any way that would prepare him to be a reformer. His head was full of gallantry and romance; he had acquired a reputation as a lover and a gambler. In effect, he was an ignorant, dissolute soldier with little thought for religion and piety. Roman Catholicism was in his Basque blood, but for him it was a matter more of culture and tradition than of com-

---

has been edited and published: *Acta Patris Ignatii, Fontes Narrativi de S. Ignatio de Loyola,* 1, ed. D. F. Zapico, S.J., *et al.* ("Monumenta Ignatiana," 1, ser. 4; Rome, 1943). The translation by W. J. Young, S.J., *St. Ignatius' Own Story* (Chicago, 1956), is cited in the text. Almost all the Ignatian sources have been edited by the *Institutum Historicum Societatis Iesu* (Rome) in the *Monumenta Historica Societatis Iesu.* Diego Laynez, second General of the Society, outlined the life of his friend Ignatius up to the year 1547; Juan Polanco, Ignatius' secretary, composed a *Life,* and a chronicle of the society up to 1556 which is rich in information. In 1572 Pedro Ribadeneira published the first *Life* of Ignatius. Cf. E. A. Ryan, S.J., "The Career of Ignatius Loyola," *Woodstock Letters* 88 (1956), 289–303.

mitment and observance. The life of the young Ignatius as courtier and soldier was far from edifying. He was a man of his times, and his times were not distinguished for moral observance. The demands of court and barracks, the centers of his youth, had exhausted his religious spirit. But two influences of this early period — the military and the chivalrous — form the style and manner of his subsequent history.[5]

The wound received at Pamplona proved to be serious; the clumsy surgery to which he submitted only increased the danger. He suffered acutely, sank close to death, and received the Last Sacraments; when he revived, it became apparent that he would be a cripple forever. The dreary convalescence in the Loyola castle was long, difficult and lonesome. Here, in the context of suffering and depression, Ignatius underwent a gradual but deeply moving experience of the religio-psychological order which radically transformed his whole way of life. This profound transformation was basic to his future work as a reformer of the church.

Quite by chance he became acquainted with the *Vita Iesu Christi* ("Life of Christ") of the Carthusian, Ludolf of Saxony (d. 1378), and the *Flos Sanctorum* ("Flower of the Saints"). The young soldier read these books and felt some urge to imitate the example which he found there. "St. Dominic did this," he reasoned, "therefore, I must do it. St. Francis did that; therefore, I must do it." But most of the hours were spent in dreaming of a great lady and in recalling scenes from the romances which he had formerly read. It was at this point that he made a discovery of some importance. The thought of worldly things, he noted, gave him pleasure that soon turned to depression, while the thought of holy things gave him pleasure that perdured. Later Ignatius described the phenomenon of this first awakening to the call of the Spirit:

> . . . one day his eyes were opened a little and he began to wonder at the difference and to reflect on it, learning from

---

[5] The heroic manner of the young Ignatius is well illustrated by his resolve (depending on the direction which his mule might take) to kill a Moor who had dishonored in speech the Virgin Mary. Cf. *St. Ignatius' Own Story*, p. 14.

experience that one kind of thoughts left him sad and the other cheerful. Thus, step by step, he came to recognize the difference between the two spirits that moved him, the one being from the evil spirit, the other from God.[6]

Here in this early period appears a basic Ignatian insight — the value of personal experience, psychological introspection and self-examination in the formation of spiritual doctrine.

The fruit of Ignatius' long convalescence was his determination to dedicate himself to God. The conviction was strong and sincere, though vague and undefined. At first he was bewildered by the overpowering experience of God's grace, but soon he began to grasp its significance and the inevitability of total surrender to it. The mind of the young Basque soldier was chivalrous, revealing itself strikingly in the heroic manner in which he formally consecrated himself at the shrine of the Virgin Mary at Montserrat. The ceremony, which took place on the vigil of the feast of the Annunciation, March 24–25, 1522, he reports in this way:

> As his mind was filled with the adventures of Amadis of Gaul and such books, thoughts corresponding to these adventures came to his mind. He determined, therefore, on a watch of arms throughout a whole night, without ever sitting or lying down, but standing a while and then kneeling, before the altar of our Lady of Montserrat, where he had made up his mind to leave his fine attire and to clothe himself with the armor of Christ.[7]

In the morning he received Holy Communion, put on a pilgrim's garb of rough material, and wore only one shoe, to favor his deformed leg; later, he let his hair grow unkempt and in general neglected his personal appearance. This abrupt total withdrawal from the world and its ways followed an ancient Christian pattern of asceticism; it was for Ignatius the beginning of his quest to find the will of God.

From March 25, 1522 to the middle of February, 1523, Ignatius lived at Manresa, a town not far from Barcelona. Here he lodged

---

6 *Ibid.*, p. 10.
7 *Ibid.*, p. 15.

in a cave, apart from civilization, apart even from the ordinary necessities of life. The religious experience of these days was crucial to his development as saint and reformer of the church. For him it was an education in the school of the Lord, an experience without which his subsequent career would have been impossible. The solitary days and weeks which this lone ascetic passed in the bleak cave provided an experiential insight into the spiritual life; what he learned was gained only at the high price of very intense personal suffering — scruples, doubts, depression, and despair. Here in the wilderness his body and soul were tested and probed to the fiber of his being. It was a self-revelation won by stark, almost inhuman, asceticism — undisciplined, unreasoned, typical of the ardent soul taking the kingdom of God by storm. Excessive penance, fasting and watching brought him almost to the edge of death. Studying day by day and examining each psychological movement, observing moments of consolation and desolation, seeing all things in the light of the gospel, he gradually came to what he believed to be a systematic ascetical method. All this he noted carefully in a little book which grew into the celebrated *Spiritual Exercises*.[8]

The last three or four months of his stay at Manresa were months of great spiritual consolation and illumination, even of ecstasy and vision. Ignatius describes one of his mystical experiences in this way:

> One day while he was reciting the Hours of our Lady . . . his understanding began to be elevated as though he saw the Holy Trinity under the figure of three keys. This was accompanied with so many tears and so much sobbing that he could not control himself.[9]

This way of reporting "the spiritual illumination which at that time God impressed upon his soul" underscores the fact that Igna-

---

[8] On the genesis and character of the *Exercises*, cf. E. Watrigant, S.J., *La Genèse des Exercises de saint Ignace de Loyola* (Amiens, 1907); H. Pinard de la Boullaye, S.J., *Les étapes de rédaction des Exercises de S. Ignace* (Paris, 1955); and H. Rahner, S.J., *The Spirituality of St. Ignatius Loyola* (Westminster, Md., 1953).

[9] *St. Ignatius' Own Story*, p. 22.

tius stands chronologically at the head of the great Spanish mystics of the sixteenth century.[10]

In mid-February of 1523 Ignatius left Manresa; a month later he was on pilgrimage to Jerusalem, to the holy places. This was a step that he had been planning ever since his first conversion. He arrived at Jerusalem on September 4, 1523 and experienced great spiritual joy in visiting the principal sites of the Lord's ministry. But it soon became clear to him that his apostolic ministry was not to be devoted to the care and protection of the holy places, that God's will was drawing him in another direction. On his way back from Jerusalem he considered carefully what he should do to bring his service to fruition; "finally he felt more inclined to study so as to be able to help souls."[11] His return to Spain in March, 1524 brought the second period of his life (1521–24) to a close.

Convinced that education was basic to his service of God, he commenced in his thirty-second year to learn the rudiments of grammar. After almost two years at Barcelona, where he studied fundamental Latin, and some months at the universities of Alcalá and Salamanca, Ignatius went to Paris.[12] After seven years in Paris (1528–35) he obtained the degrees of Bachelor of Arts and Master of Arts. He was a faithful student, sincere and industrious, but neither brilliant nor learned. This is the way that his disciple and friend, Diego Laynez, later characterized him.

In leaving Spain for Paris, the center of medieval learning, Ignatius turned his back on the great Spanish universities of Alcalá and Salamanca, which were to provide so much of the force of the Roman Catholic Reformation. In Spain he had been arrested more than once by the Inquisition for his manner of dress (like a poor pilgrim), for gathering disciples about him, for offering religious instruction, and for his theological ideas on the distinction between mortal and venial sin. At Alcalá the inquisitors,

---

[10] Cf. E. A. Peers, *Studies of the Spanish Mystics*, 1 (London, 1951), 3.
[11] *St. Ignatius' Own Story*, p. 36.
[12] For Ignatius' student days at Paris, cf. G. Schurhammer, S.J., *Franz Xaver. Sein Leben und seine Zeit*, 1: *Europa 1506–1541* (Freiburg im Breisgau, 1955), 71 ff.

thinking that he was one of the *Alumbrados* (*Illuminati*), even "threatened him with capital punishment"; his imprisonment at Salamanca gave him occasion to utter the heroic words, "There are not bars enough or chains enough in Salmanca but that I would desire more for God's love."[13] Thus the confrontation with church and university in Spain brings out a significant aspect of his character.

In effect he was silenced, but rather than submit to this oppressive, restrictive treatment, he left Spain and its universities — without, however, repudiating the authority of the church. Later, in Paris, when a friend marveled that no one molested him, he made the following pointed remark which illustrates his determination not to be frustrated in his vocation: "It is because I do not speak to anyone of the things of God, but once the course is finished the old life will return."[14]

As late as 1534 Ignatius still had only the vaguest ideas of the manner in which he would commit himself to Christ. By force of personality and the *Spiritual Exercises,* he had gathered a group of six devoted students about him;[15] in a simple ceremony in a small chapel on Montmartre they bound themselves by vow to live in poverty and chastity, to make a pilgrimage to Jerusalem, and to work thereafter for the salvation of souls. It was resolved that they should go to Venice and try to obtain passage from there to the Holy Land; if this should prove impossible within a year, they would go to Rome and offer themselves to the pope and the service of the church. When the precarious military tensions between the Venetians and the Turks excluded the possibility of the proposed pilgrimage, they were at once (June 24, 1537) ordained to the priesthood, and began in an official, public way to preach and teach the gospel. Even then they were recognized as church reformers. Thus in Venice, at the beginning of the summer of

---

13 *St. Ignatius' Own Story,* p. 50.
14 *Ibid.,* p. 57.
15 The first six Jesuits were Ignatius Loyola, Francis Xavier, Peter Faber, Diego Laynez, Alphonso Salmeron and Simon Rodriguez.

1537, a new moment had been reached; the decision to center in Rome rather than in Jerusalem ended the third period (1524–37) of Ignatius' career.

It was only in the Lenten season of 1539 that this small group began to discuss the definitive form or method of its service of God. All were animated by the conviction that their service of God should be manifested through their service of the church; and that their service of the church should be in service of the Roman pontiff. Debate centered around the more delicate question of the concrete conditions of their commitment. Should they work individually or collectively? Should their service, if collective, be under authority, or should it be unstructured service? Should they vow obedience to one of their number? No single pattern of life forced itself on this zealous group; their decision was by a free and secret ballot, and the decisive vote favored a life of obedience.[16] Under the influence of the saintly Cardinal Contarini, Pope Paul III solemnly approved the mode of life which Ignatius and his companions had envisaged for themselves. "As if animated with a prophetic spirit," the pope recognized that "this congregation would reform the church,"[17] and by the bull, *Regimini militantis ecclesiae*, of September 27, 1540, he gave canonical approbation and status to the new Society of Jesus.

In 1541 Ignatius was unanimously elected the first General of the Society despite his reluctance; he ruled until his death on July 31, 1556. In his lifetime the society grew to one thousand members, active in every part of the civilized world, on the American continents and in the distant Orient. The closing years of his career were devoted to administration; yet he did not personally retire from active apostolic work, from preaching and teaching the rudiments of the Christian faith, from hearing confessions, from

---

16 *Deliberatio primorum Patrum*, in *Constitutiones Societatis Iesu* 1, ("Monumenta Ignatiana," 1, Ser. 3; Rome, 1934), 1–7. This document is an admirable example of the openness and freedom which characterized the early society.

17 J. Polanco, *Summarium de Origine et Progressu Societatis Jesu*, 89, ("Fontes Narrativi," 1; Rome, 1943), 206.

caring for the sick, the poor, and the wayward woman. His commitment to the gospel was too deep for him to overlook his personal obligation to its dissemination. In the person of his friend and companion, Francis Xavier, he saw the gospel carried to the remote Indies, to Japan, even through the gates of China, beyond which no one had ever before preached the good news of salvation; in Francis Borgia and Peter Canisius the young society entered the theater of European history. Ignatius devoted the final stage of his apostolate (1541–56) to the development of the society as an instrument of church reform.

The generalship of Ignatius was totally absorbed in the service of the church which in the middle decades of the sixteenth century —the heart of the Tridentine age — centered in reformation. On July 31, 1548 (*Pastoralis officii*) Pope Paul III solemnly approved the *Spiritual Exercises* as "full of piety and holiness, very useful and conducive to the spiritual edification and advancement of the faithful." This was a personal victory for the men whose spiritual doctrine had been under the suspicion of the Inquisition. For years (1541–47) by trial and error he had been composing constitutions for the new society; in 1552 this new code was ready to be implemented, but with the proviso that it should be accepted only after the members of the order were satisfied that it was a reliable instrument to inspire and guide their apostolic endeavors. The first General Congregation (1556) after his death accepted the *Constitutions* exactly as their author had conceived and composed them; and later they were approved by Gregory XIII in the brief, *Quanto fructuosius*, of February 1, 1583. These two creations, the *Exercitia spiritualia* and the *Societas Iesu*, are the very heart and soul of the Ignatian reform. The Society of Jesus, the institutional element, was envisaged as the concrete expression of the *Spiritual Exercises*, the ascetical element.[18]

---

[18] On the role of the *Exercises* in church reform and the foundation of the Society of Jesus, cf. Robert E. McNally, S.J., "The Council of Trent, the Spiritual Exercises and the Catholic Reform," *Church History*, 34 (1965), 36–49; and P. Leturia, S.J., "Génesis de los Ejercicios de S. Ignacio y su influjo en la fundación de la Compañía de Jesús," *Archivum Historicum Societatis Iesu*, 10 (1941), 16–59.

II

What exactly is this book of *Spiritual Exercises* which Ignatius considered fundamental to his personal conversion, to the foundation of the society, and to its apostolate? First of all, it is in no sense a spiritual program devised against Protestantism; nothing could have been further from its original inspiration. Rather, it is a book of human destiny to be read in the light of God's grace; it is a systematic, ascetical program whose central purpose is "the conquest of self and the regulation of one's life in such a way that no decision is made under the influence of any inordinate attachment."[19] It is a program of self-reform which aims at putting life on a solidly religious basis which confirms and expresses God's order of things in this world. For Ignatius the key to the establishment of the primacy of the kingdom of God in the hearts of men is the human decision under the sway of grace. It is God who calls, but it is man who responds. Thus the history of the individual is seen as a dynamic series of personal, human decisions — progressions or digressions — in virtue of which one moves toward or away from God. Life is interlaced with a network of tensions between creature and creator on whose resolution salvation depends. The conversion of the individual never ends.

The *Exercises* outline a method for achieving perfect union with God by harmonizing these tensions with one another. The process is negative (purgation of "all inordinate attachments") and positive (the discovery of God's will). Freedom from creatures (but only from those creatures which involve a de-ordination, perversion or deprivation of the human spirit) is *de rigueur* for the full achievement and enjoyment of another, higher, ennobling freedom: union with God. The term of all human motion must be eternal life. To assist man in his quest for God's will, Ignatius devised the whole prayer pattern which makes up his spiritual program. "By the term Spiritual Exercises," he writes, "is meant every

---

[19] Cf. *The Spiritual Exercises*, trans. L. J. Puhl (Westminster, Md., 1957), p. 11. Hereafter cited as *Spiritual Exercises*.

method of examination of conscience, of meditation, of contemplation, of vocal and mental prayer, and of other spiritual activities. . . ."[20]

The Christian mysteries which Ignatius proposes to the consideration of the exercitant include the Principle and Foundation, Four Weeks (on the life of Christ from incarnation to ascension) and the *Contemplatio ad Amorem* ("Contemplation unto Love"). Interspersed at strategic points are certain "key meditations" — for example, Triple Sin, the Kingdom of Christ, Two Standards — whose function is to inculcate certain fundamental convictions. Each part of the *Exercises* has its own individual technique, psychological moment and religious attitude. A rigid, mechanical examination of conscience is specified to purify the soul and to test the daily achievement level of the exercitant. The course of the *Exercises* (generally made under the supervision of a competent director) may extend as long as thirty days, though the time element is variable according to circumstances. Fasting, penance, the use of light and its exclusion are recommended in terms of their value in creating an atmosphere of prayer. Silence and withdrawal are also prescribed. "The more the soul is in solitude and seclusion," explains Ignatius, "the more fit it renders itself to approach and be united with its Creator and Lord; and the more closely it is united with Him, the more it disposes itself to receive graces and gifts from the infinite goodness of its God." [21]

The *Exercises* are not a book to be read but a method to be followed personally and individually. The exercitant "makes use of acts of the intellect in reasoning, and of acts of the will in manifesting . . . love." He is to meditate and contemplate the central mysteries of Christianity, from creation to parousia. What is set before him is to be absorbed into the inner fiber of his life. In its purest form, Ignatian meditation is ordered so as to arrive not at abstract knowledge but at personal discovery and realization.

---

[20] *Ibid.*, p. 1.
[21] *Ibid.*, p. 10. For a modern interpretation of Ignatian spirituality, cf. Karl Rahner, S.J., *Spiritual Exercises* (New York, 1965).

"It is not much knowledge that fills and satisfies the soul but the intimate understanding and relish of the truth."[22] Christian doctrine is operative knowledge. Ignatius relates this principle to Christ. "Here [in meditating on the incarnation] it will be to ask for an intimate knowledge of our Lord, who has become man for me, that I may love Him more and follow Him more closely."[23]

But the Christian truth which is understood and relished must be grasped in a personal way. It is the truth of Christ in his mysteries which confronts the Christian who makes the *Exercises*. In the meditation on sin, for example, Ignatius asks the exercitant to return to the dread hour of the mystery, to place himself in the historical context of Christ's passion, and there to converse with the Lord:

> Imagine Christ our Lord present before you upon the cross, and begin to speak with him, asking how it is that though He is the Creator, He has stooped to become man, and to pass from eternal life to death here in time, that thus He might die for our sins.
>
> I shall also reflect on myself and ask: What have I done for Christ? What am I doing for Christ? What ought I do for Christ?
>
> As I behold Christ in this plight, nailed to the cross, I shall ponder upon what presents itself to my mind.[24]

The prayer form leads back in time to the passion in a personal confrontation — "Christ our Lord present before you upon the cross." In terms of the mystery one challenges oneself directly. "What ought *I* do for Christ?" The question elicits action more than thought; it is rooted in a very basic personal consideration: "Christ suffers all for my sins; what ought I do and suffer for him?"

---

[22] *Spiritual Exercises*, p. 2.

[23] *Ibid.*, p. 49. Note that according to the *Exercises* (*ibid.*, p. 61) Christ, in calling men to serve under his standard, "sends them throughout the whole world to spread His sacred doctrine among all men, no matter what their state or condition." For Ignatius this "sacred doctrine" is the Catholic faith.

[24] *Ibid.*, p. 28. On the position of the Bible in the *Exercises*, cf. J. A. Fitzmyer, S.J., "The Spiritual Exercises of Saint Ignatius and Recent Gospel Study," *Woodstock Letters*, 91 (1962), 246–74.

If the *Spiritual Exercises* seek to reform the individual Christian, then the totality of his life — its style, manner, inspiration, ideals, and purpose — must be prayerfully but realistically examined. To bring the life of the Christian into conformity with the faith which he professes is at the heart of Christian reform. In this context Ignatius poses the question of "making a choice of a way of life," which will establish the primacy of faith in action. The logic on which this election rests is inexorable, and is characteristic of his ascetical method. "In every good choice," he writes, " . . . our intention must be simple. I must consider only the end for which I am created, that is, for the praise of God our Lord and for the salvation of my soul. Hence, whatever I choose must help me to this end for which I am created."[25] In these few words Ignatius expresses his comprehension of the human dynamics of the *mysterium simplicitatis* which is Christian life.

It is precisely in this area of human activity that he sees the collapse of morality and goodness, and hence of the whole fabric of Christianity. "I must," he writes, "not subject and fit the end to the means, but the means to the end." The whole perversion of the right order of things — God's order — which he witnessed in his day, he traced back to this conversion of means and end. As he sensed the climate of his age it was decadent and separated from religion in its pure sense. "Persons do not go directly to God, but want God to conform wholly to their inordinate attachments. Consequently, they make of the end a means, and of the means an end. As a result, what they ought to seek first, they seek last."[26]

The imbalance could be corrected by one and only by one ultimate consideration: "to seek God which is the end." Here, perhaps more than in any other expression of his thought, Ignatius reveals himself as a religious idealist who wishes to remake the whole world in the light of gospel principles. Man need only obey the dynamics of the divine economy in which human nature, gratified with grace, drifts towards its ultimate end, God, the

---

[25] *Spiritual Exercises,* p. 71.
[26] *Ibid.*

Alpha and Omega of all. By obedience to the divine law which is built into and structured on human nature, the whole world will be renewed; properly oriented, the world will turn to the one Lord, who is "the Lord of lords."

Ignatius' approach to reform is theocentric in that it reveals once again the majesty and sovereignty of God to man, whose response is praise, reverence, and service. His program is also homocentric in that it is preoccupied with restoring, renewing, and revitalizing all human relationships of man to God, to man, and to nature. But the Ignatian reform also has cosmic import. Fundamental here is a key idea of the *Exercises:* "The other things [that is, other than man] on the face of the earth are created for man to help him in attaining the end for which he is created."[27] All creation is part of a vast conspiracy to lead man to God. Thus the natural order is sanctified and ennobled above and beyond itself; and man is given a new freedom and responsibility face to face with creatures — to use all, to abuse none. This open invitation to a full, rich participation in the material and spiritual resources of the world is extended without fear of defilement from matter or distraction from God.

Use and abuse of the world depend on choice; choice is valid only to the extent that it leads to God. Ignatius' prescription is significant: "Our one desire and choice should be what is more conducive to the end for which we are created."[28] In the ultimate analysis "what is more conducive" is the election of Christ himself, his mind, his example, his leadership, his gospel. Service of Christ is service of God. Commitment here means dedication to the establishment, the spread and the preservation of the kingdom of God in opposition to those who under the standard of Satan abuse, subvert, and overthrow it in favor of this "enemy of mankind." For Ignatius reform is a battle fought between Christ and Satan on the theater of human history through the instrumentality of man.

---

[27] *Ibid.,* p. 12.
[28] *Ibid.*

At the end of all considerations of the public life of the Lord, Ignatius specifies "directions for the amendment and reformation of one's way of living in his state of life."[29] Here we see clearly the simplicity and directness of his method which is substantially a presentation of the gospel as a challenge. The experience is not so much intellectual or rational as it is warm, prayerful, and devout. With personal affection and in the light of God's eternal truth one's actual, vital situation is carefully considered. Each one, writes Ignatius, will "reform his manner of living in his state by setting before himself the purpose of his creation and of his life and position, namely, the glory and praise of God our Lord and the salvation of his soul."[30] It is within this frame — eternal salvation — that every last contingent detail is to be examined, weighed and measured. If Christian life terminates in salvation, then every aspect of life must be Christian.

This method — personal, intimate confrontation with God's truth — is congenial to Ignatius. His ideal is the simple Christian of God's word who desires and seeks nothing "except the greater praise and glory of God our Lord. . . . For every one must keep in mind that in all that concerns the spiritual life his progress will be in proportion to his surrender of self-love and of his own will and interests."[31] There is no complexity in this *Weltanschauung*, which sees contemporary life from the point of view of its relation to eternal life. The "there and then" of the *eschata* is normative for the "here and now" of history. Neither theological nor exegetical problems distract the train of thought of this pious, uneducated layman, mystic and ascetic, as he traces out the working of God's grace in his soul.

III

Ignatian reform was church-centered. This aspect of his program is of paramount importance; apart from it his work as a

---

[29] *Ibid.*, p. 78.
[30] *Ibid.*
[31] *Ibid.*

reformer is incomprehensible. For example, in formulating "the matters about which a choice should be made," Ignatius set down the following basic norm: "It is necessary that all matters of which we wish to make a choice be either indifferent or good in themselves, and such that they are lawful within our Holy Mother, the hierarchical Church, and not bad or opposed to her."[32] And again in a special set of "Rules for Thinking [*Sentire*] with the Church," which form part of the *Exercises*, he prescribed this obediential attitude: "We must put aside all judgment of our own, and keep the mind ever ready and prompt to obey in all things the true Spouse of our Lord, our holy Mother, the hierarchical Church."[33]

The thirteenth rule enunciates the celebrated "security-principle," which brings out the authoritarian character of Ignatius' concept of the relation of the Catholic to his church:

> If we wish to proceed securely in all things, we must hold fast to the following principle: What seems to me white, I will believe black, if the hierarchical Church so defines. For I must be convinced that in Christ our Lord, the bridegroom, and in His spouse, the Church, only one Spirit holds sway, which governs and rules for the salvation of souls. For it is by the same Spirit and Lord who gave the Ten Commandments that our Holy Mother the Church is ruled and governed.[34]

Total obedience and submission to the church is inculcated because the authority principle, the "one Spirit" who is Christ our Lord is also in his church. Taken at its face value, this rule is the very epitome of Tridentine papalism.

That the Christian should center his life in the church was the *sine qua non* of Ignatian reform. As reformer, Ignatius sought by the *Exercises* to transform the indifferent individual into a perfect servant of God. He must be purged, detached and renewed; but

---

[32] *Ibid.*, p. 72.
[33] *Ibid.*, p. 157. The character of these eighteen rules, whether anti-Erasmian or anti-Lutheran, has not been satisfactorily determined. They were composed in 1537 between Paris and Venice. Cf. G. Schurhammer, S.J., *op. cit.*, 1, 232, and P. Leturia, S.J., "Sentido verdadero en la Iglesia militante," *Gregorianum*, 23 (1942), 137–68.
[34] *Spiritual Exercises*, p. 160.

it is the victorious grace of Christ that accomplishes what the *Exercises* prescribe and what the exercitant seeks. The reborn Christian enters a new life of the Spirit, but it is a life within the dimensions of the church. In fact, this new life is a commitment to the church, to its faith and morality, to its obedience. This way of thinking is fundamental to every choice of a state of life that seriously aims at the praise and the service of God.

The church, which was pivotal in Ignatius' thought, was the hierarchical church, the *ecclesia reformata et reformanda* ("reformed and to be reformed") but his reform program did not touch the structure of the church as it was known in the sixteenth century. There was no question of rewriting her law, renewing her administration, or altering her whole external appearance. Nor did Ignatius attempt to reform the theology of his day or the current order of divine worship. His renewal did not run in vertical lines, reaching from roots to branches; rather, it was horizontal in direction, reaching out to the individual Christian in his life-situation, whether his station be high or low. It was the conviction of Ignatius that if each member of the church universal were religiously and radically purified, then the whole house of the Lord would be transformed into the perfect family of Christ. His aim was not reformed laws but reformed men — reform not by justice but by charity. Ignatius' concern therefore was essentially with personal rather than institutional reform. No other possibility seemed open in the difficult days of the Council of Trent (1545–63).[35]

In terms of Ignatius' personal career, his concept of Christian renewal as a church-centered movement comes as a surprise. Arrested five times by the Inquisition, he did not repudiate (or even think of repudiating) the church which had penalized him publicly and unjustly. His psychological structure did not fit into the pattern of adverse responses to adverse stimuli. For almost twenty years he lived in the Rome of the late Renaissance popes, where through firsthand acquaintance he came to know the most deca-

---

[35] Cf. C. de Dalmases, S.J., "Les idées de saint Ignace sur la Réforme Catholique," *Christus*, 18 (1958), 239–56.

dent aspects of the style and manner of the *ecclesia reformanda*. In spite of this experience he did not turn away from it. In fact, the whole tendency of his mind was towards greater adhesion to this old hierarchical church, and the conviction burnt within him that his greatest work must be done within the dimensions of this church.

The persistence of this saintly Basque remains a classic example of the mystery of loyalty. In the midst of religious scandal that must surely have depressed his sensitive soul to its depths, he labored slowly and methodically to change men's hearts and minds by giving them a new vision of the honor and glory of God.

IV

The *Spiritual Exercises* were the fruit of the initial religious experience of Ignatius in the cave of Manresa at a time when he was neither cleric nor theologian. They express what he thought, felt, and experienced in his personal encounter with the gospel. He made the *Exercises* before he wrote them, and he was the first person to be reformed by them. They transformed him into a servant of God—without, however, explicating for him the manner and means by which he, as a reformed Christian, might serve the unreformed church of that day. The discovery of his plan of service — the concrete realization of the ideals of the *Exercises* — would be a gradual process, terminating in the foundation of the Society of Jesus.[36]

During his Parisian days, when Ignatius and his intimate circle of student friends had bound themselves together by simple, private vows of religion, their purpose was poorly defined; they could not envisage the character of the service that they might render to the church. They lacked purpose, definition, and structure — all the elecments necessary for corporate existence. In 1534–39

---

[36] Cf. A. J. Oñate, S.J., *El Origen de la Compañía de Jesus. Carisma Fundacional y Genesis Historica, Bibliotheca Instituti Historici Societatis Iesu,* 25 (Rome, 1966).

decisions were made by the small group which matured into the Society of Jesus, the organ by which Ignatius hoped to make the fundamental inspiration of the *Exercises* live in the church. By 1556 the *Constitutions* of the Society of Jesus were completed; approved by the Holy See, they were promulgated in 1559. What do they reveal about the reform of Ignatius?[37]

As they have come down to us, the *Constitutions* are divided into ten parts which provide for the increase, development, and preservation of the society.[38] No religious rule written before this time is so detailed and thorough in defining and justifying its end and means. The large amount of space (Part IV) devoted to the intellectual and spiritual preparation of its members is remarkable. It represents an attempt to adjust religious life to the complexity of the modern world which was then being born. Stress falls on intellectual and spiritual preparation, because the society is oriented to the service of God in the context of the church. "The end of the society," writes Ignatius, "is not only the salvation and perfection of our own souls with God's grace, but with the same grace the salvation and perfection of the souls of our neighbors."[39] In accord with this purpose the members of the society take three vows, poverty, chastity, and obedience, as fundamental to their gospel-witness, but also as fundamental to their church-service. And precisely because the society is church-oriented, the *Constitutions* specify a special fourth vow of obedience to the Roman pontiff and

---

[37] Cf. P. Leturia, S.J., "A las fuentes de la Romanidad de la Compañía de Jesús," *Bibliotheca Instituti Historici Societatis Iesu* 1 (Rome, 1957), 239-56 and "Roma y la Fundación de la Compañía de Jesús," *ibid.*, 285-302.

[38] The *Constitutions* have been edited and published in the *Monumenta Ignatiana, Sancti Ignatii de Loyola Constitutiones Societatis Iesu*, 3 vols. (Rome, 1934–38).

[39] Note how Ignatius' original purpose in founding the society is revised in the papal documents. According to Paul III's bull, *Regimini militantis ecclesiae* (Sept., 27, 1540), the society is founded "for the advancement of souls in Christian life and doctrine, and for the propagation of the faith." Ten years later Julius III, in the bull, *Exposcit debitum* (July 21, 1550), further defines this purpose by adding the significant phrase, "for the defense of the faith." This may well reflect the defensive attitude of the Council of Trent (1545–63); it signalizes the beginning of the polemical spirit in the society.

to his service. Obedience, because of its relationship to accomplishment, is basic to Ignatius' concept of religious life.[40]

Ignatius' definition of the life of the society shows the originality of his mind. One may well speculate what the future of the church would have been had his spirit been allowed to touch its structure. In contradistinction to the manner of religious life which had characterized the monastic and mendicant orders of the Middle Ages, the Ignatian *Constitutions* pointed a new way. The obligation to sing the canonical hours in choir was dropped; nor was a distinct religious habit specified. Monastic chapter and stability were excluded; the appointment of all superiors was placed in the hands of the General, who was to be elected for life. Its members were free in their apostolic work; they moved from city to city, from country to country, and finally from continent to continent, but under the direction of superiors and the inspiration of the goal of the society. No member was allowed to desire or to accept ecclesiastical honors, titles, or privileges; no benefices were to be held, nor was service to be remunerated. As a social unit, the order was equipped for a corporate mobility which demanded that the individual yield before the common good. No determined work was specified in the *Constitutions* of the society; its commitment would be to the needs of the church at this or that moment of history.

The whole purpose of the society is explicated in work; in fact, for Ignatius it was in work itself that God was to be sought and found. It was a veritable point of religious encounter and experience. The insight is valuable, for it elevates human activity to a new level and shows itself concretely in the conviction that the society is an instrument of service of God and man. Service means work, concrete, real endeavor in the historical order within the frame of the church. At the end of the *Exercises* Ignatius epitomized his basic thought in these words: "Love is shown more

---

[40] Cf. Karl Rahner, S.J., "Eine Ignatianische Grundhaltung," *Stimmen der Zeit*, 158 (1955–56), 253–67, translated under the title, "A Basic Ignatian Concept," *Woodstock Letters*, 86 (1957), 291–310.

in deeds than in words." Thus he could see no opposition between work and prayer. The former does not dilute the latter; work expresses, ennobles, and makes prayer real. The ascetical program which the *Constitutions* prescribe for the society allows maximum liberty of spirit, respects the human person and opens vistas of service.[41]

The stark simplicity of religious life as Ignatius conceived it is impressive. No external magnificence, no titles, no honors are tolerated. Private prayer and celebration of the low mass, with devotion and reverence, rather than liturgical pomp (as it was known in that day) are emphasized. Solid virtues are to be cultivated. There is to be neatness and simplicity of life, temperance in eating and drinking, reserve in speech and attitude, modesty in dress, authentic humility, gospel poverty, and an appreciation of the value of pure religion. This was Ignatius' ideal in designing the manner of life in the society. He was earnest in striving to recreate, restore and renew the image of the priest and the religious which had deteriorated during the medieval centuries. It is surprising to note that when his ideals are reduced to their ultimates, they coincide closely with the aspirations of Erasmus' *Praise of Folly*.[42] It may be — and I say this only by way of suggestion — that Ignatius envisaged his society, a *religio reformata*, as a model for the reform of the whole church.

It is not easy to discover the mind of Ignatius on the problem of church reform. On this delicate theme he was reticent in expressing his convictions. The remarks, therefore, which he addressed to a group of Fathers of the Society on May 8, 1555 are of consider-

---

[41] Cf. Robert E. McNally, S.J., "St. Ignatius: Prayer and the Early Society of Jesus," *Woodstock Letters*, 94 (1965), 109–34.

[42] In writing this I am aware how much the vitriolic character of the Erasmian critique of the church irritated Ignatius, who even forbade the reading of the *Enchiridion* to the younger members of the society. But the two are one in their quest for a simple, authentic Christianity within the context of the old church. Cf. R. G. Villoslada, S.J., "Humanismo y contrareforma, o Erasmo y San Ignacio de Loyola," *Razón y Fe*, 121 (1940), 5–36; "San Ignacio de Loyola y Erasmo de Rotterdam," *Estudios eclesiásticos*, 16 (1942), 235–64, 399–426; 17 (1943), 75–103.

able importance to understanding Ignatius the reformer in the broad context of church history. "On Saturday," wrote his secretary, Father Polanco, "our Father said, that if the Pope would reform his person, his house and the cardinals of Rome, there would be nothing more to do; all the rest would follow." This plan is especially significant in view of the fact that it was entertained in the pontificate of Marcellus II, with whom Ignatius had already begun to discuss the problem of reformation. The sudden death of this saintly churchman aborted his sincere efforts to introduce into the papal palace the Jesuit reform in the persons of Fathers Diego Laynez and Jerome Nadal.[43] This Ignatian plan for personal reform moving from head down radically reflects the influence of the *Consilium de emendanda ecclesia* ("Plan for Reforming the Church") of the pontificate of Paul III.

Face to face with the problems which Lutheranism had posed in the North, Ignatius was obdurate in his conviction that stern measures must be employed. A classical locus for this anti-Protestant aspect of Ignatius' thought is a letter, dated August 13, 1554, and addressed to Peter Canisius, in which he outlines all the oppressive measures which King Ferdinand might be advised to use against the heretics.[44] The reform program devised here is indeed harsh. It is an approach which is no longer valid; even within the religio-political context of that day, its validity is hard to establish. The fact that Ignatius became involved in this unbalanced program is a salutary reminder that even the saints of God are only human, and that their most noble service of the church can deteriorate into fanatical extremes.

There is no need to exaggerate the contribution of Ignatius Loyola to Roman Catholic reform; no one man does all things. But what he accomplished is impressive. His reforming spirit was most evident, most characteristic, and most effective, not in his dealings with princes and prelates, but in his formation and direc-

---

[43] Cf. C. de Dalmases, *op. cit.*, pp. 248–50.
[44] This letter is translated by J. Brodrick, S.J., *Saint Peter Canisius* (New York, 1935), pp. 211–14.

tion of the Society of Jesus. With a genuine appreciation of the value of good example, he worked to form religious priests whose lives would be a concrete expression of their Christian faith. Before the people they would represent the Roman Catholic reform; the impact of their personal renewal would lead inevitably to reformation of the church universal. Kalkbrenner, the Carthusian, described his impression of the first generation of Jesuits to work in Cologne: "They are apostolic men, filled with God's spirit and power, men of new courage and strength. Their words are like glowing sparks; they ignite the hearts . . . and in the end rich is the harvest, which the invisible Sower brings to fullness in the hearts of men." Peter Canisius epitomized all that he had learned from Peter Faber, Ignatius' friend and disciple from the Parisian days, in these words: "There is only one idea — to work with Christ for the salvation of souls."[45]

BIBLIOGRAPHY
Bangert, W. *To the Other Towns.* Westminster, Md., 1959.
Brodrick, J., *Saint Peter Canisius.* New York, 1935.
———. *The Origin of the Jesuits.* New York, 1940.
DeGuibert, J. *The Jesuits: Their Spiritual Doctrine and Practice.* Chicago, 1964.
Dudon, P. *St. Ignatius of Loyola.* Milwaukee, 1949.
Leturia, P., *Iñigo de Loyola.* Trans. A. J. Owen. Syracuse, 1949.
Loyola, Ignatius. *St. Ignatius' Own Story.* Trans. W. J. Young, S. J. Chicago, 1956.
McNally, Robert E., "St. Ignatius: Prayer and the Early Society of Jesus," *Woodstock Letters,* 94 (1965), 109–34.
———. "The Council of Trent and the Spiritual Doctrine of the Counter Reformation," *Church History,* 34 (1965), 36–49.
Rahner, H., *Ignatius von Loyola als Mensch und Theologe.* Vienna, 1964.
———. *The Spirituality of St. Ignatius Loyola: An Account of Its Historical Development.* Westminster, Md., 1953.
Schurhammer, G., *Franz Xaver. Sein Leben und seine Zeit.* 2 vols. Freiburg im Breisgau, 1955–63.
Von Matt, L., and H. Rahner, *St. Ignatius of Loyola.* Chicago, 1956.

[45] Joseph Lortz, *Die Reformation in Deutschland,* 2 (Freiburg, 1949), 140, and C. de Dalmases, S.J., *op. cit.,* p. 244.

INDEX

258